TO
VENUS
AND BACK

One Man's Quest to
Rediscover Love

TURNER GRANT

To Venus and Back: One Man's Quest to Rediscover Love
Published by Stones River LLC
Washington DC

Publisher's Cataloging-in-Publication Data
Names: Grant, Turner, author.
Title: To Venus and back : one man's quest to rediscover love / Turner Grant.
Description: Washington, DC: Stones River LLC, 2023.
Identifiers: ISBN: 979-8-218-05631-5 hardcover | 979-8-218-00424-8 (paperback)
Subjects: LCSH Grant, Turner. | Dating (Social customs) | Man-woman relationships. | Online dating. |
BISAC BIOGRAPHY & AUTOBIOGRAPHY / Personal Memoirs | FAMILY & RELATIONSHIPS / Dating
Classification: LCC HQ801.82 .G73 2023 | DDC 306.730285/092--dc23

The events depicted in this book are authentic and all people are real. Dialogue is a representation of what was spoken based on the author's recollections. Names and many identifying details have been changed to protect the privacy of individuals.

Cover design by Donna Cunningham of BeauxArts.Design
Interior by BeauxArts.Design
Rose Illustration by Turner Grant
Design Copyrights owned by Stones River LLC
Font: Minion Pro

STONES RIVER LLC

BB

"You make me better than what I am;
yet you make what I am, okay to be."

Author's Note

ON MY BUCKET LIST OF life, writing a book has probably been around number 263. That's to say, not very high. Over the years, friends have certainly suggested I write a book, but their suggestions generally had to do with some pretty tough things in my life, things I'd rather not revisit. Having said that, it's because of one of those things that this book is being written at all—my becoming widowed at age fifty-one. And while that's the *reason* this book is being written, that's *not* what it's about. This is a very personal story about dating, relationships, and the search to find love again when I expected to be doing no such thing.

The sudden loss of my wife of twenty years was the most defining moment of my life—it changed everything in unimaginable ways in an instant. And while expressions of sorrow were tremendously heartfelt from all who rushed to support my family and me, true understanding is difficult unless you have experienced the debilitating pain and trauma of great loss. Looking back, however, I realize this was the moment my particular story began.

Being lost in a world that before seemed so familiar, being disoriented and set apart from that world, were emotions I experienced in the days, weeks, months, and years following my wife's death. They were also the same emotions I experienced two years later when I first pushed myself to re-engage with the world and try, scary as it was, to seek and find my future. I had feelings of guilt too, but I knew my wife would have wanted me to find love and happiness again.

As the title implies, the search for my future was a journey—a journey that's, well … complicated. And it's a tough call as to which is crazier—what happened during those three years I was adrift and unsure as I sought to find my future as a man or writing a book about it. You see, *men don't write books like this* because men don't *read* books like this.

But by writing this book I offer a glimpse—a rare firsthand glimpse—into a middle-aged man's life when it comes to women, dating, relationships, sex, and matters of the heart.

In the title of this book, "Venus" is used in the context of the sensational book from 1992, *Men Are from Mars, Women Are from Venus.* A cultural phenomenon of the 1990s, author John Gray, PhD used Mars and Venus as metaphors for the fact that men and women *"think, feel, perceive, react, respond, love, need and appreciate divergently,"* so much so, they may as well be from different planets.

My three-year odyssey brought me into the lives of women whose views, expectations, and norms were so incredibly different and divergent—dare I say bizarre at times—from my own, that I often questioned how it could possibly be. At other times, I made connections that were so amazing and intense, I was transported away from my "normal" life. Upon my return, I felt like an entirely different person. Only in the end—after time and perspective had helped me make sense of it all—was I able to conclude what I had experienced was tantamount to a journey to a totally different world.

For my time on Venus, here are a few of the numbers and facts.

In three years, I met fifty-four women.

Let me say that again: I *met* fifty-four women, not *slept with* fifty-four women.

When I tell the story to women, they assume right off the bat that I slept with them all. In contrast, when I tell the story to men, they hear the word *met* somewhat differently. While a few jump to the same conclusion, a good number think my story is about how I *escaped* from fifty-four women—certainly an interesting contrast and commentary on the current state of affairs between middle-aged women and men.

You will read about twenty-six of the fifty-four women I met on Venus. Names, professions, places, and personal details have been changed to protect their privacy and identities. Emails, texts, and other correspondence included in the book have been edited for brevity and privacy. Conversations are from my memories of them and, while not word-for-word, the essences of the dialogues are accurate.

Given the above, the book might be considered a fictionalized memoir or perhaps a based-on-a-true-story book of fiction. But it's written in first person, what happened *really* happened, and no events are written about that didn't happen. There is no literary filler of other characters other than names given to my various inner voices. In total, it's my story, plain and simple. I'm not clever enough to make this stuff up.

I changed my name, too, both to help protect the privacy of the women but also to make the writing easier. As I discovered early on, writing about oneself is pretty hard. The sharing of one's deepest emotions, confessions, and faults is difficult. Add in embarrassing experiences and extremely intimate subject matter, and well … it was darn near impossible. But with *Turner Grant,* my pseudonym and literary avatar, I was able to put some distance between myself and the experiences I was writing about. That one little thing, much to my surprise, allowed the writing to go forth.

I strive to keep events in strict chronological order so the story unfolds for the reader just as it happened. However, from time to time, events crisscrossed or leaped back-and-forth. I describe the back-and-forth when I am able, but I also group some events or place them out of sequence to provide the best possible reading experience.

The writing of this book was a closely held secret for a number of years. I accidentally let it slip out during a conversation with a close male friend, and he asked if I wouldn't mind sharing some early chapters. Generally assuming a female audience for the book, I was curious to hear his comments. "I chuckled at the tally of women," he offered in an email. Then, from the perspective of a happily married man of over thirty years, he added, "Your world is very different from mine."

To my delight and surprise, his words captured the essence of what my story is all about: *a very different world.*

We all have in our lives certain things we never talk about and never share—that which is the most personal and intimate and rarely makes it past a hushed conversation with a trusted friend, if even that. After all is said and done, and after years of writing and all the work that went into it, I'm not sure how much the big picture on dating, relationships, and sex will change because of this book. But I do know *for sure* that between the covers of this book, one thing *has* changed—a man has spoken about things *we just don't speak about.*

Art Vandelay

"HEY, I'M CURIOUS. DOES BEING an architect help you get women?" said the young thirty-something guy.

"Ah … well … that's not something I've ever thought about," I said, totally surprised and off guard.

Only two weeks after the first anniversary of my wife's passing, a friend gave me the hard push to attend a black-tie dinner. He was on the organizing committee for an event to honor the baseball great Hank Aaron. The anniversary milestone brought on raw and painful emotions, and I said no in several polite ways. But one hook made me consider saying yes.

Way back in high school, I happened to be in Atlanta at the Braves baseball game the night Hank Aaron hit number 715 to break Babe Ruth's home run record. My ticket stub and a nice certificate from the game were framed and had hung in my home all these years. The possibility of getting Hank Aaron's signature on my certificate was a huge pull on my desire to otherwise continue shutting out the world. Eventually, I accepted, but only if he promised I would get Aaron's signature.

When the evening came, he made good on that promise.

During cocktails, I wandered around the fringes of the crowd, biding my time and staying away from everyone as much as possible; I was incredibly uncomfortable. This was my first time out at a social event of any kind since my wife's passing in 2010, and to my surprise, I was mildly panicky.

Maybe I looked sad standing alone, or maybe I stood out with my white dinner jacket in a sea of black tuxedos on that ninety-degree-plus day, I don't know, but a young couple ventured over to introduce themselves.

He was obviously one of those young, eager, Capitol Hill-type staffers who would talk to anyone he thought might be important enough to help him get ahead. We were chatting amicably enough when the question about being an architect and getting women came up. I was embarrassed by the question, partly for myself and partly for his girlfriend or wife who was standing beside him, giving him a nasty look.

"You know, like on Seinfeld. When George Costanza figures out if he pretends to be an architect and calls himself Art Vandelay, women are impressed, and they want to go out with him and even have sex. It seems like some sort of special chick-magnet dust. Is it ever like that?" he asked.

"Oh wow ... I've ... ahem ... never been asked that before," I said, smiling uncomfortably. "I don't ... well ... I know people are often *impressed* when they learn I'm an architect, and they sometimes say they always wanted to be one too, bu-u-t, I'm not sure about the 'chick-magnet dust.'"

"I've *always* wanted to know if what happened to George Costanza was true, and you're the first architect I've ever met I could ask," he said with an eager smile.

"Tell you what ... I'll give it some thought, and we can talk about it after I get a drink refill. How's that?" I said, making a swift exit.

His question, while amusing, made me uncomfortable long after the evening was over. Every ounce of my heart and soul had been about being the husband to my wife, even now, a year after her death. But the encounter foreshadowed more discomfort the following year when I dared to fill out an online form for a dating feature in *The Washington Post.* I had to answer questions about who and what I was from a dating perspective and those were incredibly difficult questions to answer. *Who was I?*

The first and obvious thing to do was to ask those closest to me what they thought I had going for me. They, of course, gave glowing responses, but really ... what else could they say?

Having not been in dating mode for twenty-four years, it was a strange exercise to undertake an inventory of myself, but I began to come up with a dating bio of who I was, where I had been, and what made me unique. Without a doubt, there were pluses and minuses.

In middle school and high school, I recall so vividly that girls seemed to be this unified gender force against us hapless boys, not unlike the fictional alien race in *Star Trek,* the Borg, whose minds are all connected and part of *The Collective.* The intimidation of interacting with anyone from the *Female Collective* was a palm-sweating and nerve-racking experience. It would take a few years into college before the myth of the *Female Collective* crumbled in my mind, and I realized we were all pretty much walking on the same shaky ground when it came to matters of the opposite sex. But the notion of women *collectively* being a group different from us guys lived on.

In high school, I was shy when it came to girls. Among the many things I was self-conscious about was my emerging tall, lanky frame. At six feet tall and 125 pounds, you can imagine the awkward-looking picture.

I was active in music and got good grades but had all of two dates in high school, both with the same freshman girl when I was a junior. I remember driving her to a dance when the conversation began to lag, and it got very quiet in the car.

"Say something," I said.

And she said, "Something."

Really? a voice in my head said.

That's it? said another.

Something?

Seriously?

This inner voice was different from my normal one, and it took several more years before I realized it wasn't just one but actually three voices. They were always in there, trying to coach and guide me when it came to women, but they also argued among themselves to no end. They were a personal posse but with three very different personalities. It took the writing of this book for me to finally give them a name—The Boys.

On my second date with the girl, it was a chilly Saturday night when we got in the car to leave another high school dance.

"Geez—I'm freezing my tits off," she said matter-of-factly out of the blue.

That meant one of two things. But with three voices in my head arguing over what to do, I panicked, ignored her, and took her home.

It wasn't until some three decades later when I ran for Congress and Facebook was an essential part of the campaign that I reconnected with classmates. I learned I *had* come to the attention of numerous girls during those years, but I was rather hapless and clueless at the time. Of course, it's not until a few decades past high school that you finally figure out that's what high school is all about—being hapless and clueless.

In college, I studied architecture, was in a fraternity, and was a top student. My shyness was still there, but self-realization of how limiting it was inspired me to push myself into uncomfortable situations in order to conquer them. I dated one girl for my entire sophomore year, and it was the first of many firsts. It was also the first time I broke up with anyone, and it didn't go well (but do they ever?). I did, however, manage to salvage our friendship the next year, and she even asked me to be her date for her debutante ball that Christmas.

Even though I dated a bit, there were no more serious relationships in college, but I had several female friends I could do things with, and it was quite nice. The experience of having many female friends continued through my adult life, and I later learned it was somewhat unique. My life became much richer and more interesting because of it, although it often raised suspicions in newly beginning relationships.

More than once I heard snarky comments. "You can't be just friends with a woman, you are so-o-o-o naïve."

After undergraduate school and a year of work in Nashville, I moved to Cambridge, Massachusetts, where I immediately found myself in an office romance with a fellow architect. She was a Yale graduate and sat four feet away from me. By day we were colleagues. By night we were boyfriend and girlfriend. It was an odd bit of role-playing but probably not unique. The relationship fell apart when we were both laid off six months later and found ourselves competing for the same jobs. That fall, I began my graduate work at Harvard.

In Harvard Square was a 200-year-old yellow clapboard house that served as an adult education center and offered ballroom dance lessons. For whatever reason, that was something I had always wanted to learn. Maybe I saw it as a way through my shyness; I can't say for sure. But I thought it would be cool to know how to dance, and I was game to learn. Little did I know that one decision would come to define my dating life from then on, and Mr. Shy became Mr. He-Dances-So-Well.

The numerous weddings that occurred in my twenties became my favorite events. Not only did I dance with single women, but I also danced with other guys' girlfriends and even wives because the men couldn't or hated to dance. The women loved it, but the men pouted or looked at me with outright contempt. As a result, I became increasingly comfortable and socially adept with the *Female Collective*.

However, on another level, I was, well … let's just say I was always the wingman, never the leading man. Five years of serious weightlifting after Harvard transformed my lanky body, but I was still plain vanilla in the looks department.

But that architect-thing seemed to change me in the eight years I was in Boston. Being well-educated, living in a fast-paced urban environment, traveling to projects around the country, and being part of the Yuppie decade seemed to make me the prototype of Art Vandelay and women noticed.

One evening at a ballroom dance event, I saw a stunning, tall, graceful woman walk in the door, and I asked her to dance. Nine months later, we moved to Washington, D.C., and eighteen months after that, I walked her down the aisle of the National Cathedral at our wedding. At our reception, we danced the night away at a grand historic mansion on Embassy Row. Five female friends of mine from Boston came down to dance with me and celebrate our wedding; it was something my late wife bragged about often.

So now, after twenty years of marriage and two years of difficult grieving, I assessed the future I was seeking to find and came to terms with my very subjective dating bio.

I was six feet tall, slim, and fit but still very much the wingman, not a leading man.

I drove a minivan and had severely thinning hair, but I didn't dress like a *dad* and was known as a sophisticated guy in general—the architect-thing I suppose.

I was a country kid at heart—an almost-redneck from the South, quite frankly—but I went to Harvard, belonged to one of the most exclusive country clubs, and even ran for Congress. I was well-read, a news junkie, and reasonably well-traveled. In the world of Washington, D.C., I could speak policy wonk and delve into politics, finance, travel, the arts, or anything else on the fly.

I was a stay-at-home dad by choice for eleven years, so I loved being around kids. I was multilingual, fluent in both parent-speak and kid-speak, and could translate accordingly with ease.

I was the most unsophisticated person when it came to food, so I never knew half the things on a menu, but my ace in the hole was a big one: I could lead any woman across any dance floor and make her look good and feel great.

I was initially blind to one characteristic I possessed—I was a one-time-married man who had faithfully carried out his marriage vows. It seemed to put me in rarified air for the general middle-aged female dating population. It gave me the good-guy seal of approval and was often my ticket out of the categories of cheating scumbag, snake-under-a-rock, stalker, and potential serial killer—things I learned all men are assumed to be in the digital-dating world until proven otherwise.

All in all, I summed myself up to be an aspiring catch, knowing full well I was no head-turner in the eyes of most women. I did have my attributes to be sure, but I knew they would only appeal to a certain segment of the general, middle-aged female dating population ... or so I thought.

YEAR ONE

The Rookie

CHAPTER 1

Crossing the Threshold

SPRING WAS FAST APPROACHING, AS were new feelings and emotions.

In the immediate aftermath of my wife's passing two years earlier—the day after Mother's Day—I took five months off from work to "right the ship," as I called it. With tremendous support from family and friends, I brought stability to my home with my twin boys and helped relatives and close friends make sense of the terrible loss. But every minute of every day was a struggle—a struggle with absolutely everything large and small.

I dreaded the end of each day and the nights alone.

But that was soon followed by dreading the beginning of the next.

In the fall after my wife's passing, my son who has a disability left home to begin a new program at a school 450 miles away in Massachusetts. My other son started high school, a time filled with … well, you know what *that's* filled with. So in only a few short months, our bustling household of four had become a very quiet household of two.

At home, I tried to establish new routines that felt somewhat familiar. Having been a stay-at-home dad before re-entering the architectural profession when my kids were eleven years old, I was a pretty adept parent at home, and that helped immensely.

One evening in October, I urged my high school son to come to the kitchen while I washed dishes, noting that it was still family time.

"But Dad, we're not a family anymore. There's nobody here."

I worked four-day weeks from September until the end of December, but when the New Year came, full-time work and home routines that seemed long-lost forced themselves back, and it was painful. The flashbacks of *before* were constant. The worry of how we would grow and evolve as a family always weighed on me. Architectural work—for those who always wanted to be Art Vandelay—is hard, intense, highly technical, deadline-driven, and demanding.

My most constant companion was my mother-in-law, Mary. In her late eighties, she was one incredible woman. She grew up in Washington, D.C., the daughter of a surgeon who, as the stories go, attended to Franklin Roosevelt during his presidency. She had been a Washington debutante in her youth and had scrapbooks full of newspaper clippings from the society pages of the day. She went to private schools and, in her late teens, attended dances every Thursday and Saturday evening at the country club where I now belonged.

In one telling of the many stories of her upbringing in Washington before, during, and after the Depression, she said her family wasn't rich. "We only had a maid, a gardener, and a chauffeur."

I looked at her with astonishment at such a declaration and she tried to soften it up. "Well, we were well-off but not richy-richy, you know."

I rolled my eyes, and she gave me a playful poke with her finger, called me a country bumpkin, laughed, then told me how wonderful I was.

She had married the son of the president of the Hudson Motor Company and moved to the tony enclave of Grosse Pointe, just outside Detroit, to start a family. Soon after the birth of her third child, however, she divorced, and all the affluence and trappings of wealth vanished. After fifty years as a social worker, she knew all the cards in the deck of life—the good ones and the bad. She was an extraordinary woman—kind, well-traveled, smart, artistic, a gourmet, sophisticated but elegantly simple too—and we trusted each other completely. Mary had moved back to Washington a decade before to be the fun-loving 'Grammy' to her young twin grandsons. Given that my own mother lived far away and was in poor health, I readily confided in and sought advice from my mother-in-law during our weekly dinners together.

With two years having passed and spring coming into full bloom in Washington, I was still struggling physically and emotionally. I realized the events of the past were dragging me down like an anchor around my neck, and I desperately needed to cut it loose.

But how? I wondered over and over.

Of course, I had several conversations with family and close friends, and they were all rooting for me to find a future of happiness. Mary's support was especially needed when I finally confided in her one evening, almost in desperation.

"Mary, I have to get the burden of the past off my shoulders and move on. I just have to. I can't carry it with me anymore ... it's crushing me."

Mary responded emphatically and with resolve. "I think you should too. Tell me what you want me to do to help." Then she added with a knowing look, "And perhaps a new woman in your life might be nice? ... Maybe?"

"Thank you," I said. "I needed to hear that from you."

"I'll make dinner here at home for my grandson and me anytime you want so you can go out; just tell me when."

And with that, I didn't hesitate. "How about four weeks from tonight?"

When I ran for the U.S. House of Representatives several years earlier, I had zero political experience but learned along the way as all new candidates do. The passing of my wife happened early in the campaign, so I never became well known in the congressional district at large. However, I did become well known in my small, immediate community, and it was here where I took the first steps into my future.

A local arts organization was having its Spring Gala garden party, a big social event. The well-heeled crowd would be there, as would all the local political folks. Given the latter, it would be natural for me to be there too.

I swear that attending my first public campaign event was easier than walking up to the table to get my nametag that Thursday evening.

I can't believe I'm doing this, I thought. I'd had little success going out to meet single women when I was in my twenties, and I couldn't imagine it going much better now.

But it was a gorgeous spring evening at an historic colonial home with terrific food, a live band playing jazzy party music under a garden-trellis colonnade by the pool, and a who's who of local people, many whom I knew and was looking forward to seeing. But I knew, too, I had to shed them and not get caught up in long conversations so as to have opportunities to meet others.

There were many stunning young women on the arms of great-looking guys, packs of beautiful, young single women looking for packs of great-looking young single guys, and groups of women who I hoped would be of the general middle-aged female dating population.

After grabbing a glass of wine and sharing some comfortable chitchat with friends around the fringes of the party for thirty minutes, it was time to head into the heart of the crowd where food was being served.

Time to dive into the deep water, pal. Let's go! said a voice in my head.

My goal for this nerve-racking evening was modest—meet one woman, have a nice conversation, make her laugh a little, if possible, be happy with a first dip-of-the-toe in the water, then go home.

With incredible luck right out of the gate, standing in front of me in the buffet line was a group of four extremely attractive vivacious women. I was reluctant to approach this *Female Collective,* but the nearest of the four chatted me up without my needing to come up with an opening line. Our ensuing small talk let me know she was there with her three friends, and her husband had been left at home. I jokingly asked if all four of them had ditched their husbands for the evening and learned two had but the other was single.

When I emerged from the buffet scrum, luck was with me again, and I landed near a wall by the pool where they stood with food and drinks in hand. The one I had chatted with briefly in the buffet line made a comment to me about "making it out safely," and I seized upon the friendly overture to join them, all the while being nonchalant—or so I hoped.

Three of the women were dressed in nice cocktail attire, but the fourth wore a faded denim jacket over a dress in a fashion-forward, I-don't-care-how-I-look sort of way. She was quiet at first, but when she joined the conversation, I could tell she was a force among the four. While running through the usual introductory small talk, she said she was in the middle of a nasty divorce and had come to this event every year before and wasn't going to "not come now!"

Her name was Joyce.

She had blonde hair, green eyes, was slender, and very attractive. I could tell by her name-dropping that she was a member of the more elite social circuit of which I was not. She mixed smiles and conversation effortlessly, and the five of us talked for about twenty minutes.

Eventually, her friends drifted away to talk with others, but Joyce stayed, and we talked for the better part of an hour.

Somewhere along the way, we talked about our kids. One of her sons was really into computers, and I shared I had a son who was too. My high schooler had recently built his first computer, and I offered to send some photos that might be of interest to her son. I casually pulled out a business card for her to write her email address on … and she did!

I must say she was a nonstop talker, mostly about herself, but she eventually shifted the conversation to ask questions about me that went much deeper than casual conversation. She asked about my two sons, how they took the death of their mother, how I supported them in the aftermath, and how I handled all the responsibilities now as a single parent. The more we talked, the more interesting Joyce became, and, if I was reading her correctly, she seemed to be interested in me.

She had an MBA from one of the top schools in the U.S., and her soon-to-be-ex was a vice president with one of the local Fortune 500 companies that call this area home. She had given up her career to be the corporate wife and seemingly lived a high-income good life. She had a full-time nanny for the kids who freed her up to be out often with her girlfriends. She had personal everything from trainers to cooks. She noted numerous respite getaways in the U.S. and frequent travel to envious international destinations. She said the reason for her divorce was a cheating husband and left it at that.

After an extraordinary hour of just the two of us in deep conversation, the sun began to set. The twinkling party lights and illuminated pool cast a magical aura onto the evening. I was thinking the night was probably a wrap— mission accomplished and then some—and she seemed ready to catch up with her girlfriends. We said warm goodbyes and parted ways.

At home that evening, Mary was waiting for a debriefing.

"So, how did it go? Did you meet anyone?" she asked with an inquisitive smile.

"I *did* meet someone," I said, "but I think she's way out of my league. She's big bucks, a soon-to-be ex-wife, and accustomed to living the good life I can't offer. Kind of like what you had growing up."

"Oh pooh!" she good-naturedly interjected and put on a fake-frown expression. "Now I don't want to hear that from my wonderful son-in-law! You're quite a catch for any woman."

"Thank you," I said from the bottom of my heart. "I don't know. We'll see if anything comes of it. Even if nothing does, it was wonderful to be out in the world again. Thank you so much for your help."

I got a big, happy hug from Mary and she left for home.

I immediately began to think of my next move. I certainly wanted to see Joyce again, but given my baby-steps and her current situation, it needed to be simple and low-key. Without waiting the usual amount of time to pass to keep from appearing too eager, early the next morning I anxiously sent off an email.

EMAIL SENT: Nice to Meet You Last Night

> Joyce,
>
> Thanks to you and your friends for helping make my evening enjoyable last night. Attached are a few in-progress and finished photos of my son's PC. This was last T'giving when he had time to work on it. Amazing our kids seem to know how to do things like this out of nowhere!
>
> Be in touch – Turner

In the world of dating, as everyone knows, the elapsed time between sending a message and receiving a response—be it a letter, email, text, or whatever—is crucial and revealing. So how fast would she respond and what would she say?

Two hours later, her email response popped up on my phone.

EMAIL RECEIVED: Nice to Meet You Last Night

> Turner,
>
> It was very nice to meet you as well. I really enjoyed talking with you. Thank you so much for sending me the photos of your son's computer. How amazing! And yes, it's so interesting what they can do on their own. I love his keyboard. I am definitely going to show these to my son—I could see him trying to reproduce it right away!
>
> I hope we have the opportunity to chat again. I'm glad you enjoyed your first spring event! —Joyce

This is good, really good, I thought.

Even as I thought about her constantly, I intentionally let the entire next week pass before sending another email on Sunday.

EMAIL SENT: A Casual Dinner Invitation

> Joyce,
>
> My son is going to be up near Philadelphia this coming Friday on a school trip, so I was looking to have a very easy, casual bite to eat at my club after work. Wondered if you might be up for joining me? Very easy, very casual.
>
> All the best, Turner

EMAIL RECEIVED: A Casual Dinner Invitation

> Turner,
>
> I would be happy to have dinner with you this Friday. Let me know what time you were thinking and I'll see if I can get there by then. If not, we can plan for another day. I hope all is well.
>
> Joyce

More emails were exchanged, and to keep it even more relaxed, I told her I would probably play nine holes of golf beforehand. I said I'd meet her at the bar in the informal dining area at six thirty.

She knows I'll be in golf attire on a warm day, so that's very casual and she'll dress the same. It will be more like hanging out together than a date, right? … Yeah, that's it! Or at least that's what I kept telling myself to keep my nervousness in check.

The day finally came with great anticipation and nine holes of golf never went so badly. It wasn't a matter of keeping score of my strokes, it was keeping track of how many extra balls I had left in my golf bag—six at the beginning.

I lost them all …

In the woods …

No pressure.

It's my nature to be on time or early for an appointment, and this was no exception. I finished my round a full hour early, cleaned and polished myself up, then waited for her at the bar.

She came from the opposite direction than I had expected, and when I saw her, she positively took my breath away. Here I was in golf shorts and a polo shirt, and there she was in a goddess dress with layers of sheer fabric floating toward me. The I-don't-care-how-I-look woman was caring big time and had spent a lot of time preparing for this jaw-dropping moment.

Close your mouth and say hello to your date for the evening, I heard a voice say to me.

She looked gorgeous and positively heavenly.

She smiled and came immediately near to say hello and offered an unexpected hug. We ordered drinks and then walked outside. The terrace dining area was immediately adjacent to the spectacularly landscaped golf course, and the spring smells of early evening and perfect weather portended a special night. Over drinks and dinner outside, the conversation never stopped.

A few curious things were notable during the first half of the evening. Even though the conversation was lively and interesting, it was mostly driven by her continuous train of thoughts, almost like a verbal stream of consciousness. She looked at me as she talked, but her eyes frequently fluttered up in a way that made it seem like she was talking more to herself, and I just happened to be there. It was like she simply wanted someone to talk to, and I was *it* for the evening.

But then, just like when we first met, she abruptly and deftly transitioned into questions about me, my family, and my being a widower, offering comments of great understanding and empathy. It was in those particular moments, with her inquiries and insightfulness, that I found her extremely attractive.

After dinner, as dusk was settling in, we walked to a bench overlooking the landscaped golf course. The moonlit star-sparkled sky above enveloped us, transporting us away from the rest of the world.

She shared more about how her life and marriage had come crashing down at the discovery of her husband's affair. He made over a million dollars a year—as I had speculated during our initial meeting—and she led a charmed life she feared would disappear after the divorce. Her house was on the market. A settlement had been crafted, milestone dates had been established for various things, and her husband and his lawyer were making everything difficult. Life seemed precariously uncertain.

We went on to share intimate, close-to-the-heart conversations about loss, life, and more for almost two hours. I kept waiting for her to say it was getting late and she needed to go, but she gave no indication of wanting to leave. The club closed at ten and it was now after eleven; the whole place was quiet, dark, and empty. We had been sitting on the bench alone late into the evening, and I was having a wonderful time.

I told her we should probably see if we could get out because the club closed up tight at night. After walking to her car, we shared a nice, caring hug.

Then, the thought of whether there would be a kiss came to mind.

Why are you even thinking twice about it? I heard a voice say. *This gorgeous woman is in your arms. Kiss her already!*

No kissing, said another. *She needs a man to talk to, not a man to make a move on her. She's in a tough place; life's too hard and complicated for her right now. Besides, you're still coming out of your own emotional woods and … by the way … you're delusional if you think you've got any chance with her.*

Then a third voice jumped in. *If you want to kiss her, then kiss her. Just be nice.*

With so many thoughts and unexpected chatter going on in my mind (it was like being in high school all over again), I hesitated. After thinking it through, I didn't think either of us was ready for such a thing unless she indicated otherwise. It would have been easy to kiss her, but certain things weren't adding up. I had doubts about anything coming of it, and I wasn't ready to get involved with anything complicated.

The lifestyle she had become accustomed to and wanted to continue having required financial means far above mine, and she would figure that out soon enough; I just wasn't her guy, it seemed to me. She was also very into herself, and I was too often a sidebar in our conversations. But when she did shift her attention to me, it felt incredibly good. She reached inside me with ease, and I liked it when she did.

There I was, conflicted to be sure—so no kiss, just a hug to reassure her that she was indeed a very nice and deserving woman.

I had been keeping a cousin in the family, Wendy, in the loop about my impending date, and she eagerly requested a debriefing the next morning on the phone.

Wendy and my late wife were first cousins but more like sisters growing up. She was equally devastated by my wife's death and had been among the most wonderful and supportive of my large, amazing, in-law family. She helped my children and me immensely in the weeks, months, and years after my wife's passing.

Wendy was from a prominent, old-moneyed Washington family—original cliff-dwellers, as they're called in our nation's capital. She, like both my mother-in-law and my wife, was a Washington debutante. She married the handsome and charming son of a South American diplomat, moved there after her wedding, and had four wonderful children. But extramarital affairs over the years destroyed their marriage. Being a Catholic country, divorce wasn't legally possible where she lived, but since she still had her United States citizenship, she researched and arranged to come back for a divorce. She found the state with the quickest divorce timetable, Nevada, and moved there to live for six months. She was granted a divorce from him, but since he wasn't a U.S. citizen, he wasn't given a divorce from her. So in this odd situation, she was divorced from him, but he was still married to her. She could legally remarry, but he couldn't.

Wendy was an outgoing, gregarious, and wise woman made so by her nature and life experiences. In my book, she had a combination of qualities that put her in rarified air. In addition to being caring, supportive, wise, and savvy, she was one cool chick with vibe and verve in spades.

"I have to say, it went pretty well," I said as we talked on the phone, "but it felt so strange being on a date after twenty-four years. Still, it was really great, she's gorgeous, and it was pretty darn nice spending time with her. But I have to say, I think she's trouble with a capital T and it's probably going to be a pretty fast burn."

"Why's she trouble?" Wendy asked.

"Because she's in the middle of a nasty divorce, life for her is crashing down, and I'm trying to get past the crashing down part of my life. Ideally, she's looking for a new million-dollar man to replace the one she's losing, and I'm not that. Plus, she's really into herself," I said.

"Yep, you're right. If she's right in the middle of a divorce *and* she's really into herself, you don't need to get involved with anything like that. You need something much simpler," she said. "What's the fast burn part? Hot romance and sex?"

"No, a fast burn in that it will probably be over in two weeks." Little did I know my prediction was wildly optimistic.

"Would you go out with her again?"

"Absolutely. I'd love to see her again," I said.

"I thought you just said she was 'trouble with a capital T'?"

"I know, but I enjoyed being with her, and she's gorgeous. Is that a bad *guy* thing to say?" I asked with a bit of apology in my voice.

"No, dear. I know *aesthetics* are important to you as an architect," she said gently but mockingly. *You men are all alike* was the unspoken message.

But then she added, "Then ask her out already! This isn't a commitment to marry her, for goodness' sake. If you enjoy being with her, then spend time with her. If it's over quick, then it's over quick. Relax and enjoy the ride. You deserve it, dear."

"Okay," I responded. "Thanks, Wendy."

I emailed Joyce within minutes and said I enjoyed our evening and would like to see her again. Apologizing for the short notice, I proposed getting together tomorrow evening, on Sunday. She wrote back quickly.

EMAIL RECEIVED: A Thought

Turner,

That sounds wonderful and I'd love to go, but I told a friend I would do something with her that night. I must sound quite boring, but I don't have any plans tonight. Perhaps we could do something this evening if you are free.

Joyce

Yes! a voice in my head shouted.

Given our enjoyable long conversations the night before and still wanting to keep it fairly easy and casual, I suggested we go to the National Mall in Washington. We could take a nice long walk to someplace for dinner, then walk back and catch a light show that was scheduled for that evening at the Hirshhorn Museum of Art.

She liked the idea and then offered an invitation for poolside wine and hors d'oeuvres at her house before we went out. My anticipation needle went zooming off the charts!

She wanted me there at five, but always being early, I drove around the neighborhood until a few minutes after.

As I pulled into the long driveway, I saw a large house surrounded by lush landscaping. It was what I had imagined, and I tried to guess what the interior would be like. I felt like a dork pulling up in my minivan—not a cool set of wheels for Art Vandelay.

She came to the door and looked absolutely stunning once again. A big smile came to her face and another embrace followed. As I walked inside, I was jolted by the near-empty house. *What the heck happened to all the furniture?*

She explained things were going in and out as negotiations with her soon-to-be-ex progressed, but it seemed more like everything was just going out. We walked through all the rooms on the main level, then out to an empty screened porch. The deck overlooking the pool was unfurnished and leaves were strewn about. This was a large property, one that required weekly care. It was probably happening only once a month now at best. The pool looked great, however, and there were two chairs and a small table with wine, glasses, cheese, and pate carefully laid out.

She said she spent all afternoon trying to find just the right wine and hors d'oeuvres for us to eat. I was overwhelmed by how much thought and preparation she had put into our second date.

She's putting on her A-game, so be ready, said a voice in my head. *This has "a night to remember" written all over it!*

I tried to act cool and nonchalant, but I felt hopelessly awkward and nervous being there alone with her.

Soon enough we were on our way to the National Mall in Washington on yet another exquisite, late-spring evening. She was really into art and design, and the light show on the exterior stone walls of the Hirshhorn Museum would be great. We parked near the museum and proceeded to stroll across the Mall to the edge of downtown to find a place for dinner.

Walking across the middle of the great lawn, I stared at the Capitol building. I had told her the story of my run for Congress, and she knew how important it was. At that moment, she grabbed my hand, and my heart skipped a beat.

Things had moved to another level, and it felt wonderful as we walked hand in hand.

Dinner was so much nicer than the evening before. Sitting next to each other at the corner of the table instead of across from each other was an intimate arrangement she chose. She often leaned in so close when talking I could feel her breath and smell a hint of her perfume. When she gently laid her hand on my arm, sparks flew and my heart raced. Pauses in our conversation made the silence more desirable than words because she would look into my eyes and fix her gaze.

We finished our wonderful time together at dinner and walked back across the Mall to the museum. The air was cooler with the sun going down, so she walked close as we held hands, touching the side of my body with hers. As we came to the same point in front of the beautifully lit Capitol dome, I became quiet as I stared at it.

"Don't worry," she said. "I know you'll get there someday. I just know you will. You're strong and passionate. And you have to admit, I would be great arm candy for you on the campaign trail."

And with those words, I paused …

"You would indeed. You're such a beautiful woman, Joyce. How lucky would I be?" I told her, squeezing her hand and pulling her even closer.

Then, just like the night before when I contemplated kissing her, the same chorus of voices erupted in my head.

Can you believe she just said that? Is this some sort of proposal? Where is she going with this? This is nuts! one voice said.

Then another jumped in. *This is not right! This is trouble, pal, that capital-T thing! You were right, I'm telling you! Are you L-I-S-T-E-N-I-N-G, T-U-R-N-E-R?!*

Run! was the final word from inside my head.

Wow! Those voices. I haven't heard from these guys in a LONG time, I thought.

Lost and pretty much forgotten, they were clearly back. It was The Boys, and just in time. But where had they been for so long?

Oh … yeah, I haven't been on a date in twenty-four years, I reminded myself.

Our inner voices—we all have them. How could we live without them? For me, there were three, and at times like these, they came together to make up my posse. But their voices seemed a little different now—a little wiser perhaps.

First, there's Darrell, the crazy, fun-loving, kind-of-goofy redneck who talks big but turns tail at the slightest sign of trouble. He rarely looks before he leaps. His two most-used phrases are *Let's do it!* and *Oh shit!* Remember the goofball Jethro from the old TV show *The Beverly Hillbillies*? That's him.

Then there's Charles. He's my version of Art Vandelay. He fancies himself as Mr. Urbane, erudite, sophisticated, and above everyone else. Heck, he's a friggin' snob most of the time, and he takes risks because he thinks he can do A-N-Y-T-H-I-N-G. But here's the thing—without him and the risks he's pushed me to take over the years, I wouldn't be where I am today.

Lastly, there's Little Turner. He's the original, shy, Southern country boy, but now a wise middle-aged man given all the hard knocks and experiences of life. More often than not, he was content to remain silent and let Darrell and Charles dominate conversations, but when he spoke ("still waters run deep," so the saying goes), the other two would shut up and listen.

As I walked with this beauty in front of the illuminated Capitol dome, my heart continued skipping beats as The Boys tried to knock some sense into my head. My recollection of the conversation immediately after is a bit fuzzy with The Boys yelling at the top of their lungs.

It turned out the light show wasn't scheduled for that night after all. As I apologized for blowing that part of the evening, she began some good-natured ribbing and flirting.

"I bet you did that on purpose just so you could have me alone here in the dark, didn't you?" she said.

She mockingly pulled away but held tight to my hand. I pulled her back and gave her a hug and an ever-so-slight kiss on her cheek.

As we pulled into her driveway around midnight, I turned off the engine, and the "are-you-going-to-get-invited-in" thought crossed my mind.

There was no pause in her voice. "Would you like to come in for some tea or something for a few minutes?"

We walked inside, and she closed the door behind us. She immediately turned and kissed me.

I think it was more drama-filled than my actual first kiss when I was sixteen years old. It was wonderful.

Two more long kisses followed, along with a closer embrace. Our hands began moving about, caressing each other's bodies. Completely in the moment, I whispered what I was feeling and thinking.

"That's my first kiss, Joyce … it was wonderful."

And with those words, she stopped.

"Oh, that's a lot of pressure to put on me!" she said, pulling away. "I'm not sure about this."

"I'm so sorry! I shouldn't have said it," I said quickly and awkwardly, trying to get the moment back.

"No, no, that's okay, but it's a lot of pressure," she repeated. "I'm not good with pressure."

Then the nails to the coffin came hammering in fast and hard. "I mean, you're such a *nice guy*, you really are. But I should probably be meeting other men too. It's all too much pressure."

Flameout … and doww-nn he goes! snickered Darrell.

We kissed again, and I could sense her wanting to … then not wanting to anymore.

"I really should go to sleep. It's late," she said.

One more kiss on her part, but it wasn't a goodnight kiss—it was a *goodbye* kiss.

We talked on the phone the next day, and it was nice enough, but I said something that triggered the same response from her again.

"Careful, remember … no pressure!"

What the hell? said Charles. *It's like she's accusing us of doing something terrible. 'She' was the one flirting last night and who kissed 'us,' but now we're the one putting on too much 'pressure?' That's really lousy.*

We talked about my stopping over the next weekend on Sunday evening, but she would let me know the time when it was nearer.

As you can guess, my texts and emails the next week were no longer answered quickly. Sunday came, and by mid-afternoon, there had been no text message from Joyce for three days.

Don't you dare send her a text! The ball's in her court. Stop being such a lovestruck wuss, The Boys said, bashing away at my longing heart.

Finally, at eight in the evening, I sent a text and she responded immediately.

> **ME:** Are you still up for getting together tonight?

> **JOYCE:** Oh sorry. Out with my girlfriend. Another time, okay?

And that was it; it was over.

Wendy and I had a long debriefing soon after. She acknowledged my premonition skills for knowing how this would go.

"Impressive and insightful," she offered, "for a man."

But then she said the most important words of all. "That's okay, dear, you did well. You've crossed the threshold, and that's all that matters. The future is yours."

CHAPTER 2

All the World's a Stage and So Was This Date

"DAD ... HOW DO YOU get a girlfriend?"

It was mid-June and two weeks after my last date with Joyce. Matters of the heart were now back in my life with all the aspirations, longings, cross-currents, frustrations, and disappointments that come with them.

So why am I interested in doing this again exactly? I asked myself.

Because you are, was the answer from The Boys.

My desire for a strong, personal, romantic connection had been rekindled simply by the passage of time. And while time hadn't healed all wounds, it had healed my heart enough to where I was open to, and interested in, having a person in my life, and that was huge. It was also apparently on the mind of my sophomore son for the first time in his life.

Sitting across from each other at the dinner table, I knew he hadn't come to this moment lightly. He had inherited my shyness as a kid, plus he was in full teenager-mode now. He was typically silent unless I could pry out a reluctant "yeah, no, maybe" or an "I dunno" from him.

"How do you get a girlfriend?" I repeated.

"Yeah."

"Is there someone in particular you have in mind?"

"No, just curious."

My initial thought was that he was feeling like he needed one in the same way he *needed* certain things in high school—the right clothes, an iPhone, a car … and now a girlfriend. So for the moment, I went from being the rather hapless, middle-aged, second-time-around-dating dad to the sage girlfriend-expert for my son.

"The first thing to do is be involved in activities at school so you can meet and interact with lots of girls. You're doing that pretty well already," I said. "Next, you're going to have to talk to them, which I know can be pretty hard. That's why doing things you like anyway will make talking to them feel more natural and put less pressure on you. From there, you'll start to make friends with a few girls, and at some point, you'll find that you're attracted to one or more. You'll know soon enough if they're interested in you and things will just go from there. But the scary part is you have to put yourself out there in ways that can be uncomfortable. It's not easy to do that, I know—believe me, I know."

I then told him about how girls can seem like they're all part of a single impenetrable group of solidarity—the *Female Collective,* like the Borg in *Star Trek.*

"Yeah, that's what it seems like," he confessed.

"Even though it may feel that way to you now, they're not a unified group. In fact, it's just the opposite," I said. "They can be pretty mean to each other, and you'll want to stay out of the way of that stuff as much as you can."

"Oh yeah, I've seen that. They're really weird sometimes."

So we did two things together to increase his female understanding and acquisition skills.

First, we watched the movie *Mean Girls.* It was a movie about high school girls, social cliques, and how rough-and-tumble it is for girls. It's a movie, of course, but it realistically showed that girls are *not* a *collective* and in it together against the boys. It's every girl for herself.

The other thing we did was watch several episodes of the TV show *The Bachelor,* which I had already been hooked on for a while. This was a real eye-opener for him. He was appropriately appalled at all the off-the-wall things the women did to try and get the guy. He couldn't believe how grown-up women acted, schemed, and backstabbed each other. Conversely, when we later watched *The Bachelorette,* he couldn't believe what doofuses the guys became in trying to get the girl. He vowed he would never do that.

I knew how far both men and women would go to find love and, unbeknownst to me, I was about to do some pretty off-the-wall things myself.

But given that men and women coupling is a basic primordial human need and a requirement for life, we are wired to do whatever it takes, I suppose.

For months we laughed and screamed at the TV on Monday nights. It turned out to be a great father-son activity. But it also made me do some serious thinking too. As ridiculous as it was, *The Bachelor* was another way of doing what I was now trying to do—make a connection and possibly more. My mind began to come around to the idea that any opportunity to meet someone of the general middle-aged female dating population was worth grabbing.

Enter *The Washington Post*.

Every weekend for years, I read *The Washington Post Sunday Magazine* and its *Date Lab* feature. In a small, two-page spread, readers got to be voyeuristic flies-on-the-wall as two people were matched by the *Post* and went on a blind date on the magazine's dime. Anyone with even the slightest bit of sanity would never consider doing it.

Mostly it was singles in their mid-twenties to early-thirties, but now and then it was an older couple. It was justifiably terrifying but also an intriguing idea. Since I was coming around to being in the opportunity-seeking business, I thought, *why not?*

You know when you're in a certain frame of mind and you see only the upside to something, to the point of being euphorically positive that it's the right thing to do and that *nothing* could go wrong? Well … that's where my head was as I filled out the online application.

There were two things I was specific about when filling it out.

First, I wanted a person who understood what it meant to have a significant loss in their life. It wasn't that they had to be widowed, but being able to grasp the magnitude of a significant loss was important. I thought a person with that insight would understand me better, understand the big picture of life in the way I was beginning to, and they might be less inclined to treat me the way Joyce had.

The other was that I wanted someone my age or a year or two younger. My late wife was ten years older—a May-December romance—so I knew age was irrelevant in love and long-term commitment. It wasn't that I was ruling out a relationship with an older woman, but to be comfortable in this *very* uncomfortable dating scenario, I preferred to keep age out of the equation.

With the understanding that this could be a significant moment, I hit the send button, and off it went. A day later, I received an email from *Date Lab* saying they would be in touch if they had a match in the next year.

For the rest of the summer, I thought about ways to get out and about, both to do things I enjoyed and to find new ways to meet people. I participated in a mixed-doubles tennis night sponsored by a local club that led to a date of sorts. I say *of sorts* because I asked a woman I met to join me one weekend on the golf range at my club, but the reality was I had little interest in her. I did it because there was such a strong feeling inside of needing to do *something*, but I ended up forcing something I shouldn't have. I felt pretty crummy about it afterward, especially when she showed up wearing what was obviously new golf attire from head to toe for the *date*.

Down, boy! Be patient, The Boys said. *It's not a race, and you don't want to end up being a jerk, in a lousy situation, or both.*

Then, in the waning days of summer in late August, I received a phone call at the office. "Hi. Is this Turner Grant?" the woman inquired.

"Yes, it is," I said in the hesitant voice I usually used when a total stranger called and knew my name.

"Hi, Turner. This is Joanne with *Date Lab* at *The Washington Post*. I don't know if you remember, but you applied to *Date Lab* a few months ago."

"Yes, I remember."

"Great! Then I wanted to find out if you're still interested in being matched with someone and going out. If you are, would you be available to go next week?"

"Ahem … yes, I'm still interested … but no, I can't do it next week. How about in two weeks?"

"Oh, okay. Let me check with the other party and see what she says. I'll get back to you," *The Post* reporter said.

Stunned momentarily, I did the next logical thing—I texted Abby on the other side of the office.

ME: Need you!

ABBY: Coming!

Abby was a work colleague who, over the course of the last couple of years, had become a close friend and confidante. When I finally returned to work five months after the passing of my wife, she checked on me every day. "How are you doing? How was last night? How was the weekend?"

Abby was ten years younger, married, and we shared similar attitudes and outlooks on many things in life. You know that kind of person; they just get it, and they get you. Years later, someone remarked upon meeting her for the first time, "She's like the little sister you never had, and you the big brother she never had."

It was true, and we considered each other best friends, foxhole friends—the person you want around and can lean on when times are hardest, but also the person you've gotta have there when a celebration is in order. Through her divorce shortly after my loss, I did my best to return the support, understanding, and caring she had provided me during my darkest days. As she began to venture out into the dating world, we shared stories, commiserated, and, on occasion, defended our respective genders when the other had an outrageous experience on a date. She was the first to declare she was going to write a book about her dating experiences and quickly arrived at the title *Kissing the Frog!* I later admitted, after one horrendous and truly unbelievable experience she shared, that I could no longer defend the male gender; we were indeed despicable scumbags.

Abby now popped up around the corner with a Cheshire-cat grin on her face.

"What's up?" she asked with inquisitive eyes. Requests like this from each other were never without a good reason.

Abby knew I applied for *Date Lab* back in June, but like me, when nothing happened, she pretty much forgot about it. When I told her about the phone call, she lit up.

"Oh my god, are you serious?! Are you going to do it?"

"Yeah, I think I am. Why not?"

"Well, I can think of a few good reasons why not, but okay," she said sarcastically.

"Wow, you gave me up pretty quickly there," I said, a bit surprised.

"What do you want me to say? I would never do it, but you're the risk-taker. Do it if you want … then come hide out at my house when it's published!" she said, laughing. "But I want to know all the details *before* it's published and you go into hiding."

"Oh, you will," I said, laughing. "You will."

Joanne from *Date Lab* called back a few days later to say we were good to go two weeks from Monday. They would call beforehand with the details, but I wanted to know a little more—a lot more—about what I was getting into.

"Can you tell me more about how this works now so I have an idea of what's coming?"

"Oh sur-r-r-re," she replied. "We'll call you either at the end of the week before or the morning of your Monday evening date—they're always on Mondays—and give you the details, including her first name. We'll tell you the restaurant and the time, which is usually six thirty. When you arrive, you'll go to the host or maître d' and tell them you're with *The Washington Post,* and they'll make introductions. We give you a credit of one hundred and twenty-five dollars at the restaurant, so you won't have anything to pay at the end unless you go over, then that's on the two of you.

"We also drop off a disposable camera, and you can't finish the date without at least six pictures of the two of you together. The next day, we'll call both of you to get your thoughts and details about the date. As the story is written for publication about two weeks later, a reporter may call back to ask follow-up questions. Any desire you have to see the other person again is totally up to the two of you, but we'll ask and report in the story if you've communicated since the date and if you have any plans to see each other again. You'll also be asked to rate the date on a scale of one to five."

"So this is a blind date that a half-million or so readers will see … with at least one picture?" I said, like I didn't already know.

"Yep, that's the deal! You still okay with this?" she asked.

"Yep, I'm good with it."

The Boys, however, couldn't hold back any longer. *And why exactly are we "good with this?" It's got "we're going to regret this" written all over it.*

It was a fair question, one I wondered about too.

If I were being honest with myself, I felt a palpable need to push forward. I didn't know if it was my trying to break away from the past, or, if it was because I'd experienced a few nice but fleeting moments of romance with Joyce and I wanted more. Perhaps it was a bit of both. Either way, I was determined to do this.

Later that week, I had dinner with Mary. She knew I had applied for *Date Lab* back in June but had forgotten about it too. I went over all the details again, along with the new information I learned.

"Gee, Turner, isn't there an easier way to do this?" she asked.

"I'm sure there is, but I'm game. Why not?"

"You're amazing, Turner, and a little crazy too. But I think you're wonderful. You just remember that," she said kindly.

She offered to come over and make dinner for my son that Monday evening, then hang around until I got home to hear details of the date. She was thoroughly enjoying seeing me get back out in the world, and she liked the idea of being in on a secret that would later appear in the pages of *The Washington Post*.

****

The end of the week before the Monday date came, and I didn't hear from *Date Lab*. I was annoyed and a little concerned. Since I didn't know where I would be meeting her for dinner, I wasn't sure how to dress. Our office tended to be casual dress for daily-office wear unless you were meeting a client, so I would make it a *client day* with a coat and tie and hope I wouldn't get too many questions about who I was meeting with.

I followed my usual routine of arriving at the office early on Monday, but I was on pins and needles waiting for the phone call from *Date Lab*. The morning seemed to drag on forever, but finally Joanne called.

"Hi Turner. Your date for the evening is named Rachel and she's really looking forward to meeting you. We made dinner reservations for the two of you at six thirty at Filomena near your office in Georgetown. Remember, they'll make introductions when you arrive, and I'll be calling you tomorrow morning to find out how the date went. Have a great evening!"

Rachel ... I like her name, I thought after nervously hanging up the phone.

A busy work schedule helped keep the jitters in check, even as Abby came over several times during the day to throw in some good-natured ribbing. As late afternoon eased into early evening, coworkers drifted out, and I went to the men's room to freshen up and take one final look in the mirror.

Okay, Turner. Screw this up and all of Washington will know, The Boys lectured. *We'll have to go into hiding for a year. So, whatever you do, whether you like her or not, don't do or say anything stupid!*

I made my way down the back stair, out to the alley behind our building, and onto Wisconsin Avenue where I crossed the street to the restaurant.

The entrance descended one level to the main dining room, which had windows overlooking the C&O Canal. As I arrived at the maître d' stand, I quickly scanned the dimly-lit space.

Standing off to one side was a well-dressed woman. Her attention seemed more focused on the dining room than looking like she was waiting for a date to arrive. Another woman stood a few feet away, but she was younger than I imagined my date would be, even though she was nervously looking around for someone. With apparently no one there to meet me, I approached the host's stand.

"Hi, I'm Turner Grant, and I'm with *The Washington Post.*"

The host looked confused, then another fellow approached and they quietly exchanged urgent remarks in Italian. They both looked back and forth at me with worried looks on their faces, seemingly not knowing what to do.

As I stood there a bit annoyed, a woman approached from behind. "Hi. Are you Turner?"

I quickly turned around and said, "Yes … Rachel?"

She was the woman focused on the dining room a minute ago.

"Yes, so nice to meet you. I don't know what they're talking about there, but it seemed like someone needed to take charge. I hope that was okay."

"Perfect," I told her as she smiled warmly.

She was slender, average height, nice-looking, very well-dressed, and outgoing; I was relieved. *This is going to be a very nice evening,* I immediately thought …

… but nothing more, Darrell jumped in to add. *No sparks. No attraction. She's a dud.*

Then an argument broke out.

Hey, hey, hey … you can't judge so frickin' fast! You have no idea how this will go until you get to know her! snapped Charles. *She looks nice!*

But you know if it's there or not, and it's not! Darrell shot back.

And then Wendy's voice came in from nowhere to give her two cents. *"Yes, dear ... but you're not saying you'll marry her. Just have dinner with her and ENJOY IT FOR CRISSAKES!"*

To some degree, everyone was right. While there was no instant attraction, I also knew the *Date Lab* setup was a different ballgame altogether, and I needed to let it play out.

Little Turner had the final word and calmed everyone down: *Just enjoy the evening.*

A man from the restaurant approached and graciously introduced himself as the manager. "Oh, I see you've met. I'm sorry not to have introduced you. Please accept my apologies," he said with a warm smile and gracious manner.

"Welcome, welcome, welcome. We are so excited to have you here! My name is Anton, but everyone here calls me Soprano. If you would please, allow me to take you to your table."

Soprano led us through the mostly occupied main dining area to a private dining room. It had a long table that could have easily seated twelve but was set for two. It was separated from the rest of the restaurant with wrought-iron screens, but you could peek in and out through the iron latticework. It felt like a gracious dining room in someone's very Italian home, and Soprano explained that was exactly the ambiance they had designed it for.

After we were seated, he went on to explain that many famous people had sat right where we were sitting: Presidents Obama, both Bushes, and Clinton; Paul Newman, Sylvester Stallone, and so on.

"We had an owner and management meeting to discuss what we should do for you since we've never hosted a *Washington Post* event. We decided we would treat you like family and ensure, to the best of our abilities, to give you a memorable evening with us. Please order anything you want from the menu, but also please allow us to treat you to a medley of specially prepared tasting dishes. I know *The Post* has given you a limit of one hundred and twenty-five dollars, but we don't want anything to take away from a marvelous evening, so anything above that is on us. Please, please, simply enjoy the evening and stay with us as long as you like."

As he stepped away to give us our first moments together alone, Rachel and I looked at each other with delight and surprise.

"Wow! How lucky are we?" I said.

Rachel was easy to talk to, and we immediately put each other at ease, but I couldn't shake the fact that anything I said or did might appear in the published story for friends, family, and strangers to see. Ever since my run for Congress, I had been wary of the press, and even in this venue, that feeling crept uncomfortably into the evening. I mostly spent dinner moving from one guarded moment to the next, unable to relax and simply enjoy her company.

We asked each other the usual first-date questions.

"What do you do?"

"Where do you work?"

"Where do you live?"

"Where are you from?" and so on.

The *Date Lab* matchmakers had gotten the main things right. She was two years younger and widowed in her first marriage. We shared the basic details of our losses, and it was incredibly hard to not feel deep emotions as she shared her story, even though it had been twenty years earlier. She was several years divorced from her second husband, a sordid tale of bad behavior and love turned to anger.

We ordered appetizers, main courses, and a bottle of sparkling wine to start, but as soon as the menus were taken away, tasting plates of delicious food began to arrive. Several different bottles of wine "specially selected for you" came out during dinner as well. We both realized we were going to get inundated with food and wine, and we might be embarrassed by how much we *couldn't* eat, in addition to perhaps needing to be carted out at the end of the evening. Doggie bags, or large doggie boxes, might be needed, along with taxis for each of us to get home.

Even though the evening was young, Soprano had taken up the *Date Lab* charge to take pictures of us with the disposable camera. From my vantage point at the head of the table, I had already seen him twice through the iron trellis, snapping pictures of us like paparazzi lurking behind shrubs; he was now back again.

We were about to enjoy the first of several appetizers: arancini. Neither of us had had them before, and they looked like small fried hockey pucks. As I picked up my fork to cut a piece off mine, she picked up hers with her hand in an unsure way to take a bite. If this were a breakfast hash brown at a fast-food restaurant, that would have been fine, but since we were in a white tablecloth restaurant, she looked odd and awkward holding a small fried hockey puck in her hand. As Soprano was about to take what I thought would be an unflattering photo, I suggested a fork might be a good way to approach it. My gallant intentions were taken as the opposite, I would later find out.

The evening proceeded along nicely for almost two and a half hours, even as my apprehension kept me on guard. We shared a lot in common: being in creative fields, having teenage children, and more. Being in a private dining room was quite special, and everything was marvelously done by Soprano and the staff. When dessert came, we shared a gelato, and Soprano plied us with several aperitifs.

We were ready to end the dinner but not the evening, so I suggested we go for a walk along the waterfront. She asked a few questions about architecture, and I happily shared some thoughts. Since it was late on Monday night, we had the riverside park mostly to ourselves. It was a pleasant but too short of a moment during our time together.

I walked Rachel to her car, told her how much I enjoyed the evening, and said it would be nice to see her again; she said the same. We exchanged numbers, and I offered her a hug and a kiss, which she readily accepted and reciprocated.

I sent a short text to her that night and an email early the next morning, thanking her for a very enjoyable evening.

EMAIL SENT: Thank You for a Great Evening

Rachel,

I sent you a text message when I got home last night. Not sure if you received it, but I wanted to thank you for a fabulous evening and wanted to know that you got home okay. I can't imagine a better time. Wasn't that great with the VIP treatment they gave us?

As I mentioned to you last night, I have a busy week of work and travel, Amherst tomorrow then back up to Boston for the weekend with my son. I'm not sure how we top that first date, but we'll have to think of something.

I hope the rest of your week goes well.

Be in touch,

Turner

I heard nothing from her that morning and became increasingly annoyed at the lack of any response to my text or email.

A reporter called from *Date Lab,* and we talked about the date. I recounted the flubbed introduction by the maître d' and my first impressions of realizing the evening was going to be nice but that I felt no real sparks when we first met. I walked her through our conversations, the way the restaurant gave us the VIP treatment, the walk along the river afterward, the exchange of numbers, and the brief kiss. Each *Date Lab* story made a point of noting whether a kiss occurred at the end of the date.

Then she asked the two final questions each story ended with: How would you rate the date on a scale of one to five, and have you contacted each other about going out again?

I wanted to be positive, so I gave her a four. I then told the reporter I had texted Rachel last night and sent an email early this morning but hadn't heard back. Thinking out loud as we talked, I surmised that a lack of response probably told me all I needed to know about how it went for Rachel, but that was okay. The reporter said she would be talking to her next and would be happy to pass along her positive or negative impressions of the evening.

Truthfully, seeing her again would have been fine, and not seeing her again would have been fine too. Even though there was no apparent chemistry during our date, I thought the circumstances put too much pressure on me to relax and fully enjoy her company. Seeing her again outside of *The Washington Post's* watchful eye could offer a chance to get to know Rachel in a more comfortable atmosphere and explore any possibilities. Or perhaps, it would be me pushing something that wasn't there for the sake of moving forward. It was hard to know. But the whole experience was one that I did, enjoyed, and got through.

Another foot in front of the other and moving forward, I thought, patting myself on the back.

Near the end of the workday, I finally received an email from Rachel, but surprisingly, it didn't say much.

"Wow! Lukewarm at best," Abby said after reading it. "Given your enthusiastic email to her and the evening you described, that's surprising. Ready to hide in my house until all this blows over?" Abby snickered and grinned.

"Yeah, I think maybe I am."

The following Monday, the reporter from *Date Lab* called to ask some follow-ups. She asked several questions about when I had lost my wife, if I had gone out on any dates since it happened, and a few other questions. When I finally cut to the chase and asked what she was after, she shared Rachel's comments that I seemed to be reserved and holding back, and possibly that it was still too soon and not totally comfortable for me to be out with another woman. I told her it was true that I had only been on a few dates, but my reserve was more about trying not to make unflattering quotable quotes that would end up in the story. I reiterated that I thought she was a nice woman, but there were no real sparks when we met, so perhaps I unconsciously tried to keep expectations down.

"So you have no interest in seeing her again?" the reporter asked.

"Oh, just the opposite," I replied. "It'd be great to get together again and not be under the watchful eye of *The Washington Post*, but based on her tepid email response last week, I'm not getting the sense she's interested."

"Well, actually, she'd like to see you again," the reporter said.

"She told you that?" I responded with surprise.

"Yes."

"Oh, wow, that would be great. Then I'll certainly get back in touch with her. Thanks."

Shortly after the call, I emailed Rachel.

EMAIL SENT: Have You Met Your Deadline?

Hi Rachel,

How did (is?) the deadline crunch go (ing)?

Turner

Five days passed before she bothered to respond.

EMAIL RECEIVED: Have You Met Your Deadline?

> Turner,
>
> How has your week been? I finally got my magazine to print (big sigh of relief) and now have to confront all the other things on my desk. I know you have been very busy as well. How did your trips go?
>
> Let me know if you would like to get together next week for dinner.
>
> Rachel

I responded, telling her about my week and noting that I would love to get together for dinner without feeling like the press was watching, and apologized for being rather reserved on our blind date. I wrote that I couldn't make a weekday evening the next week, but would she be free Saturday night?

I never heard back from her again.

You know the deal—even if you don't care about seeing someone again, you don't necessarily want to be the one on the receiving end of silence or a no.

I told Abby what happened and showed her the email exchanges, and she offered her support as she had so many times before.

"Seriously, I don't know what her problem is. I guess we'll just have to keep our fingers crossed that the story isn't so bad when it comes out on Sunday."

By then, I had started corresponding with a woman on an online dating site. We had our first date the Friday night before the story was published. When we met and began to exchange dating stories, I confessed that I had just done *Date Lab*.

"Nooooo! … you didn't! I could never do that! You're brave, really brave. When does the story come out?" she asked.

"Sunday," I said.

"Nooooo! Oh my god! Is it going to be okay?" she anxiously asked with a big smile.

"I don't know, it could go either way. I wish I could hide until getting an 'all clear' sign from someone."

"I'll look at it and let you know. I usually get the *Sunday Post Magazine* delivered with my Saturday morning paper. I'll send you an email with either an 'all clear' or 'don't come out,'" she said, happy to be in on it.

"That would be awesome!" I replied.

Early the next morning, before I went out to get my Saturday paper with the same *Sunday Magazine,* I got an "all good, you're okay" email from her. Relieved, I got my paper and opened it.

As I read, I wasn't particularly thrilled. It wasn't bad, but it wasn't good either.

In the introductory summaries for each of us, *Date Lab* noted that I was "looking for a younger woman," without the qualifier "for this date." I immediately regretted my comment about when I first saw Rachel, saying "there were no sparks," because the reporter used that as my general impression of her.

"U-u-u-gh!"

Then Rachel was quoted as saying that perhaps "we talked a bit too much about the loss of our spouses."

Continuing with Rachel's recounting of the date, the reporter wrote about the arancini appetizer moment and my comment suggesting she use a fork instead of her hands. She had clearly taken offense and was quoted in the article as concluding, "He was probably conservative."

Well that's lousy, offered an indignant Charles.

On a positive note, Rachel described our walk after dinner on the Georgetown waterfront and our conversation about architecture as being really enjoyable.

The one photo in the story was what I feared—a lousy photograph that only a disposable film camera could produce. It was a picture taken by Soprano when Rachel and I had nuzzled our chairs close together and put our arms around each other. That was a nice moment in the evening, but it was a moment lost in the bad photo.

Rachel gave me and the date a three-point score out of five, and the story made the date seem much less enjoyable than it was. Though I was fairly disappointed in how it played out in print, I was still glad to have done it.

The last thing to deal with now was: Who would see the story?

Surely my friends and others my age wouldn't have the time or interest to read a feature that's mostly about twenty- and thirty-somethings on blind dates, but that was wishful thinking.

I went to the office the next day to put in some overtime; it was empty except for one older senior architect who was generally quiet and kept to himself. He and I had both been there working for a few hours when he went around the corner to leave.

Still at my desk and unable to see him, he said from the other side of the wall, "I'll give you one thing; you've got a lot of guts."

A few people emailed me over the next few days and thought it was both great and brave. The neighbors teased me a bit, but it was all good. One or two others thought it was a continuation of my campaign for Congress and I was just seeking publicity.

A few more slightly embarrassing moments occurred at the meetings of organizations I belonged to. At one there were about forty people in the room and the meeting was about to begin as I walked in. One of the women said very loudly, "Turner-rr! ... Saw you in the *Sunday Po-o-ost*. Ni-i-c-c-ce!"

The room erupted into murmurs, chuckles, and toothy grins all around.

Unbeknownst to me, there were online *Date Lab* groupies, mostly middle-aged and older women. They eviscerated me in their online discussions. My comment about wanting a younger woman brought out the heavy guns, and I was verbally obliterated.

One woman did a little online research and came to my defense. "I read his wife's obituary, and she was ten years older than him, so give the man a break. Maybe he just wants a woman his age or younger to be able to enjoy more of life with."

Over the next three months, the *Date Lab* story was a fifteen-minutes-of-fame kind of thing, one I mostly tried to ignore. But to a broader circle of friends and acquaintances who had been unaware of how I was doing, it was a huge neon sign: after over two years of darkness, I had found my way back into the light of life.

CHAPTER 3

53 WWM

IN THE 1980S, PERSONAL DATING ads proliferated across the country. The magazine Bostonian and the tabloid The Phoenix were prime-print real estate for the personals in the Boston/Cambridge area where I lived. If you were in your twenties like I was, single and dating, you read them out of voyeuristic curiosity and in the off chance someone's ad might catch your eye. For most of us, the chances of summoning up the courage to respond were slim.

Nonetheless, I did respond once and met an "entrepreneurial-minded 26 SWF" for a drink at The Parker House Hotel. She turned out to be a meek, painfully shy legal secretary, and it was like trying to carry on a conversation with a closed book. I never mentioned a word about it to anyone, and the experience killed any interest in doing that sort of thing again. I did, however, continue to read the personal ads when they came out. How could you not?

A new language of acronyms and urban slang was created by these short ads since you were charged by the number of printed characters. Simple ones like the above-mentioned SWF (single white female) and SWM (single white male) were fairly easy to understand, but everything became an acronym. Sometimes office conversations revolved around deciphering the more baffling ones. Here are a few:

DWF – divorced white female
SBM – single Black male
SBF – single Black female
SJF – single Jewish female

MWM – married white male (and usually noted, "seeks mutually beneficial relationship")

BBW – big beautiful woman (with no male acronym equivalent)

BBBW – big Black beautiful woman

SWFSM – single white female into sadism and masochism

HWP – height and weight proportional

DDF – drug-and disease-free

Combinations of acronyms made your sexual orientation clear:

SWM seeks **SWF**

SWM seeks **SWM**

SBF (single bisexual female) seeks **SWM** or **SWF**

One day during lunch in the office library, six of us twenty-somethings were stumped by an acronym we couldn't figure out: 45 WWM.

"A forty-five-year-old what?" we wondered.

"Working white male?"

"Willing white male?"

"Wanting white male?"

"White woman male?

Being so young, we were rather clueless, but decades later I not only came to know what it meant, I became one—Widowed White Male.

Yes, I had become the unknown dating acronym from the 1980s as I contemplated the digital-age version of the personal ads—online dating.

After my fast burn with Joyce in the spring and the submission of my online application to *The Washington Post's Date Lab* early in the summer, the notion of online dating had crossed my mind, but it felt like something too extreme, totally radioactive, and quite frankly, an embarrassing-to-admit sort of thing to do. To all who asked if I was contemplating it, a fast and definitive no was always my response. But it seemed everyone had a friend who had done it, and in fact, I knew people who had done it with success.

I soon learned I was totally out of step with the times. The baggage previously associated with the old personal ads and early online dating had fallen away. Lots of terrific people were doing it, and I needed to figure out how to get past my hang-ups.

It was a warm evening at an end-of-summer block party in August when I talked to a neighbor about putting myself out into the dating world. As we noshed on hot dogs and sipped cold drinks, I shared with a mother about my age that I had applied to *Date Lab* in June. Once her wide eyes of surprise calmed down, she asked if I was going to do online dating. I gave her my standard no for a response, but she was by profession someone who was paid to get people to think her way—she was a lobbyist on Capitol Hill. She effortlessly slipped into lobbying mode.

"You know, Turner, don't say no so quickly. I have a friend who did it, and she has been with this guy for two years now and she is so-o-o-o happy. Seriously, you should think about it. Everyone is doing it. There's nothing wrong with saying you're doing it. I think you'd be silly not to try. Just tell me, what have you got to lose?" she said in her most reasonable-sounding and persuasive voice.

"Okay … I'll think about it and maybe take a look," I said.

"eHarmony is the best," she said. "That's what my friend did. Look at that one first. Okay? Just that one."

"Okay, okay-y-y," I said, trying to turn her back into my friend instead of the darn-good arm-twisting lobbyist she was.

But later that night, all my fears and anxieties rose to the surface—fear on par with, say … an unleashing of the powerful forces of doom that could destroy the earth—as I went to the eHarmony website to have a look. To my surprise, the homepage looked friendly and welcoming. They touted their research-based method of matching based on their extensive questionnaire and algorithms. If true, then maybe there *was* something to this after all, but I hit my first roadblock with the very first question.

"What is your first name?"

I immediately froze as the cursor on my computer screen silently blinked.

Should I use my real name or a fake name? If I used a fake name, how would I explain it? I could see a woman using a fake name for the sake of safety, but a guy doing it would just be creepy.

Even though I *reeeee-ally* didn't want to, I eventually typed in T-u-r-n-e-r.

Then, who was I and what was I seeking?

I'm *A Man Seeking a Woman.*

Then my zip code.

My email address.

I proceeded along with all the personal information—location, age, religion, and such—before getting to the real questions that would be used to algorithmically make my matches. The list was lengthy, and I admit to being reassured by the in-depth nature of them. Another dating service I used later (OkCupid) was more detailed about personal habits, likes, dislikes, and sexual preferences. Yet another (Match.com) was basic data, a photo, then you were dumped into an unfiltered online meat-market.

After working on the long questionnaire, I finally got to where I had to write something about myself and answer a few questions that would be posted with my profile. I hesitated here for the longest time.

I wanted it to be interesting, but I also didn't want to reveal anything about myself. The idea of putting such personal information online where anyone could see it, especially for dating purposes, was unsettling. Thinking about it further, I realized I was as worried about someone who knew me seeing it as I was a stranger seeing it, maybe even more.

ABOUT YOU: Widowed white male, 53, 6 ft tall, Ivy-educated architect
LIKES: Tennis, Golf, Karate, and Ballroom Dancing
MOST INFLUENTIAL PERSON IN YOUR LIFE: My late wife
THREE MOST IMPORTANT THINGS: My family, kindness, good design
FINAL THOUGHTS: I'm a unique combination of a private yet outgoing person who has stepped out onto the public stage and enjoys engaging the community. Adventure really is the spice of life.

In addition to the brief description, I had to answer a dozen or so questions that could only be viewed by a woman if we matched and began to communicate. Together, this was pretty much the entirety of the inaugural online dating profile of Turner Grant. To say it wasn't flashy is an understatement.

It took time and significant evolution for my online dating profile to advance from very little into something more confident and interesting. I later questioned whether this evolution worked for or against me, but over the next three years, with incremental practice and trial and error, my dating profile evolved to read like this:

Southern fellow who honed his craft in Boston. Widowed, architect, Ivy-educated, and recent empty nester looking forward to the exciting opportunities I see ahead. I don't define adventure as skydiving (although it keeps life interesting and fun). I define it as those things that alter the course of your life and/or the lives of others. Good design and having a real sense of style are important to me. Fairly well-traveled and looking forward to more. I'm the kind of guy who goes well from jeans to black tie (a white dinner jacket for the summer). I like fast cars, smart women, and … I love to ballroom dance.

I'm definitely an old-fashioned, romantic sort of guy. I want to hold hands as we walk. I want to steal a kiss (or two) as we turn the corner. I want to feel the fast heartbeat when the chemistry is great.

I'm a rather unique combination of reserved but outgoing, private but someone who has stepped out onto the public stage as well. I pulled back significantly from my emerging political life after the loss of my wife (to focus on family), but I remain involved locally and at the state level.

This more interesting guy didn't emerge onto the online dating scene until much later. Right now, on this late-August evening, I was dealing with the guy who was hesitant and full of second thoughts. After reading it through twenty times or so, I uploaded the one really good picture of myself—my official campaign photo from my run for Congress—hit the submit button, and it was live.

The next morning, I eagerly logged on to my account and saw eight matches—wow! As I read through them, I was struck by the similarities.

"Seeking a man who is honest …"

"Seeking a man who is honest …"

"Seeking a man who is honest …"

"Seeking a man who is honest …"

"Seeking a man who is honest …"

"Seeking a man who is honest …"

"You should be drama free …"

"I seek a man for whom life is an adventure …"

As a proud member of the male gender, I resented this blanket judgment, but I knew the rap had some truth to it. In my three years on Venus, I heard frequent stories from women about husbands who cheated or, in control of the family finances and unbeknownst to the wife, lost or spent every penny and put them in bankruptcy. I even heard more than one story about husbands who led double lives. I would meet a few women who, as they euphemistically phrased it, "strayed in their marriages," but that was as far as I could go in getting the other side of the story.

A woman once asked me that if *they* worried about men who lied and cheated, what did *men* worry about in *women*. My response was that men worried about a woman being some sort of psycho-emotional nut job, a woman who—when she got going—could become emotionally or psychologically unhinged and/or otherwise unbearable to be around. A guy would feel the urgent need to flee and, I assume, sometimes into the arms of another woman.

Reading through the profiles of my eight matches, they were generally modest in revealing details about themselves. Besides the must-have quality of honesty, the bar was otherwise set pretty low for the men out there.

"You should have a car, a job, and a stable life," they often noted.

You qualify, Turner, The Boys said sarcastically.

Without a paid subscription, I couldn't see the women's photos, so it quickly felt like a worthless exercise. But a few days later, an email arrived from eHarmony letting me know a woman named Marilyn had sent me a message.

With eHarmony there were several ways to communicate. You could send a *wink* or a *smile* to let the person know you were interested, or you could initiate what was called an *icebreaker,* the sending of three or four preselected questions to a person of interest. Once you both shared your answers, the next round of preselected questions was sent. After three rounds of Q&A, you were then invited to send a personal message to the other through the website. You could, if you chose, bypass everything and send a message directly to a person of interest, and if they accepted, they could read the message and write back. It could be a back-and-forth dating-dance ritual, or you could cut straight to it, and someone had now done that with me.

Of course, this was the *gotcha* moment, because to open the message, I had to pay up. So I signed up for a month's worth of service and all was revealed.

Marilyn was a career diplomat at the State Department. Her brief note said she liked my profile and would be interested in talking. She included her cell number and email, which surprised me. I hadn't yet established that I wasn't a cheating scumbag, snake-under-a-rock, stalker, or potential serial killer. Her profile said she was fifty-two, and her photos showed a nice-looking woman with nothing odd or outrageous. I responded, and we arranged a time to talk that Tuesday evening.

As soon as she said hello, I was struck by the fact that her raspy voice sounded more like she was seventy-two than fifty-two. However, she was a smart, accomplished woman and, except for the sound of her voice, I was put at ease by her confident and engaging manner.

We went through what would become over time an almost rote recitation of children, jobs, and why we were single and looking to date. She had been divorced for a few years from a man who was widowed, which explained an intuitive understanding of widowhood I had picked up from her early on. She was extremely nice and gracious, and our forty-five-minute conversation was going well until she offered up advice for being widowed and dating.

"You'll need to get rid of all the pictures in the house of your wife who died. That just won't work for any woman to be seeing those around. I'm telling you; they really have to go."

"Well, right now those pictures are pretty important for my children. She's their mother."

"I understand," she said, "but it will be a problem for any woman you bring into your life. You'll need to make some changes. It will be really important for a successful relationship."

Fuck you! shouted Darrell. Subtle he's not.

I agree Darrell, said Charles, *but I'm afraid there may be some truth to what she's saying.*

Easy does it guys, said Little Turner. *Except for this, she seems pretty nice.*

Sadly, in time, I would come to learn that Marilyn and Charles were right, not just about the photos, but about the "ghost of wife past" in general.

She shared a few details about what her widowed ex-husband had done, and it was clearly more than photos of his late wife in the house that had been a problem. However, I got her point, even though it rubbed me the wrong way.

Moving the conversation along, I asked how long she had been on eHarmony and confessed she was the first woman to contact me. She said she had been back on for several months after taking a break, and it had generally been hit and miss.

I then asked what about my profile prompted her to get in touch.

"Well," she said, "first, your profile suggested you're kind and sensitive but not a player, employed in an interesting job, not living in the boondocks, and good-looking. You didn't boast about being fit, your love of sailing or motorcycles. Very refreshing and all good. I also liked the adventurous aspects of you … and your answer to the question about a first-date kiss, 'You know when it feels right or not.'"

We finished the call by talking about getting together for a drink in the next few weeks, but her comments about my ditching the photos of my late wife didn't sit well, so I put off getting together. Also, *The Washington Post Date Lab* had called and my blind date was set to happen soon. Feeling stymied at how to go about juggling different women, dates, and the emotions that went with them, I was further pushed off from wanting to meet Marilyn anytime soon.

****

With my paid subscription, I could now check out the other matches from the past three days. Their appearances ran the gamut, but I found myself drawn to those who had a real sense of personal style. I also saw *glam photos* for the first time, professional photos for women to use in their dating profiles. They were much too good, much too staged, much too fake, and quickly deleted.

One woman, whose photo instantly attracted me, was from France. Her playful picture was of a woman with dark hair partially falling into her face, with large, bright eyes peeking through in a flirtatious manner. She had a huge, illuminating smile, and the entire picture exuded sophistication, playfulness, and an excitement for life. It was captivating.

I tried out eHarmony's *wink* feature and sent her one. Her name was Claudette.

It took less than thirty minutes to hear back from her. She sent a direct message, thanked me for the *wink,* and asked if I'd like to talk. So much for the carefully choreographed getting-to-know-you steps eHarmony had crafted. Women wanted to get right to it. We scheduled a call for the next evening on a Wednesday night.

When I called, I discovered an outgoing and commanding conversationalist. She told me she worked in the art industry and at the Louvre in Paris before coming to the States about twelve years ago. That explained her sophisticated sense of style which was so obvious and appealing in her photo. She now worked for an international student exchange company. But she was not one for beating around the bush with idle chitchat. Once we got past the kids, jobs, and our being-single stories, she got right to the point in her heavy French accent.

"So tell me, are you ready?" she asked.

"Ready for what, dating?"

"No, to have someone in your life."

"Well … like I said before, I'm just beginning to get back into the dating world, so I'm not totally sure how ready I am, but I'm certainly willing to see and explore what the future might bring."

"What sort of answer is that? Either you are or you aren't," she said.

"Are you ready?" I asked calmly but annoyed.

"Yes, of course I am. I've been divorced and alone now for four years. I'm ready right now. I want someone," she said forcefully.

Yeah, uh-huh. This'll get you there, said The Boys.

"Well, I've told you pretty much my situation. If that doesn't work for you, then I certainly understand," I said.

"I see you're a tennis player," she said, abruptly shifting the conversation. "Do you want to play tennis with me?"

"Ahem … sure … would love to. I rarely get a chance to play," I said.

"You want to meet and play this Saturday at my club?"

"Yeah, that'd be great," I responded, genuinely interested in playing but with caution lights flashing all around.

"Good," she said, then added. "And maybe between now and then you can think about if you're ready to have someone in your life. Let me know when we meet."

"Ahem … oh-kaaay," I responded with exaggerated sarcasm which she totally missed.

We discussed the time and location then finished up the call.

"Great talking to you, nice to meet you," she said pleasantly, which, after her grilling, caught me off guard.

After she hung up, I tossed the phone on the sofa like a hot potato.

What the fuck was that?! The Boys shouted.

After a few more WTFs, The Boys went on to a few rounds of *Run, Forrest, run! Run, Forrest, run!*

I knew I was probably walking into an ambush with live fire, but curiosity about a woman who thought this was a reasonable way to have a first conversation with a guy made me curious as hell. I knew it would be a lesson in something. Call it *Online Dating Boot Camp 101.*

That evening, I mulled over the two conversations I'd had while thinking about the blind date still to come in five days with *The Washington Post's Date Lab.* If the phrase "dipping-my-toe-into-the-dating-waters" was apt, then a footnote clarified that the waters weren't puddles. This was deep water, with potentially rough surf, unforeseen riptides, and venomous creatures poised to attack at any time.

But I had another kind of discomfort too. I recognized that my sense of being—of who I was—had everything to do with the still strong connection to my late wife. My identity, in my head and my heart, was all about her. She was still the only love-of-my-life. How was this getting-out-there thing supposed to work in moving my life forward?

I talked about it with Abby.

She had met my wife at our office holiday party six months before her death. The party was at a cooking school we designed in downtown Washington and had only recently opened. Everyone divided up into teams for a cooking lesson on how to prepare our holiday-party dinners. Abby was there without her then-husband, so she joined my wife and me to make a team of three. That evening over cocktails, a fun-filled cooking adventure, and dinner, Abby saw up close how special my wife was and our unique connection.

As I discussed my feelings of discomfort, there was little new Abby could offer except kind support as the emotions of loss once again moistened my eyes.

We talked about Marilyn and Claudette too. She confirmed there was a bit of truth in what they both said, but that Marilyn wasn't very tactful in how she told me to get rid of the photos, and Claudette was downright weird. Abby predicted a disaster on Saturday.

At ten thirty in the morning, I arrived at the tennis club to find Claudette already waiting outside on the court reserved for us.

"*Bonjour!*" she offered, along with a half-hug and double-cheek kisses.

"*Bonjour!* Hi, Claudette, great to meet you. Thanks for the tennis invitation. This will be fun!"

She was tall and slender and had a tomboyish look about her. But the sexy, attractive woman I saw in her profile picture was *not* the woman standing in front of me. She had to be ten or more years older than her photo, and she had changed—a lot.

For the past twenty years, I had played tennis once a year at a weekend church retreat and that was all. With her twelve-inch thick case of multiple tennis rackets, I figured she was at least a twice-a-week player. That was confirmed during our initial, but short, chitchat conversation and our first few volleys. She was like a panther, quickly and gracefully covering the court. I am a fairly good advanced intermediate player, and I thought I would be able to get my shots in, but she was good, really good, and would no doubt crush me.

Both on and off the court, The Boys gleefully added.

Ten minutes into our volleying back and forth, the skies opened up and it began to rain. The game was a washout. Disappointed, we decided to at least have lunch and grabbed a table inside.

She wasted no time asking once again if I had figured out whether I was ready to have a woman in my life, and I gave the same answer as on the phone.

"Oh … hmmm … I see," she said.

Dropping this line of questioning for now, we proceeded to have a pleasant conversation. But as lunch was coming to an end, she circled back to her main focus and drilled right back in.

"Okay, so look. You're wasting my time and every other woman's time if you don't know if you're ready to have a woman in your life. I mean, I can play tennis with anyone—and I can beat you anyway. I know this. You should just stay home until you can decide if you're ready. Okay? You need to know this. Any woman will tell you. It's not just me. I'm not trying to be mean—others might—so you need to know. So, will you let me know if you decide you're ready?"

Seriously?! The Boys asked.

"So … you're saying you'd be interested if I could figure this out and was ready?"

"Of course I would. Why wouldn't I be? I just told you I was ready."

"Sure," I said, genuinely astonished but with the most poker-faced sincerity I could muster. "I'll let you know if I figure it out. Maybe we can play tennis again too."

"That would be good. You're good. I can tell these things," she said in a more modest and retreating voice.

Okay, dating gods, what am I supposed to be thinking here? I wondered as she stared at me with an absolute deadpan serious look on her face.

She likes me, and if I ever get my act together, she'd like to see where this might go?

I'm not objectionable, and if I ever get my act together, she'd like to see where this might go?

I'm a living, breathing man, and if I ever get my act together, she'd like to see where this might go?

Who the hell knows? The Boys shouted. *Let's end this now!*

We said our goodbyes and I breathed a sigh of relief. I felt like I'd just dodged a bullet—well, maybe been slightly grazed—with this stern and humorless woman from Paris.

****

The rest of the weekend came and went, as did my Monday evening blind date with Rachel for *Date Lab*. Three days later, I was able to catch up with Wendy. We hadn't talked much since late spring and my dates with Joyce, but with impeccable timing, Wendy was in Georgetown that last week of September.

When we talked on the phone about getting together, she was positively giddy about consulting on and being privy to my online dating activities. She arrived on a Thursday evening, and with a newly opened bottle of wine, we settled onto the sofa with my iPad, and I walked her through the eHarmony app.

As I tried to explain the whole process, she finally shouted, "Just get to the pictures already!"

"Geez," I said with a satisfying smirk. "You sound like a guy!"

"Open 'em, damn it!" she said, grabbing the iPad.

The homepage glowed with thumbnail pictures and the names of each woman, and Wendy was momentarily riveted. Then she began opening each one quickly and without hesitation, more than forty women in all.

She was decisive and brutal.

It was hilarious to watch, and The Boys laughed all night.

I thought I might catch some grief once she saw my choices, but we were mostly on the same page as she sorted through them.

"Nope. Don't like her. Nope ... Nope ... Nope. Oh good god, no! Ahem ... she's okay. Hmmm ... she's kind of pretty. I could see you with her."

I felt reassured and safe in her hands.

Then she came to Marilyn's profile and paused for a moment.

"Oh ... I *like* this one! Who's she?" Wendy asked.

I explained her background at the State Department, that she was divorced from a widower, that we had talked on the phone last week, that she said all the pictures of my 'dead wife' had to come down off the walls, and that her voice sounded like a seventy-two-year-old.

"Huh? She what? Sounded old? That's strange," Wendy said before pausing to consider for a moment. "I wonder if she used to be a smoker."

"Don't know, could be. Kind of sounded like that sort of thing," I said.

"And she said all the pictures had to come down off the walls? Well ... I still like her," she said. "I *really* like her. Are you going to meet her?"

"We talked about having a drink, but the pictures off the wall thing really hit me the wrong way, so I've been stringing her out in emails. But I thought you might like her. You think I should meet her?"

"Oh yeah, I do, I *really* like her," Wendy said.

With that strong recommendation, I ramped up my communication with Marilyn.

****

Marilyn and I began to correspond by email almost daily for several weeks, discussing everyday things and much more. I was surprised at how quickly we established a comfortable relationship given we'd never met. We shared things you don't share with perfect strangers, and in the process, we became fast friends. We both had challenging schedules, but we finally found a Friday evening for drinks at the Ritz-Carlton right across from my office and not too far from the State Department.

The Ritz-Carlton was built inside an old brick industrial power plant in lower Georgetown, and the lobby had a cool, hip, modern design I liked a lot. There was always a fire going when it was cold outside and, with soft sofas and cushy chairs in cozy groupings against the brick walls, it was the perfect setting for a first date. It became one of my go-to meetup places during my time on Venus.

I found a sofa and table for us near the fire, and Marilyn arrived a few minutes later with a smile and great cheer about her. It felt wonderful to finally meet her in person. We exchanged a warm embrace and a nice first kiss, then settled down into our warm, cozy sofa cocoon.

It was like being with an old friend but with a twist, since this was the first time we had laid eyes on each other. We let the real pleasure of meeting wash over any awkwardness for the next two hours.

Marilyn was attractive, smart, well-spoken, full of optimistic energy, warm, engaging, and just plain nice. Wendy was right; Marilyn was a real catch. She easily checked off many of the must-have boxes on my list.

This is awesome, I thought, but The Boys were more cautious.

Marilyn and I sat close together, our animated talking punctuated by laughter, lots of arm touching, and even the sharing of snarky, letting-your-guard-down comments, the kind you only make when you're feeling comfortable and safe with someone. The evening was firing on all cylinders.

When we got around to talking about our dating experiences, I didn't have much to share. Far from being taboo, I learned quickly that dating was *always* a topic of conversation. And as I mentioned in the previous chapter, this particular date coincided with the hours-away publication of my *Date Lab* tell-all. I had to let her know, but I wasn't sure how she would react.

She couldn't have been better about it.

Marilyn positively howled with laughter. She understood the trepidation and sense of foreboding I was feeling for when the *Sunday Post Magazine* would hit the stands. When she told me she got an early delivery of the magazine on Saturday mornings and offered to prescreen it for me, I knew how cool a woman she was.

We enjoyed each other's company immensely, which made it all the more uncomfortable when I realized that, for me, anyway, there was no romantic chemistry whatsoever; The Boys were right in being cautious. She was a kindred spirit to be sure, but I couldn't picture myself with her, and it left me frustrated and flummoxed. This was the first time, but not to be the last, that my head and my heart would not be in sync.

I was torn as to what to do. Given how great Marilyn was, it didn't make sense to not give it another chance with a second date. I offered a tender goodnight kiss, which she gladly accepted and returned, and the evening ended wonderfully.

Early the next morning, I received the "all clear" email from her about the *Date Lab* article.

Wendy was anxious to hear how the date went with her handpicked match. I filled her in on all the details, mostly all good of course, but also that the chemistry never materialized. She reluctantly accepted the bad news.

"That's the way it goes sometimes, but it's still too bad," she said with sympathy and understanding.

Marilyn and I kept in touch after that, but neither pursued the other with much energy. A few days later, I contacted her and offered a last-minute invitation for dinner that evening. She had other plans, declined, and the emails stopped altogether until we exchanged Thanksgiving greetings. Another two weeks passed before I emailed her about getting together. She again declined, this time with a goodbye.

EMAIL RECEIVED: Hey There

> Turner,
>
> That is such a nice invitation, but in the last month or so, I have started to see someone I met through work. I think I should explore that for the time being. I hope you understand.
>
> Marilyn

EMAIL SENT: Hey There

> Absolutely, I understand. I wish you only the best of luck. We all deserve to find happiness. Stay in touch. You are a class act all the way.

EMAIL RECEIVED: Hey There

> Right back at you!

****

The one photo on Stephanie's dating profile was of a slender woman, who I surmised had probably been a stunningly beautiful woman in her youth but was now trying to play down her natural beauty, for whatever reason. She wore no makeup, had plain shoulder-length hair, and showed only a hint of a smile. I saw an incredibly attractive, understated woman. Her profile was equally understated and cryptically short, but reading between the lines, I could tell she was a woman I definitely wanted to meet.

As we exchanged messages over the next few days, it became clear we had a connection in common—an architectural client of mine at that very moment. After that realization, our messaging conversations became easy, casual, and friendly. In one message, she confessed how lonely her life could be.

Now when a woman says she's *lonely,* guys are programmed to think she is suggesting sex. I was surprised by her choice of words and found it hard to believe that was her intention. I put it aside for the moment, but still!

We arranged to meet at Starbucks on an October afternoon.

I am not a coffee drinker, and Starbucks is not my hangout. Already nervous about meeting someone of more than casual interest, I arrived early to grab a table and figure out what I could order to drink as she sipped her favorite drink.

Like most Starbucks stores, the space was too small and crammed with people on this chilly, rainy fall day. I had no idea where we might sit to have a private get-to-know-you conversation, but I also knew darn well this was not about being private. She chose this public location where she would feel safe from ... well ... me. Until proven otherwise, I would carry the cheating scumbag, snake-under-a rock, stalker, and potential serial killer label. This was my first experience being treated like I carried this tag, and I have to say, it felt pretty lousy.

I ordered a tea and hovered around several tables, waiting for someone to leave, all the while giving the entire room a look that screamed, *You've all been here friggin' forever. Leave already! I need a table more than you. Get out!*

Continuing to scan the cafe, I saw two people in the middle of the room rise imperceptibly. I slashed and dashed my way through the cramped little shop to grab their small table before someone else could beat me to it. As the stream of people continued into the store, I fended off a half-dozen inquiries of, "Is this seat taken?"

Finally, Stephanie arrived, and we greeted each other with warm smiles and a half-friendly, half-reserved hug. She looked just like her picture with that understated quality I found incredibly attractive.

She ordered coffee, then sat across the table from me; we were at one of five tables aligned in a row that divided the room in half. As we began to talk in the noisy room, we had to lean in to hear each other. We were oddly far apart while too close to the people next to us for a private conversation.

A movie image immediately came to mind—a prison visitation room with a row of prisoners on one side of a long table and the visitors on the other. She, of course, was the visitor, and I was the prisoner.

I made a note to myself to avoid the prison-visitation-like Starbucks meeting places in the future.

That aside, we talked for the next two hours, and the conversation never lagged. A sign for me whether a conversation is going well is my ability to make the other person laugh or at least smile. Laughs were fleeting—she wasn't that kind of person—but when I did make her smile, it lingered on her face in a fetching and attractive way.

We easily could have talked longer—certainly a good sign—but it was four o'clock and we both needed to leave. As I stood up, relieved at how well it went, it was then, almost as an afterthought, that she asked two questions that would not only stop our budding relationship a few days later, but questions I would also soon learn most women on Venus wanted answers to.

"What do you want? Where do you see yourself in ten or fifteen years?"

Frankly, I was stumped by the questions.

I babbled out something incoherent as I described maybe having my own architectural firm or possibly even successfully making it to Congress in ten or fifteen years.

The reality was I had no idea about either, and that was a problem.

Quickly pivoting from her questions, we traded email addresses and I walked her to her car. We shared a much nicer hug than before and talked about getting together again.

That evening and over the next few days, we exchanged several chatty emails, and I asked her out for Saturday night, suggesting dinner and a movie. She excitedly accepted, and I noticed the beginning of little pitter-patters in my heart. But when I asked her preference for an early or late movie for Saturday night, her response made my pitter-patters pause.

EMAIL RECEIVED: Saturday Night

> Turner,
>
> Let me think about it and I will shoot you an email later in the day tomorrow.
>
> Stephanie

After ten enthusiastic email exchanges over four days, she was hesitating.

Charles was on it immediately. *She's going to make up an excuse to cancel the date, lover boy.*

Darrell was more to the point. *We're about to get dumped.*

Her email arrived the next evening.

EMAIL RECEIVED: Saturday Night

> Hi Turner,
>
> I hate to do this to you, but I am going to cancel our date for this Saturday. To be perfectly honest, I met someone last night who is more in my phase of life … empty nester, winding down in his career, looking to travel, etc. The more I have thought about it, that is really what I am looking for right now.
>
> I did really enjoy meeting you and best of luck in your search for "what's next."
>
> Stephanie

The Boys and I sulked for days.

****

Margaret was the fifth woman I met, and it went the distance of my then-personal-best with Joyce in the spring: two dates … sort of.

The several photos in Margaret's profile were of a youthful, slim, attractive brunette in her late forties, very much the girl-next-door type. She worked for a local commercial developer and said she enjoyed architecture.

Having just been dumped by Stephanie and still feeling bummed, I wasn't in a particularly caring mood or interested in dissecting Margaret's online profile in detail. She looked great, and that was good enough. I quickly sent off an *icebreaker* to her—as well as several other matches—and moved on.

Looking at my rapidly growing group of online matches—now getting close to fifty—it was clear I needed some sort of online dating-management system to deal with them all. Even though I was only weeks into this, I had already learned it was an incredibly time-consuming process. In brainstorming strategies, as cavalier as it was, a shotgun approach seemed to be best. I started firing off lots of *winks, smiles,* and *icebreaker* invitations and waited to see what came back. If they responded, only then would I spend time reading their profiles in depth and decide if I wanted to pursue them.

Margaret quickly accepted my *icebreaker,* but our initial communication progressed slowly and deliberately over several days before we exchanged emails and took our conversation into the real world. I took that as her being more cautious and, frankly, it was more of what I had expected in meeting strangers online. I extended an invitation to meet, and we arranged a Saturday afternoon date at a restaurant near her condo in Washington, D.C.

Walking inside to meet her, I was nervous. After Stephanie's recent brush-off, I worried about not being what Margaret expected, not being able to answer her questions, and just about everything else that could go wrong.

After my friend Abby divorced and hit the online dating scene, we debated what to call these first meetings. Were they dates or dating interviews? We agreed it depended on the setting, the time of day, and if there was any apparent chemistry.

When Margaret arrived and saw me, she quickly offered a business-like handshake. The sense from her was, "Let's meet but keep our distance."

This was clearly, a dating interview.

Although put off by her formality, I offered a comment about the beautiful fall day outside to break the ice. It worked well enough, and we talked for about an hour and a half.

She looked just like her pictures, a pretty woman with a great smile, the kind of woman men would notice on the street. The usual first topics were covered in due course, and I learned she was divorced and had a college-age son. We talked about architecture, which was quite enjoyable. I hadn't met anyone yet who cared much about it, except for the guy two years earlier who asked if being an architect helped me get women.

I didn't give much thought to it at first, but Margaret left the table about every twenty minutes to check her messages, or so she said. After the third time, I wondered if she was excusing herself to make a phone call to a friend.

Okay, I'm here with him, and I need you to come and get me out of here, now! was one passing thought.

As the hour and a half began to wear thin, we both started giving signals of needing to go, but I was caught off guard by the way she concluded our *interview.*

"I just want to make something clear that I hadn't in my profile," she said. "I'm not looking for a romantic relationship. I'm only looking for friendships. Would that be something that's okay with you?"

Dumped into the friend zone, chump! The Boys exclaimed with laughter.

"Oh … um … you mean someone—a guy—just to do things with … just as friends?" I asked.

"Yeah, like that," she said with some hesitation, but a look that said, *What's not normal about that?*

"Well, actually … I have a number of women friends and … we're just friends in the way you describe, so … I know what you mean, I think. So sure, I'd be interested in that … like going to the movies together as friends and things like that?"

"Yeah, exactly," she said.

Okay, this just got weird, The Boys muttered.

Driving home, I was left scratching my head.

She went through all of this just to find a male friend to do things with? I wondered. *Or did I just totally flame out, and this was her way of letting me down gently?*

We stayed in sporadic touch, and a month later, just after Thanksgiving, we made a date … um, arranged a time to go to dinner and a movie together, on a Saturday night, as friends. But I had decided a friendship wasn't what I was looking for. I resolved to see if she was being straight up about the friend thing or if there was any sort of relationship possibility below the surface.

We went to dinner at my club and then to an artsy movie nearby. During dinner, she continued to excuse herself every twenty minutes to check her messages. Leaving dinner for the movie, I lightly touched her arm from time to time as we passed through a door or crossed a street. It was a natural, gentlemanly gesture from me, but I also did it intentionally to see her response. Walking into the dark theater, I gave another slight touch to her elbow.

This time, she turned around quickly. "I want to make sure you're still good with what we talked about—just being friends."

I lied so as not to make a scene. "Yeah, sure."

Throughout the movie, she continued to slip out to check her phone every twenty minutes. By the time the evening was a wrap, I was ready to say goodbye to Margaret.

****

In the days after my rejection from Stephanie, I sent Susan a *smile* with little thought. She also had only one picture of herself on her profile, that of a smiling, nice-looking, youthful woman, surrounded by other women in a group-party picture. It looked like it could have been a college sorority photo. If she were in her late forties as noted in her profile, then she was an *amazingly* youthful late forties. It was hard to tell much else about her because everything seemed fairly generic in her written profile—perhaps similar to my too-brief profile. So it was based on the one picture alone that I put her into the yes-category and reached out to her.

She similarly chose the *icebreaker* Q&A, and nothing unusual arose during the back and forth. She was originally from Colorado, which made me think she would be more laid back and open to new people, so that was a plus. She was divorced with two grown children who were in different parts of the country. I invited her for a casual Sunday lunch at my club two days after another first date with someone else. I was beginning to get comfortable with multiple meetings and dates on a single weekend, a change that happened shockingly fast.

I thought meeting at my club was a good idea for several reasons. First, it would make a good first impression that I was a member, and women might more readily accept my invitation. Second, I knew people were always delighted to visit, and I was happy to share an interesting and personal part of my life for a few hours. Third, it would be my treat and would eliminate the awkwardness of who would pay the check or if we'd split it. Finally, it was just a wonderful place to be among the families and lively activities in the fall and early winter months. Along with the Georgetown Ritz, the club became my go-to place for first-meeting dates.

This date, however, was about to end before it even began. When she arrived, I wasn't sure it was even her. Her eyes and smile resembled the online photo, but she was like a thirty-year-older version of the person in the picture. She easily could have been the mother of the women in the photo. Maybe that *was* an old college sorority picture she had used.

The Boys immediately cried, *Foul!*

I was more than annoyed too.

What did she think was going to happen at this particular moment?

In addition to my disappointment and annoyance, I felt she had breached an unspoken understanding of honesty and integrity. Perhaps that was too much to expect in the online dating world. Maybe this was a sample of things to come.

****

Taking stock five weeks into my fall rookie-dating season, I had had seven first-meeting dates.

In the pre-internet world of dating and my life decades before, this number of encounters would have constituted a year's worth, not five weeks' worth. But as I was beginning to learn, such was life in the digital-dating world.

One thing I figured out quickly—and it had already begun to bother me— was that online dating tended to work against having a conscience. It provided a continuous stream of faces, matches, and opportunities that could lull you into a mindset of casualness and thoughtlessness in the way you thought about and treated other people. In the months to come, I learned you could discard a potential match without giving it a second thought; casually send a note to a potential match with no intention other than to see if they would respond and then do nothing if they did; continuously arrange for first-date meetings to increase the *number met* that you could then recite to others; and you could too easily drop off the face of the earth and disappear with nary a word or, in online dating parlance, *ghosting.*

"I had three dates this weekend alone," seemed to be a common number recited by others. I hit that number, too, on several occasions. The most I ever heard of was a woman who had six first-meeting dates on one weekend that started on a Friday night. She cited having met three hundred men in two years before finding someone she finally became serious with.

In short order, I read hundreds of online dating profiles and could place them into several general categories. There were nice women simply looking for nice men. Some women wondered if a decent man even existed (i.e., "Seeking a man who is honest"). There were the man-haters who, instead of listing qualities they were looking for in a man, wrote angry dissertations of what their ideal man should *not* be. Of course, some women only wanted the hunkiest and hottest of men, and I need not apply. Others would settle for nothing less than to be swept off their feet by a man of travel and adventure. There were also the ones who were looking for wealthy men to be "generous" to them. And lastly, a few women were looking for men of means who could match their financial success.

It was a never-ending point of fascination to read the lists of must-haves and must-not-haves from the women of the general middle-aged female dating population. Here are just a few:

"A man who is honest" (always at the top of the list).

"No baggage" (another top-of-the-list one) or "You must be drama free."

"You should not have kids, or they are grown and out of the house."

"You must be fit and care about a healthy lifestyle as I do."

"Vegans need only apply."

"I love all animals and I don't eat meat, and you should be like-minded."

"I like to hunt, even for Bambi."

"Seek a partner like a Labrador Retriever: loyal, reliable, and tolerant."

"I want a man whose only focus will be me."

"If you need a woman to focus on you 24/7, look somewhere else."

"I love the feel of a vibrating road hog between my legs" (a love of riding Harley motorcycles).

"I will only date men who are monogamous."

"You should know that I will date other men until, if, and when we become serious."

"Not looking to be serious until after we have lived together."

"You must care about the environment and believe it is up to all of us to do our part."

"If you are a tree hugger, then go hug one and delete me."

"I like to dress up and go out on the town, so have something besides jeans in your closet."

"If your closet is full of suits, then you should hang with them and not me."

"Don't contact me if you are just looking for a hookup."

"I want a man who can fog up the car windows at the end of a date."

"Don't fuck me then not call me."

My lists of must-haves and must-not-haves were only vague ideas at best. Feeling adrift about everything in life, I found it hard to be certain about anything. So being open to new opportunities, new people, and new things seemed to be a reasonable way to go forward. Of course, being so uncertain would have implications—big implications—but having been on Venus for only six months, I was just beginning to scratch the surface.

CHAPTER 4

Flashback

A SAVE-THE-DATE NOTATION IN MY calendar for an upcoming Friday night said *Fall Soiree.* It was a seasonal companion for the local arts organization's spring event where I had *crossed the threshold* into my future, such as it was, and met Joyce.

I found myself seeing this upcoming event as a positive one, considering it to be a mini-milestone of sorts. With such trepidation in approaching so many *firsts* over the past few months, I was now about to have my first *second.* I took it as a you've-come-a-long-way moment. It still seemed everything I was doing was forced and often awkward, but I was moving forward; no small feat, I kept telling myself.

I told Abby about the evening, and she nonchalantly wished me luck. I told her I was a bit nervous about the event, both because I wondered if I would meet anyone *and* if Joyce might be there. She was keen to know if I saw Joyce, but otherwise, I could give her the lowdown at work on Monday.

Turner's dating life was now back-page news. *A good thing,* I thought.

The *Fall Soiree* differed from the Spring Gala in that it was mostly indoors. Guests could mingle not only with each other but also with artists whose works would be on display. This year, it was being held in one of the many oversized, look-a-like McMansion-type houses that are everywhere.

Making my way to the check-in table, I tried my best to relax and be at ease, but my nerves were ever-present. Unlike the spring event, I didn't know many people here, so I didn't have the same safety net of friends to start the evening with. At a bit of a loss for what to do, I did what anyone might do in this situation—I grabbed a glass of wine, then took a few laps to check everything out.

The large house was crowded with lots of well-heeled people. Dress was work attire for some, but those who outfitted themselves to be noticed—women wearing dress-to-kill cocktail attire—were here in force too. All-in-all, it felt like a festive, end-of-week party rather than a fundraising event, more like what a *soiree* implied. It had a great ambiance, a this-is-the-place-to-be sort of vibe.

It wasn't long before I saw Joyce. She was about to walk through a doorway and into another room. She wasn't with her three friends from the spring event but was on her own and seemingly taking the same laps around the house as I was. I wasn't sure if she had noticed me, but since she was going in the opposite direction, I watched her disappear.

I was now in the largest room of the house where artwork was on display. Tall folding partitions zigzagged through the space. Since I enjoy and appreciate art, I took my time looking through the fifty or so pieces being shown. I made small talk with several people along the way, then came upon some friends and paused in my art crawl to catch up with them. As we chatted, Joyce came back into the room and headed in our general direction. She was part of a line of people perpetually snaking back and forth through the room. When she got near, she momentarily paused and stepped over.

"Hi Turner, how are you? Great to see you. Enjoy!" she said, nervously gesturing to the art in the room.

"Hi Joyce. You too," I said.

She then quickly rejoined the moving line of people, and just like that, it was over—awkward, polite, and swift. Turning back to my friends, I realized my nerves had calmed and, now breathing easily, I could *finally* start to enjoy the evening.

By this time, the house was in complete party mode. Guests filled the rooms, music was playing, food was being served, and artists stood near their work, ready to offer explanations of artistic expression and inspiration. Rounding the corner of one display, I saw two attractive women chatting with each other. One glanced my way, made eye contact, and smiled with an expression I took as an invitation to say hello.

"Hi, how are you? Are you both enjoying the evening?" I said.

"Yes, it's wonderful; it's fabulous," one said cheerfully, turning toward me in a way of gesturing me to join them.

The Boys said, *Go!*

The two middle-aged women seemed to be together, but it was Frances who greeted me and took the lead in the conversation. We introduced ourselves, then she introduced me to her friend Kim.

As Frances and I talked, I found out she was in sales and marketing, thus a pro at engaging people and working a room like this. Kim was quite content to listen as Frances talked, probably knowing well that this was what her friend did all the time and better to just let her go on. Frances noted this was a work event *and* a social event for her, so she had left her husband at home and invited Kim to accompany her.

Kim slowly joined the conversation, and the three of us went into full cocktail-party small-talk mode. It was the kind of conversation you typically have to scope out a situation like this. A few minutes in, you might decide you want to stay, or you excuse yourself to go refill your empty glass.

My glass was empty, but I was going nowhere. The Boys made sure of that.

Over the next fifteen minutes, Kim and Frances asked many questions and I shared a lot about myself: where I was from, college, the kind of architecture I did, cities I'd lived in, family, kids, what had brought me here tonight, etcetera. Soon, it became more than cocktail small talk; it became getting-to-know-you talk. Given the conversation was quickly going deeper than I expected and I had already shared that I was widowed, I became worried they might ask questions I preferred to avoid.

During the previous two years, I had worked out a mental script I used to introduce myself to new people. If appropriate, it included a simple and straightforward way of letting them know I was widowed fairly recently. Stating it the way I did allowed me the flexibility of bowing out of any situation I found uncomfortable or uninteresting. It caused little discomfort to whomever I was speaking with, and after brief condolences for my loss, the conversation usually moved on.

Kim said she, too, was widowed and had lost her husband in 2001. My guess was she was five to six years younger than I was, and my heart went out to her for having experienced such a loss in her mid-thirties. Knowing this put me at ease to some degree, now confident that certain questions wouldn't be asked about my wife's passing that could be uncomfortable and emotional.

If anyone ever asked how my wife died—and a few would from time to time—I simply told them she died of heart failure. If they pressed, I had a long-answer script I used.

To my surprise and discomfort, Frances asked and pressed me to delve into the long answer. Some years earlier, my brother-in-law discovered a genetic defect that made him susceptible to various heart problems. He suggested his brother and sister get tested as well to see if they carried the same defective genes. My wife was tested and found she also carried it, so she had the same susceptibility, which eventually took her life.

Since I was no fan of this line of questioning, it never crossed my mind to ask Kim how she lost her husband.

Frances continued to lead the conversation. She repeatedly offered up interesting facts about Kim, who didn't hesitate to jump in but rarely initiated conversation. After about forty-five minutes of standing together and getting to know each other fairly well, it was clear Kim was holding back and Frances was on a mission to draw her out.

I was able to figure out from the various details of our conversation that Kim wasn't married or dating anyone, and it came as a real surprise. Kim was a woman of substance, depth, beauty, and brains and possessed an elegance that would turn heads in any room. It didn't make sense that this incredible woman was unattached after all these years of being widowed.

When I mentioned somewhere along the way that I was a ballroom dancer, it became *really* clear what Frances was up to. She quickly offered up that Kim, too, was a ballroom dancer, and (even though I wasn't supposed to see it) Frances gave Kim a double-raised-eyebrow look, then an eye shift several times from left to right in my direction as if to say, *Hey, what about this guy? ... He's a dancer? ... What do you think? ... Come on, Kim!*

During the silence of this unspoken communication, I stood uncomfortably, doing my best to pretend I wasn't seeing it. Then, trying to quickly move past the awkwardness, I turned the conversation to something else.

We spent the entire evening together in enjoyable and often animated conversation. At one point, we noticed the sizzle in the soiree was fading and it was getting late. We exchanged business cards, offered friendly hugs goodbye, and promised to be in touch.

All I could think about on the drive home was Kim. Frances thought we should go out, and I agreed. We had a lot in common, our conversations were interesting, easy, and pleasant, and I was attracted to her brains and beauty all wrapped up in her elegant but understated manner.

I emailed Kim late Sunday evening and extended an invitation for dinner. It was nice to know someone well enough to ask them out for a pleasant evening instead of yet another first-meeting date/interview. She emailed back early the next day, accepted, and suggested a few possible dates a few weeks off.

For my part—with one son in a different state, single parenthood, and a demanding work schedule—I was beginning to wonder how this time-intensive dating thing was going to work out. I could be available for a couple of weeks, then not have a free minute for the next two. But in an exchange of a half-dozen pleasant emails, we settled on a Saturday night toward the end of October for our evening together. She couldn't have been nicer, and I was beginning to do that imagining thing everyone does when a little bit of fondness for someone begins to take hold.

When the week of the date arrived, we exchanged emails almost daily. Over just a few messages, she threw out date ideas that got progressively more elaborate and pricier. Our original plan for a casual dinner and a movie evolved into a very nice dinner and Kennedy Center tickets for the Washington Ballet.

I was keen to go out with her, but the original idea of an easy casual evening had now morphed into what looked like a $400 first date—not my typical first-date budget by a long shot. Given suggestions and indicating preferences, I wondered if perhaps it was a sign she wanted this to be more special than a typical first date. It made my anticipation of an evening together grow—*this is going to be a great evening with a terrific woman*, I thought.

Dressed in coat and tie, I headed into the city in the early evening to pick her up. When Kim came to the door, she looked fabulous, showing the innate style she possessed and that I liked so much. Dinner was at a Watergate restaurant across the street from the Kennedy Center, but we first had to navigate the traffic in Washington on a busy Saturday night.

As we drove, I tried picking back up on several conversations we had started at the soiree and in our emails. We weren't more than a few minutes in the car, and I was in the middle of updating her on one of my projects, when she stopped me cold. "I'm sorry, but what is it you do? … And where exactly do you live?"

"What?" I said, reacting as though I hadn't heard her correctly.

"Sorry, I don't remember what you do," she said with a sense of confusion in her voice.

I paused.

"I'm an architect ... I work here in Georgetown, right over there," I pointed.

I paused again ... and received no response.

"Remember the art soiree several weeks ago? Where we met?" I added, baffled, confused, and grasping for a toehold with this strange turn of events.

"Oh ... right ... sorry ... I don't know why I didn't remember," she said haltingly. It wasn't clear that she did remember.

All of a sudden, I felt like an intrusive stranger in the car with her. It was odd and uncomfortable. I felt embarrassed and foolish at first ... and then really annoyed. All this time planning for and looking forward to our evening together—our $400 evening no less—and I'm getting, "I don't remember what you do ... And *where* exactly do you live?" and, "Oh right, I forgot about where we met."

The confusion in my mind is hard to describe, but I had to figure out something on the spot. It crossed my mind to cancel the date and take her home, but the ballet tickets had been paid for and the *what-would-you-do-with-those* thought nixed that option. With no better idea than to keep going, I went through a sort of mental rebooting process to try and find a new common point from which we could take a second try at the evening.

We parked the car at the Kennedy Center and walked across the street to the restaurant. It was a cool, crisp evening, really nice for what we had planned. The restaurant looked elegant and inviting, but things were moving along on a minute-to-minute basis, and I was working hard to figure out what to say next ... and what not to say.

When drinks arrived at our table, I offered a toast to a nice evening and good company. What else could I say? *Gee ... nice to be with you, but it would be great if you remembered who I was and why you agreed to go out with me?*

I continued trying to figure out where we were still connected and where we needed reconnecting. So much seemed like new ground that needed to be covered, but I tried to keep it easy and comfortable. While sharing an appetizer, the evening finally seemed to be moving in a better direction. I touched on various topics and she began connecting the pieces of me back together, at least that's what I thought.

We talked about more personal things we hadn't discussed at the soiree and had a fairly long conversation about our families and children. The moment seemed appropriate to finally ask how she lost her husband since she knew (or did she remember?) how I lost my wife.

"He was on the one-hundred-and-first floor of the World Trade Center on 9/11," she responded simply, but with a mindfulness of the gravity of what she was saying.

At first, I paused; then my mind froze.

I know I offered my heartfelt condolences for her loss, the tragedy, and the trauma she must have experienced, but the truth is, my mind raced and my heart sank in a rapid confusion of images, feelings, and flashbacks that gripped me inside.

… the image of the second plane hitting the tower as I watched it live on TV, then the face of my wife when I found her the day after Mother's Day. I heard the voice of the police officer ordering me not to touch her, but I ignored him and ran around to where her face was covered and pulled off the blanket. I remembered the momentary suspension of time, the strangest feeling I have ever had, of standing in the shadow of my life as I knew it, and then of being yanked away into some never-experienced dark and terrible place, where the outside world ceased to exist in my consciousness. After an unknown suspension of time, a rush of pain and anguish tore through me … I faltered … my knees buckled … then I broke down and cried uncontrollably.

When I looked at Kim, I wondered what her experience must have been like. I imagined her at the exact moment, utterly helpless and in horror, watching the towers collapse on live TV. The disbelief that this could be real—it just can't be—then that same overwhelming emotion and anguish tearing and ripping through her, and finally having her entire world yanked away in the flash of a moment that never ends.

I wondered how she handled conversations to protect herself and her children in the days, weeks, months, and years that followed. I know I went silent at first, and then I created a blurry narrative that intentionally left much of what happened unexplained. A bit later, I created a story, a story to protect the memory of my wife and to protect my children from yet more trauma from that day, the day their mother died. But Kim's loss was a horrific national event, public at every turn with no place to hide, while mine was private. I couldn't begin to imagine what she experienced.

I had hard discussions with Mary, my brother, my clergy, and my wife's therapist in the immediate hours after her death, ultimately deciding not to tell my children that their mom had lost her lifelong battle with depression and had taken her own life. I discussed some vague findings of the police report with my children days later, but I did not, could not, reveal the truth until quite some time later when Mary calmly suggested it was time they knew.

For years to come, except to family and a handful of close friends, a mysterious genetic heart defect had claimed her life, and that was the only way I could talk about her loss in the outside world. On the rare occasion when I did share with someone what happened, I usually got, "I thought there was more to it. Now it all makes sense."

And then they would look at me—or at least it *felt* like they were looking at me—trying to find any visible cracks or damage in my soul or my psyche.

Kim made sense to me now, too, with an emerging narrative that seemed to reconcile everything I hadn't been able to figure out before: her reticence at the soiree; why Frances was trying mightily to draw her out that night; how it could be that no man had scooped up this incredible woman; and finally, that she seemed so distant tonight and hardly knew who I was.

When I had told my mother-in-law that I needed to move on because the burden of the past on my shoulders was crushing me, I had a feeling of being under an unbearable weight of trauma, loss, and lonely grief. That's what I now saw in Kim.

She was still struggling and carrying that weight with her for over a decade. Right or wrong, this was how my mind assembled the pieces of the puzzle in the seconds after she told me of her husband's death on 9/11.

Back in the moment with Kim, I thought, *I'm going to make this as nice an evening as possible,* and then offered a simple toast.

"To those we will always love and forever hold close in our hearts."

We softly clinked our glasses, and she seemed to appreciate the thought and words.

No pall hung over the evening—quite the contrary. The moment of sharing what happened on 9/11—and my unexpected flashbacks—came and went, and the evening was very nice. She maintained a polite posture throughout the evening—physically, emotionally, and conversationally—with the same reticence as at the soiree. If her friend Frances had labored to bring her out, it seemed any efforts I made were falling even further short.

Kim had mentioned several times how much she adored the ballet, and the production of *Dracula* was spectacular. I glanced over several times during the over-two-hour performance. She sat stoically with her hands resting motionless on her lap. I never saw a change of expression on her face during any of the dramatic scenes or particularly wonderful dance sequences when I thought perhaps a hint of a smile might show.

After the final curtain call and a standing ovation, we began the descent from the balcony. Our conversation was happy and animated as we talked about the fabulous performance. After getting in the car, I asked if she'd like a drink or cup of coffee somewhere nearby. I was pretty sure she would decline, and she did.

We drove to her home, I walked her to her door, and we thanked each other for the nice evening. We exchanged a polite hug, and I wished her goodnight. *And happiness too,* The Boys added.

As I turned around on the sidewalk to walk back to my car, my one wish, in that moment, was that she had enjoyed the evening. I knew I would never see her again, but I hoped above all hopes, that she would be okay.

CHAPTER 5

The One and Dones +
The Three-Date Rule

A FEW YEARS AFTER SHE had recovered from her marriage and divorce from brash billionaire Ted Turner, actress and activist Jane Fonda was asked in an interview how their relationship began.

It was no small question.

The world of popular culture was shocked when the news had broken over a decade earlier that the two were even dating. In many people's minds, Ted Turner was an old-fashioned, Southern male chauvinist whose views about women had them being eye candy, making babies, or being the little woman in the kitchen.

Jane, besides her movie career and other successful business ventures, was admired by many women as a flag-bearing icon of the woman-hear-me-roar movement. Many women felt sold out when she married Ted Turner.

I remember being curious as well. I never would have imagined them as a couple.

So how did it begin?

Jane's response was shockingly simple for two such complicated individuals. "It began like all relationships do; it began with sex."

Of course, that's a hugely important part of a relationship. *Let's not be coy about this,* Jane was saying.

The online profiles of women I read usually noted the need for "chemistry," but what they really meant was *sexual* chemistry—heart-beating attraction, excitement, and more. I was all-in for finding chemistry—sexual or otherwise—but except for the second date with Joyce, there was no chemistry to be found on Venus. Meanwhile, whatever planet Abby's dating life was on, she was garnering much more attention in this area.

The Monday after my date with Kim, Abby came to my desk with her tea in hand to say hello and hear how it went. Abby's heart sank when I told her about Kim's husband and the World Trade Center on 9/11. Retelling the story put us in reflective moods for much of the morning. The sadness I felt for Kim's loss on that terrible day and the helplessness at being unable to help her in any meaningful way would stay with me for quite some time. The memory of the evening is still quite vivid, even today.

Four hours later, however, my reflective mood was shattered when Abby came flying around the corner from her side of the office. Lunchtime was ending as she strode up to my desk. She had an expression that combined a smirky smile with a sense of absolute exasperation.

"What is it with you men anyway!" she shot at me, trying to keep her scream to a whisper.

"What? What happened?!" I responded with worry and concern.

"You men! Where do you get your brains from?"

"W-H-A-T … H-A-P-P-E-N-E-D?" I asked slowly, trying to calm her down. "Is it an office thing or a dating thing?"

"It's a dating thing, of course!"

Abby had been out in the dating world for about six months since her divorce, and we shared our dating stories with few details spared. She was doing mostly online dating with Jdate for Jewish singles, OkCupid, and Match. com. I had to admit that the stories she came back with were pretty off the wall at times, but I'd never seen her worked up like this. I couldn't imagine what happened.

Some of the surprises I could chalk up to age differences. She was in her mid-forties, and I was in my mid-fifties, and each generation has differences in relationship expectations.

"Okay," she began. "You remember I told you about this younger guy down in Richmond, about thirty-six years old?"

"Ye-ahh," I responded carefully.

"… and I've told him he's probably too young for me, and he's too far away? Well, he keeps calling me."

"You haven't met this guy yet, right?"

"No, we've just talked on the phone a few times."

"But you keep taking his calls?"

"Well, yeah, he really seems to like me."

"Oh-kayy," I continued cautiously.

"Well, I just got off the phone with him, and you won't believe what he said!"

"Can't wait to hear," I said, with a small grin beginning to emerge.

"He says he understands that older women have more needs, you know, sexual needs than men the same age ..."

"Oh-kayy," I said again, not sure I wanted to hear what was coming next.

"... and that he's fine with that and understands. Then he says ... if we were dating, and if I wanted to, I could bang anyone in the office whenever I wanted, and it would be okay with him!"

"W-H-A-T?!" I said with an expression of *eweeee!*

"What is it with you men?! Where does this crap come from?!"

"Wow! Okay ... you got me. I can no longer defend the male gender. I give up."

****

With Abby's regular reporting of her dating exploits and my busy dating month of October, it felt like I was in it up to my eyeballs as November arrived. Yet, because of various parenting responsibilities and the Thanksgiving holiday, the month was looking like it would be date-free.

With this welcome pause from the go-go-go dating scene, I considered what I had learned in the last few months about the general middle-aged female dating population, the unwritten rules and the reality of the digital-dating world, and myself.

First, each woman I met was clearly on a mission of their own design; there was no *Female Collective* at work. Each had to be taken individually, and no general assumptions could be made.

Second, they mostly made it clear—some more than others—that they were in this to find a mate and there was no time to waste. After the preliminary niceties upon meeting, it was usually quickly down to business.

Third, sex was a primary issue (how could it not be?) but a back-burner dating subject, almost taboo.

Fourth, regardless of how many pre-communication steps were taken or how much direct communication occurred by email, texting, or phone calls, until I met them in person, I had no idea what a given woman might be like. Had they been truthful in their profiles and what they said? How much was everyone building themselves up, and how much was genuine? Everyone seemed to have studied the same dating playbook and mostly came off the same in the pre-meeting stages. Nice conversations, appropriate compliments, and generally good and timely communication carried the day. Only when we met in real life, however, would the real person emerge and the chemistry—personal, sexual, or any other—be measured.

Fifth, I found that for me—and I suspect for the women too—when meeting in person for the first time, it could be over within a matter of seconds. I knew immediately whether it was a *yes*, a *no*, a *maybe*, or whether those little voices in my head—The Boys—were shouting *Wow!*

My French connection was pretty much over in the first few seconds. My *Date Lab* blind date was a thumbs-down within a nanosecond, as was Susan, the woman whose profile picture turned out to be thirty years old. When I met Stephanie at the Starbucks that day in early October, she was an immediate *yes* for me, but I was clearly a *maybe* for her and a *no* days later.

If the woman was deemed a *maybe*, then the next decision point would come about five or ten minutes later. She could remain a *maybe* or become a *yes* or a *no*. She also could go from a *yes* to a *maybe* or even a *no*. Only once, much later, did a woman go from a *maybe* to a *Wow!* on the first date.

If she were a *Wow!* right out of the gate, she pretty much stayed a *Wow!* for at least the first date. Of the nine dates in the first six months on Venus, seven were one-and-done dates—a pretty poor rate of success, it seemed to me.

Am I doing something wrong? I asked myself every time.

But in talking to Abby almost daily, and Wendy more infrequently, I was assured that my dating compass was working fine.

The dating-free month of November turned out to be a busy pre-dating month, with new online matches, countless *winks* and *smiles*, and repeatedly answering the same getting-to-know-you questions. The stage was set for December and the New Year, top months for dating and romance.

Michelle was a Washington, D.C., attorney. During our online pre-communication phase, I discovered a gregarious, intelligent woman with a quick wit. She was a year younger than me and a partner at her law firm.

We exchanged a series of slightly flirtatious and humorous messages on the dating site before switching over to email. She had no hesitation engaging in a lively back-and-forth correspondence. Given my recent experience, it was refreshing to have a woman jump in headfirst like this. In short order, we scheduled a phone call for the next day, a Saturday morning.

The call started with a wisecrack remark that we thought was terribly funny, and an hour of great conversation followed. It was clear that Michelle was successful and at that midcareer point when you can be on top of the world—and she was. Her quick, sharp humor and worldly views were on full display. She was great.

A real *Wow!* thought The Boys.

After the call, we exchanged emails about how great it was meeting each other on the phone and quickly made a date for the following Saturday night at my club. She asked me to pick her up at her home in Georgetown, unheard of for a first online date so far.

The week leading up to our date featured another phone call and a constant stream of emails. Michelle dug unexpectedly deep into my answers to the questions on eHarmony, pulled up all sorts of stuff, and poked pretty good fun at me. She told me how to find her answers to the same questions—from serious to silly—and it was almost scary how many were similar.

Our answers to one particular question about how long it would take for each of us to get over a breakup caught my attention. She answered "a few days," and I answered "a month or more." I poked back at her in one of our email exchanges.

EMAIL SENT: Ketchup on Grilled Cheese?

> … only a few questions we differed on. But if we became a couple and we broke up, seems it would take me longer to get over it than you—how could you get over me so easily? I'm so sad.

EMAIL RECEIVED: Ketchup on Grilled Cheese?

> ... you make me laugh! I too noticed that most of our responses were the same. It's kind of refreshing that we seem to be in sync, with few minor exceptions but obviously, these exceptions are more significant ... I mean, heck, we've already become a couple, broken up, and now you are sad :-(Are you as witty in person as you are in writing? I am REALLY looking forward to meeting you :)

I parked in front of her home early Saturday evening and went to the front door. Michelle answered wearing a welcoming smile and offered a nice hug. She was fashionably slim and nicely dressed. I would call her well put together and a woman who made herself attractive but not a natural beauty. However, with all the disappointments lately with stunningly attractive women, I found myself relieved to have her as my date this evening.

She invited me in and gave me a quick tour. The decorating was smart and could have easily been from an interior design magazine.

Our conversation was as lively in the car as it had been during our phone calls and emails, and this was unusual too. In the last few months, I had discovered most women could be chatty on the phone, in texts, and in emails, but then pull back, becoming subdued and cautious upon meeting for the first time. Her boldness continued to be refreshing and attractive.

I gave her the requisite tour of the club before settling in at our table. We didn't order for a while, as she seemed content to enjoy our conversation and the vibrant atmosphere of the crowded dining room.

I did, too, for a while.

It was the usual first-date Q&A at the beginning, but after drinks and dinner arrived, Michelle got down to business and became more pointed in her questions. Sometimes she would stay on one subject for a while and drill down, while at other times, she would veer from one subject to the next somewhat randomly. But her questions were always specific and probing. What did you do when you found out such and such, or why did you think you had to do such and such?

After a while, it began to feel like I was in a verbal tennis match with a hard-hitting player intent on keeping me on the run all over the court. It was all I could do to come up with quick answers to her rapid-fire questions and then respond again to her follow-ups. An hour later, I was exhausted, frustrated, and ready to be done with this unexpected inquisition.

Then, out of the blue, I answered something that contradicted an earlier response, and she pounced. With her eyes wide open and a finger pointed at my face, she shouted, "Ah ha! Ah ha! You said earlier, yada yada yada! … yada yada yada!"

Ah ha, what? I thought, staring dumbfounded at her.

The inquisition had seemingly reached its climactic moment. It felt like a courtroom drama I had seen a thousand times. I was the accused killer and had been caught in a lie at my murder trial while I was on the stand. But it had to do with something I said about peanut butter, of all things, forty-five minutes earlier.

This was nuts in more ways than one, and The Boys woke up from their slumber.

Ha, ha! Sucks to be you! they shouted in laughter.

I brushed off her accusatory finger-pointing with some amusing remark, but I was far from amused. She continued to look at me with an "I win" smirky grin affixed to her face, her eyes bugged out, and an expression of "gotcha!"

We spent another half hour or so at the club, and then I drove her home. Sitting back in my seat, I waited for any clues as to what her next move might be. But she sat still and silent looking at me, seemingly content to remain in the van. With that, I moved toward her and leaned in for a kiss. She was ready and willing, and we locked lips and then some. I made it a doozy that went on for quite some time.

With a grin on her face and half out of breath, she pulled back and said, "Wow! That's one heck … of a first-date kiss!"

I pulled back, too, thinking I would say something nice before wishing her goodnight, but to my surprise, I blurted out, "You know, you ask way-y-y too many questions. Goodnight … and good luck."

****

About two weeks after my date with Michelle, I had a date with the youngest woman I would meet during my three years on Venus. Her name was Cathy. She was forty-two years old, and her online profile was fairly generic. From her photos, she was a nice-looking woman with long auburn hair and a fantastic smile. She was an analyst, which in this town, usually means CIA, NSA, or some other super-secret agency. Our early communication phase was unremarkable.

The most attention-grabbing thing about her was that she was interested in me at all. I could fairly easily group all the women who were matches into one broad age category, but she was well outside of it. Her profile status was never married, but she had one child at home. I wondered if she decided to have a child on her own with a sperm donor or something.

Definitely a question to be answered.

Arriving early at the Ritz-Carlton for our afternoon date, I grabbed a cozy little seating group that would give her the option of either sitting beside me on the sofa or directly across from me. Waiting for her, I did the usual wondering about someone I was to meet for the first time.

Would she look like her pictures? was the most obvious thought. I was looking forward to the great smile in her photos.

But why is she interested in an older guy like me, and how old is her child? were questions that kept nagging.

Sitting there facing the entrance, I saw her come through the door and into the lobby. When she saw and recognized me, I thought a smile would soon appear on her face. Instead, I was taken aback and realized something was seriously wrong. Not only was there no smile—if my reading of her was correct—she wasn't happy to be here at all.

Uh oh, Darrell whispered, *you're screwed!*

She walked quickly but not as if she wanted to greet me as soon as possible. It was more like she was in a hurry. Her facial expression was terse, and her lips were tight and horizontal.

I rose from my seat, stood with a smile to greet her, and thought for sure she would offer a smile back.

She didn't.

We shook hands, and she sat down across from me, not beside me.

"Hi," I said as warmly as I could. "So nice to meet you."

"Yes, you too," she responded, terse and businesslike.

This is going to be bruu-tal, Charles chipped in, all The Boys now laughing and yukking it up.

I asked if she'd like to have something to drink and said I was going to have hot tea to warm up a bit. I then commented on how cozy it was with the fireplace right beside us and all.

She declined the drink offer, ignored the "cozy" comment, and ordered a glass of water.

As we launched into the usual questions, I found myself having flashbacks to one of the few hostile job interviews of my architectural career. It happened almost twenty years earlier not far from where we were sitting. During the interview, it seemed I could say nothing that this senior partner wouldn't criticize. He even dismissed my Harvard degree as being pretty useless in Washington.

I asked where she was from, about brothers and sisters, and family in general. She had grown up nearby and had plenty of family in the area. But she zipped through her answers to my questions and got right to the point.

"Look, I have a babysitter with my son, so I'm in a bit of a hurry. He's four years old, and I adopted him. Can I ask you about your family?"

"Ah-h-h, sure," I responded warily.

She asked me not only about my children and how I had raised them but also about my mother and father and how I was raised. She frowned upon learning that my parents were divorced, but I seemed to score points when she found out I had been a stay-at-home dad for eleven years.

Over twenty long, painful minutes, it became clear I wasn't there for the usual compatible-mate interview but instead a daddy interview for her son. She said she wanted a father figure in their lives but wasn't necessarily looking for a relationship that might lead to anything.

She was clear, serious, tight-lipped, and to the point the whole time.

This needs to end, and it needs to end now, said Charles.

As gracefully as I could, I noted that I didn't want to keep her babysitter waiting, and it had been nice to meet her. She seemed content to wrap it up; from the first handshake to the last was a mere forty minutes.

Declining my offer to walk her out, she stood up and dashed out. As I plopped back down into the sofa, I was stunned.

Flabbergasted, The Boys asked, *Is this what we're in for? Really? Please tell us it's not.*

Sadly, it was, because this was a *special* day—my first two-date day.

That evening, I met Leslie, an attractive, dark-haired woman who was an accomplished doctor. In our pre-communication phase, she wondered out loud what my Myers-Briggs score would be—a clue of things to come.

We met at my club for dinner and for ninety minutes she told me all the things I was doing wrong that would ruin my eyesight, make my bones weak, make my skin wrinkle, and shorten my life. According to her, I was generally an unhealthy and uninformed doofus. She had two dogs that I had noticed in one of her online profile photos, and she made the point several times that they were much better than any man could be.

What could possibly be running through this woman's mind? The Boys said with their hands up in total surrender.

I concluded that beating up on men and being a total jerk—*jerk* being a term usually reserved for men—were *likes* of hers, but ones she'd left off her online profile.

****

Notwithstanding Michelle, Cathy, and Leslie, other recent one-and-done dates had been pleasant and drama-free but with the same unsatisfying result: nothing. Considering the trend, I made what I thought was a significant course correction on the dating-ship Venus: first dates would be followed by a second as long as the woman seemed interested and our first date hadn't been a disaster, a situation I was now reflexively braced for.

Doubting that lightning and that magical moment would ever strike twice—like when I first saw my wife-to-be on the ballroom dance floor—it seemed to me, this time around was going to be a more deliberate process of seek and discovery to find that special person. Making an immediate *no* decision based on only one date might not be the best way to go about this, I reasoned. A single date had too much pressure on it with the rapid-fire checking off of must-have quality boxes, always feeling like I was on the clock, trying to guess what a total stranger was thinking about me, and often second-guessing what I was thinking about them. This decision drew mixed opinions from The Boys, Darrell being the most opposed.

Embarking on this strategy of at least two dates, I then became aware of something previously unknown in my earlier dating years: the unwritten but *well-known-to-everyone-else* Three-Date Rule.

The Three-Date Rule says it's make-or-break time on the third date. Either there's a high level of mutual attraction with a longer dating future in the cards—maybe even a lasting relationship—or confirmation that nothing is going to happen, and it's time to move on.

If a kiss hadn't yet happened, it needed to on the third date to move forward, and thoughts of sex came into play.

Conversely, if a relationship starts with sex on the first date, then getting to the third date is a real milestone. It's a sign that it's about more than just the sex—you genuinely like each other and have an incredible connection, or so the *Rule* says.

Sex on the first date isn't a sign of a future together, of course. It's a sign the sexual chemistry between you is zooming off the charts and sex is the obvious next step. Or perhaps, you both got smashingly drunk.

Halfway through my time on Venus, I started using OkCupid for online dating. They gave personal but optional questions to answer that would automatically be shared with any match. One category of questions was about sex, and one prominent question asked, "How many dates would you typically go on before considering having sex?" I was amazed at how many women answered this question openly, and the third date was far and away the most common answer.

Having the benefit of several women friends (including Abby) also in dating mode, expectations within the Three-Date Rule were thought about and talked about *all* the time. It was carved in stone and written with blinking neon lights.

****

Mid-December brought a date with a school administrator, a nice woman named Sandy. Like me, Sandy was fairly new to online dating and was appropriately cautious. Immediately upon meeting her, I could tell she was a warm, kind, and lovely woman.

Divorced for several years, Sandy told me yet another story of lies and deception about an ex-husband; these stories would never stop surprising me. She had arrived at a nice place in life with a great job she loved, and a home that I'm sure was as warm and inviting as she was. I would describe her as the mom or schoolteacher that every little boy wished they had. It was a pleasurable two hours together.

After walking to her car, we exchanged a brief, but nice kiss. Lingering in the after-moment—that little intimate moment that hangs in the air just after your lips part—she offered, "I want to say there is nothing about you that gives me any pause or concern. I just want you to know that. I have no concerns at all, Turner."

It would seem I had passed the "you're not a cheating scumbag, snake-under-a rock, stalker, or potential serial killer test," and she wanted to let me know.

Isn't that special, The Boys said sarcastically.

When I shared this with Abby on Monday morning, she immediately deadpanned, "I understand her perfectly, Turner. Perfectly. That's why you're my friend. Because I have absolutely no concerns about you in any way, none at all. I just want you to know that."

Then she smirked and gave a hearty laugh. "What can I say?"

Given my self-imposed second-date mandate, we went out again shortly after. It was a *no* with certainty by the end of the date, but not without regret. Sandy was a super nice person who easily could have been a great friend, but I sensed in her an attraction to me that I couldn't reciprocate. Rules being rules, that was that with Sandy.

****

Another evening in December was filled with anticipation, as I was to meet a woman who had grabbed my attention with her profile photo. Think of the Olympic figure skater from the seventies Dorothy Hamill, blonde instead of brunette (and yes, perhaps I did have a crush on her at the time, like many other adolescent boys) and you pretty much have her. Kate was a natural beauty originally from Texas. Our first date was dinner at my club on a chilly Friday evening.

Kate arrived thirty minutes late, as she got lost finding her way there in the dark. But even as she was apologizing, her perpetual shining smile never left her face, and her easy manner and carefree spirit were infectious—at least for the moment.

93

I gave her a tour of the clubhouse, and from there we went to the more casual dining area with a warm fire ablaze. It felt nice being with her, and The Boys started whispering, *maybe yes?*

Kate had been divorced for four years. She worked in advertising, had two grown children, and lived in the upscale Washington, D.C., enclave of The Palisades.

As we had drinks and began dinner, I became aware that Kate's smile hardly ever wavered. It was certainly nice to look at, but—after looking at her for two hours—it finally struck me that it was more like a perpetual toothy grin than a smile.

How can smiling seem so peculiar? I thought.

When it never stops! The Boys blurted out.

Turn her off! they begged.

Even when I asked several serious questions, her grin sort of hung on as she gave her answers. It started to feel a little weird. No one can be that happy— or rather, grin—all the time.

At some point, I decided to ask a variation of the question that had tripped me up with Stephanie two months before. "Where do you see yourself in the future?"

I figured if anything could diminish the toothy grin, having to give a thoughtful answer would do the trick.

With a contemplative furrow of her brow but her grin still intact, she answered, "I have absolutely no idea." She then tilted her head slightly and fixed her gaze at me with her happy grin turned up to a thousand watts.

The answer alone would have been fine, given my inability to answer the question, but with her unflinching grin and tilt of her head, Kate came off as a ditz.

A rather high coefficient-of-blonde, don't you think? offered Charles.

This aside, the evening was pleasant enough, she seemed interested in me, and it certainly wasn't hard being with a blonde Dorothy Hamill. At the end of the date, we exchanged a nice hug and kisses on the cheeks. I walked away thinking she was a *maybe* ... maybe.

Early in the new year, I picked her up at her home on a Saturday night for dinner and a movie. She looked as nice as before, but the grinning thing had thankfully diminished.

Dinner conversation revolved around how we spent our Christmas holidays, our families, and what each was doing at work. Normal stuff for the most part, and everything felt comfortable. I was game to see how she might respond to a little bit of flirting, but she never offered a hint of interest.

With the chemistry either reluctant to come out or just not there, The Boys thought she was now a *maybe no*. But on the drive back to her house, there was a mutual and smooth transition into talking about going out again.

Opening her car door in front of her home, she didn't ask me to come in, so we exchanged a brief kiss right there. With absolutely no fireworks at all from the kiss, we simply wished each other goodnight.

Three weeks later, we had our third date. My first *third* date with anyone.

Kate had two tickets for a gallery show and brunch at The Phillips Collection near Dupont Circle in Washington. As an art lover, I thought it was a great suggestion and checked off the "likes art" box.

We met at the gallery and spent the next hour and a half doing a somewhat polite museum crawl. In truth, with no apparent chemistry and what felt like forced pleasantries, the date was over not more than five minutes in. The pivotal third date had done its job of sorting things out.

During my time on Venus, the Three-Date Rule was more of a red stoplight than a green go-light. Relationships that went beyond three dates were typically *Wow!* from the first date. It was also, for me anyway, a rule that kept me honest most of the time. If I were considering asking someone out on a third date because I had nothing better to do, I knew it could be taken as a sign of further interest, thus I had to tread carefully. The few times I broke the rule for no reason other than I wanted to, I left some hard feelings in my wake, which I always regretted.

****

In the months between December and March, Kate was one of fourteen women I met. Among the fourteen was another Parisian connection. It went the two-date minimum but turned out even worse than my first French encounter back in September. Among the more memorable quotes, "I don't hold hands or even think about kissing because then it's just all about sex! sex! sex!"

And then there was, "Why didn't you bring me flowers? This is our second date!"

The second date had been a forty-five-minute lunch meetup in her office cafeteria at the International Monetary Fund. I had made an arm-touching gesture when she stopped the conversation cold to make her emphatic statement against public displays of affection because it all just leads to "…sex! sex! sex!"

Clearly, she wasn't in the Jane Fonda dating camp.

Dating during these four months was a real mix and churn process. My current method of total dating immersion was yielding nothing but frustration and a lot of wasted time. I questioned not only my judgment in picking matches to meet—it seemed awful—but also the whole notion of meeting someone for any reason at all. It felt like who I was as a man, at my age, and for my circumstances, was totally out of sync with the general middle-aged female dating population. Being a hopeless romantic only made matters worse.

I talked to Abby and Wendy. While they sympathized, they urged me to press on.

"You haven't been back out there that long," Wendy said one evening on the phone. "Don't give up. Someone out there is going to be a very lucky woman. I so-o-o-o want you to find happiness, dear. We all do. No one deserves it more than you."

After giving it a lot of thought, I realized that perhaps I had set my match filters too narrow; I decided to open them all up and expand the dating-distance radius as well, from twenty-five to fifty miles.

****

While expanding the filters brought in new and interesting matches, meeting women through eHarmony wasn't the only way I was putting myself out there. During my time on Venus, I met two women through Facebook. It happened that the first meeting with one of them took place around this time but was well over a year in the making.

I first saw Diane when she appeared in a Facebook video posted by a male friend. She was a colleague of his in the tech industry, and he was congratulating her on a business accomplishment. Even then, a good six months before I pushed myself out into the dating world, I couldn't help but notice her. She was awesomely attractive, well-spoken, poised, and with a strong personal sense of style—my type if there ever was one. I searched for her on Facebook and sent her a message of congratulations. From there, we exchanged messages about my friend and had an extended messaging conversation over several months. Not a few messages a week sort of thing, but a few messages every month or so. She sent a Facebook friend request at some point, and I accepted.

Over the year that followed, as I finally emerged from the grief of my loss and rejoined life again, I noticed Diane's Facebook posts were all about optimism, life, and reaching for goals. It was just the sort of thing I needed. She often started the morning by posting an optimistic message for the day. I wondered if she was some sort of motivational speaker or something on the side. Whatever it was, seeing her on Facebook always left me happier than the moment before, and I wondered if perhaps this was a sign.

So it was of great concern when, around Christmas, she posted words alluding to tough times and sadness. This was not the Diane I knew. Something had happened; something was wrong.

I suppose being a survivor of someone who took her own life and knowing what preceded it made me more sensitive to this sort of thing, so I texted Diane on Facebook Messenger.

> **ME:** We are only FB friends, but I saw your rather pensive posts today. R u ok?

> **DIANE:** Thanks, Turner. Several things happened all at once last week in my family and relationship. You are the only one who noticed.

> **ME**: I specialize in helping damsels in distress! Let me know if you'd like to talk.

DIANE: Haha! I clearly am a damsel in distress! But things are better now. Thanks for reaching out. I hope you and your family are doing well. Have a great day. Stay in touch.

Through the end of December and into the New Year, we exchanged occasional messages. I told her one of my New Year's resolutions was to invite her to meet for coffee or tea. She readily agreed we should meet, and we picked a weekend afternoon.

After warm greetings and hugs, we went right into a conversation about everything. We knew a fair amount about each other, but two hours together allowed us to fill in the details. A successful professional and a dedicated mom, Diane was also very health-conscious and outspoken on many issues. She was traffic-stopping beautiful and had a persona of perfection—perfectly dressed, perfectly made up, and perfectly well-spoken. It was the kind of perfection that made you aware of everything about yourself that wasn't.

I asked her what happened in her relationship—if she didn't mind my asking—that had gotten her so despondent back in December.

She said her boyfriend had been getting increasingly upset about the time she was spending with her teenage children and *not* with him. She said he was getting angrier about it and questioned her motherhood, parenting skills, and commitment to the relationship. She was being put in a position of having to make choices she didn't want to make, so with great sadness, she left the relationship. It had been a tough decision, and she was despondent at the time of her post.

Diane was obviously a devoted mother to her kids, no less so than I was a father to mine. Of course, your children come first. If anyone questioned me about my need to be a parent to my children, that would be fatal to the relationship.

We ended our time together with a warm embrace. Feeling little heart-flutters, I asked her out for a Saturday night.

I picked her up at her house and we drove to my club. I talked about having a casual dinner to keep the evening light, but after giving her the tour and then sitting in the more formal clubhouse, a casual dinner didn't quite seem to fit the mood of the moment. She was dressed perfectly, as usual, so I requested a club blazer to slip on, and we went into the formal dining room for a candlelit dinner.

This is more like it, I thought.

Atta-boy, said The Boys.

I hoped she would appreciate the more elegant setting and gourmet menu. I knew the chef would send out samplings of various delicious little bites before and between courses, and they were always a treat, even for a guy like me who was so unsophisticated in the food department.

After taking our drink order, the waiter came out with the first of several tasting treats from the chef, one for each of us.

"Napoleon of Potato Crisp with Tuna and Foie Gras Confit with a Black Truffle Vinaigrette," said the smiling waiter. They looked delightful on the two little plates.

Upon hearing the description, however, Diane stared at them as though rat poison had been put down before us.

I knew she was health-conscious and was involved in the promotion of nutritional supplements. I knew, too, that she questioned what constituted healthy eating, but the expression that came to her face was something to behold.

First, she glared in silence at the labored-over, artistic-looking plates put before us. Then, like a little picky-eater child, her nose wrinkled and her upper lip curled up ever so slightly. Picture someone doing an Elvis facial impersonation with one side of the upper lip curled up, and you have it.

"NO," she emphatically declared.

Not, "Thank you, no."

Not, "Thanks, but no thanks."

Not, "How wonderful, but not for me right now."

Just, "NO."

By the way she spoke, she not only declined the offering, but she also rendered judgment on it. It was an uncomfortable moment. The waiter fumbled with what to say and do.

"Umm ... shall I take it away?"

She continued to look at the little plate in silence.

"YES," she finally responded.

My remaining little plate looked conspicuously lonely and awkward on the white tablecloth as its rejected mate was sent to the food gallows via the garbage disposal.

I guiltily consumed mine, even as she told me not to worry.

I didn't say, "Yum, that was delicious," as I might normally have. Instead, I ate in silence, and my worry grew with uneasy anticipation of the evening ahead.

I caught the waiter during a made-up trip to the men's room and told him, "No more treats from the chef unless we order them."

Perhaps now being more comfortable with me on our second date, Diane didn't hold back. Conversations with her elicited more statements of opinion and moments of pause that felt rendered in judgment. I have to say her views weren't off the wall; quite the contrary, they were generally just and right— almost perfect, really. It was the sense of judgment that came with everything that was the problem.

Diane was a picture of perfection in beauty, accomplishment, beliefs, morals, justice, injustice, optimism, truth, and kindness, and she was true to her principles through thick and thin. A lot of perfection was sitting there across the table, but it was from a different place than where I sat.

Her sense of perfection came with judgment of your imperfections, making you feel like ... well ... when you're confronted by two eager Mormon missionaries looking at you with bright eyes, perfectly cut hair, black ties, and crisp white shirts (even on ninety-degree days). At that moment, you feel pretty darn imperfect, but you know they come from some form of alternate universe with very different points of view.

As much as I admired Diane for all that she was and stood for, it was clear— well before the main course ended—that she was not for the very imperfect Turner Grant.

CHAPTER 6

Kiss Me Not, Kiss Me Now

WITH MY DATING-PREFERENCE FILTERS OPENED up, by mid-January, I was averaging eight to fourteen new online dating matches a day.

Talk about self-inflicted pain. I mean, we are talking fifty to seventy honest-men-seeking women each week. It was nuts.

I deleted matches more often than not and cavalierly sent out *winks* and *smiles* to see what might come back. Only a few caught my attention and were worth a closer look. But even with those, by now I was beginning to loathe the whole process. It was mind-numbingly repetitious, time-consuming, and unexciting. Each profile, although with slightly different words, seemed to read the same: "I'm special, looking for someone special, so we can be special together."

Ugh!

Each time, it felt like I was throwing my ten thousandth dating dart into empty space. Looking back, it felt like the very definition of the proverbial abyss—the online dating abyss, that is.

So when a particular photo caught my eye one dreary February morning and The Boys yelled *Stop!* I was unexpectedly yanked out of my dating gloom.

With her large, brown, almond-shaped eyes, I guessed she was Middle Eastern. She had an incredible twinkle in her eyes and a closed-mouth smile that hinted at a certain kind of reserve. But it was a pixie-esque reserve, and it was incredibly sexy. It was a professional studio-type photo—obviously done for her job—but it was a good one, and I was smitten.

101

Her profile said she lived five miles away, was my age, and was involved in the public relations business. She, like most women who now caught my eye, had a great sense of style in her personal appearance.

Her name was Caliana.

She spoke three languages: English, French, and Arabic. She had no lists of must-haves or not-haves for guys, which was unusual. With little else to go on, it was her one photo I found myself looking at again and again, in search of more clues about her.

I resolved one thing in my mind almost immediately—there was no way I was going to go through the excruciating pre-communication process with her. I wanted to reach out to her directly and let her know she had caught my attention.

But how to do it and what to say?

It couldn't be a bunch of made-up lines; I'm not that clever. After mulling over how to go about it, I finally decided I'd be fearless and honest with her. Wasn't that what women said they wanted? This would certainly test the declaration of the honest-men-seeking women of the general middle-aged female dating population.

I started composing my message, and much to my surprise, it all flowed out pretty quickly and easily. It went something like this:

> Hi, Caliana,
>
> I know this breaks the rules, but I saw your profile and picture. I thought I would take a chance and write to you directly; I hope you approve. Quite frankly, I thought your photo was captivating and the brief information about you left me very intrigued. I would love to meet you.
>
> Feel free to Google 'Turner Grant Congress,' and you'll find me pretty easily—there are no secrets to hide. If you are then as intrigued about me as I am about you (and I hope you are), might we meet?

I offered an invitation to meet for lunch at my club on a Sunday. I hoped that between her finding everything there was to know about me online and the club invitation, she would be intrigued enough to say yes.

She was, and she did.

She thanked me for writing and said she considered it charmingly bold that I would be so direct. She added she was more than impressed with what she read online about me and was flattered by my invitation.

Okay, note to self. The honest/direct method is a good way to go.

Since I knew so little about her, it felt a bit like a blind date for me, albeit with one photo in hand. She, of course, had all kinds of information on me. My entire life story was out there on the internet.

But it all felt good—really good—and really exciting. I thought it might be a turning point, a breaking out of the online dating abyss I had fallen into. It was time to do this my way rather than someone else's way, and I was psyched.

****

I saw Caliana through the front windows of the clubhouse and watched as she came inside. Caliana looked incredible. The photo I had found so captivating just a few days before now came to life—she was positively radiant.

She was dressed with a restrained elegance I fell in love with immediately— her clothing, her makeup, her accessories, even the way she carried herself exuded a personal energy that made the spacious and refined grand sitting room positively glow with her presence.

When she saw me, she quickly walked over and gave me a nice and polite hug. She smiled broadly with the incredibly cute, sheepish grin I had seen in her photo—shy but knowing, willing but holding back. She spoke with an accent and charmed me with each word she spoke.

She was a woman who oozed femininity.

The Boys took notice in a way they hadn't since Joyce nine months before. *This woman is in a league of her own,* Charles said, speaking for all The Boys.

Chatting as I slow-walked her through a tour of the club, we maintained a polite friendliness, all the while trying to hide what seemed to be coquettish feelings on both sides.

Making our way to where we would have lunch, we sat down at a table near a blazing fireplace with a clear view of the winter landscape outside. Families with children were scurrying around the large dining area. A happy, winter-holiday vibe permeated the space, taking away any pressure of formality.

Smiling at each other, we took measure of the moment.

We made the obvious remarks about how unusual this was, and how we were both taking a chance. I then added that she knew a lot about me, but I knew nothing about her.

"So, may I ask what you do?" I said.

The Boys immediately gave me grief. *Oh, that's really smooth, Turner. Wake us up sometime, say ... in the next twenty years when you get somewhere with her.*

She worked at a public relations company, was divorced, and had several grown children in the area. Given her outward appearance and personality, I imagined she won over anyone she came in contact with during her work. She grew up in a Middle Eastern country but was part of a minority there. The story she then went on to tell was one of the most amazing I had ever heard firsthand.

While in her early twenties, during a period of devastating civil war, she escaped the fighting by literally walking out of the country over mountains and difficult terrain, with battles all around. She escaped alone, while her family chose to stay behind. Over several weeks, she made her way through two countries before finding safety. Then, with the help of friends, she made it to the United States. Caliana stayed away from her home country for many years until it was safe for her to visit her family, which she now did often.

For the next twenty minutes, she shared details that were personal and painful. I listened quietly and carefully and asked several questions, which she answered. I was left both frightened for her and awestruck. What she had done on her own as a young woman, in what was then one of the most dangerous places in the world, was nothing short of astounding.

She met a man a few years later in Washington, married, and began a family and career.

When she finished her story, I expressed my utter amazement and admiration for what she had done and endured. Nothing in my life could compare to what she had experienced; it was jaw-dropping.

To break the seriousness of the moment and take the pressure off her a bit, I shared a silly story about ice skating with my young boys and how I was in constant fear for my safety.

"It was terrifying too," I said.

She got the silly joke, laughed with a sense of relief, and smiled so very sweetly.

What an amazing woman, I thought.

Slowly working our way through lunch, the conversation switched over to me. She was keen to know what had happened to my wife. While staying with the story of heart failure, I otherwise truthfully conveyed the details of saying goodbye to my wife one morning and being widowed by lunch on that terrible day, and then of the two years that followed. Shaking her head often, I knew she understood the pain, shock, and devastation of how my life had been turned upside down.

In fact, she seemed to understand my experience better than anyone I had met in the last nine months. Her experiences living on the edge seemed to have given her many of the same filters about life I now had: a greater appreciation of how precious time and life are; an ability to discard things unimportant and irrelevant; and an intense appreciation of family and friends. It seemed we understood life in a similar way, although we couldn't have been more different.

When I finished my story, we sat across from each other in silence for a few moments.

It was now her turn to speak first.

"You know, I took a chance coming here today. I just had this feeling I should meet you. I have to tell you, Turner, I'm awfully glad I did. I feel like we have this connection even though we were strangers two hours ago."

Her gorgeous eyes then locked on mine, and she looked deep inside me.

I smiled.

She smiled.

"I'm really glad you came, too, Caliana. I feel the same. But don't ever meet a strange man like me again. What would your mother say?"

She laughed and playfully tilted her head back in a relaxed and flirtatious way.

That sealed the moment.

As we walked outside, the chemistry between us was palpable. Stopping by her car, she turned and gestured for a hug, which I happily offered, and then it became a momentary embrace. She then tilted her head back to one side, offering me her cheek, which I kissed.

"Can I see you again soon?" I asked.

"I would really like that," she said.

Back home, I waited not more than an hour before emailing her and suggesting a second date on Saturday night.

Caliana wrote back, saying she would love to see me again, and suggested cocktails at a recently renovated hotel bar that she said had a cool, international design atmosphere. That week, we emailed each other every day, checking in and expressing how much we were looking forward to Saturday night.

I logged on to eHarmony and clicked the setting that stopped any more *new* matches from being sent.

With any luck, I was now done with this stuff.

****

The soaring space of the hotel lobby, bar, and lounge was stunning and impressed this discerning design snob. The minimalist bar was made of backlit onyx marble panels and framed like a stage with a soaring, two-story, wood-paneled proscenium arch. Classic modern furniture with leather and chrome, along with suede sofas, made up various cozy sitting groups. Dim but dramatic lighting highlighted many other well-executed design details.

It was sparsely occupied and felt like the perfect place for a rendezvous on this cold February night. I arrived first and seated myself in the corner of one of the L-shaped sofas when she texted.

> **CALIANA:** I'm on my way to you.

> **ME:** Can't wait to see you! May I order a drink for you and have it waiting?

> **CALIANA:** How thoughtful. I'll have a Bellini.

> **ME:** Ordered and on its way!

> **CALIANA** :-)

When she arrived, she walked quickly toward me, smiling and looking stunning once again. She had on a mock-fur jacket, eye-catching snug silk slacks, and high heels; she looked immaculately sexy and wonderful.

"You look FAB-ulous!" I said.

"You look quite handsome yourself," she said in a quick retort. "It's so nice to see you."

We exchanged kisses on each other's cheeks, a short embrace, and I directed her to the corner sofa.

She came around the table to the inside corner of the sofa and sat to my left. If she wanted to, she could put her legs up on the sofa extending out from the corner. She kept her coat on when she sat down, and I snuggled up next to her. She then snuggled up a bit more next to me.

As we looked at each other, trying to figure out how to begin the conversation, I offered up a silly question to hopefully make her laugh. "Can I get inside that coat with you? It's so cold tonight."

She laughed. "You want to get inside my coat with me? That might be difficult."

"Never mind. It was just a thought."

"Well, we could try. There's probably enough room in here."

She proceeded to unbutton her coat, slip her arm out, then put the coat around my shoulders. I snuggled in with her, tugging the coat around to my other side. We grabbed each other's hand and entwined our arms so that my left arm was over her right breast. She put both legs up on the sofa; I moved in closer still, putting my left leg up beside hers, and we melted into each other.

"So is this okay?" she asked, with a knowing smile.

"I think it works pretty well," I said, with the same expression back.

The Boys were holding their collective breaths with excitement.

Where might this go? they discussed. *Don't forget, this is a h-o-t-e-l, Romeo!*

With her large eyes shyly looking at me, she said, "I've only just met you and here we are like this. You've rather got me cornered. Should I be worried?"

"If it's too much, we could sit over there," I offered, pointing to a cocktail table and stools not far away.

"No. I think this will work if you promise to be good."

"I *might* be able to promise that," I answered in an unsure tone of voice.

She smiled approvingly with just a touch of mock-fear—this woman who walked over the mountains in wartime.

The next two hours were magical. Snuggled into each other and partially entwined on the sofa, flirtatious and suggestive banter mixed in with more questions about each other—our lives, our families, our jobs, our dreams, travel, and more. We were positively lost in one another in our private togetherness on this cold February night.

Finally, I decided it was time to make a move, but nothing on the sly, I decided.

"I have a thought I'd like to run by you, if that's okay?"

"A thought you'd like to run by me?" she said coyly. "Okay."

"My thought is, I would like to kiss you right now."

She paused momentarily, then said, "Oh … that's not something I can do."

What?! The Boys said, caught totally off guard and unsure if she might be joking.

Does she have a cold? Is something more coming? Or is she serious about this?

We had been sitting here, body to body, wrapped in the cocoon of her fur coat, with me nuzzled into her breasts in a dimly lit lounge, having suggestive conversations for almost two hours.

"I really can't do that until I know you much much better," she said.

She's serious!

My head and heart went into a confused state.

"You don't kiss or don't like to kiss?" I asked.

This was new territory, and I tried to mask my fumbling search for an understanding. *Was this a cultural thing? A personal choice? Or what exactly?* I wondered if something really bad had happened before.

"No, I like to kiss." Then she repeated, "But I have to know you much much better before kissing you. That's just the way I am."

"Well …then could I ask for you to let me know when that might be?" I said, trying to save the moment and our evening together.

I also heard the voice of my second French encounter from six weeks earlier saying, "Holding hands and kissing just leads to sex! sex! sex! No! No! No!"

"Of course," she said, fluttering her eyelashes over her gorgeous eyes.

"Well … ahem … is it okay for us to be like this?" I asked flirtatiously but also seriously. At this point, I wanted to know what her ground rules were.

"I like it. Don't you?" she said softly.

"I hope I don't really need to answer that question, Caliana."

"No. I think you've answered it pretty well already," she offered with a knowing look.

We talked for another hour, wrapped up together on the sofa until just after midnight. Nothing about our intense chemistry had diminished, but navigating her ways had become decidedly unsure for me.

We walked out of the hotel, arms firmly around each other, tightly pulling the other close. Standing by her car, we shared a nice long embrace and lingering kisses on each other's cheeks and then said goodnight.

As I drove home, I wondered how to proceed. All the dating etiquette rules I knew were out the window. *Now what?*

This foreign beauty had captured my heart in so many ways, but I needed to figure out how to go forward with her. After a lot of thinking and back and forth with The Boys, Charles shared what he thought was the best way forward. *Seems to me good old-fashioned courting is what's required.*

It wasn't something my generation usually did, but it seemed to make the most sense.

****

Along with coming back into the world of the living after two years of grieving, I was also taking baby steps back into politics, but this time at a local level. I was running for an elected position in my community. I was just getting a handle on how I needed to campaign for the seat when, four days after my date with Caliana, an invitation came my way.

The local chamber of commerce was having its annual gala at the headquarters of a nearby Fortune 500 company, which would feature speeches by a few local notables. It was the perfect event for me to meet, greet, and campaign for votes, so I needed to be there.

But it was late Wednesday morning when I got the invitation, and the dinner was for Friday night; I would have to scramble to get a ticket. I was now so used to going to everything alone, I kicked myself for not thinking that Caliana might like to go too. I quickly sent her a text explaining the situation, and she texted back in less than a minute.

> **CALIANA**: Yes! It would be a great opportunity for me to meet important people for my business, and I get to be there with you! :-)

> **ME:** Thrilled you can join me. Can't wait!

> **CALIANA**: I really owe you one. Thank you so much!

Might that kiss be forthcoming? I wondered.

The keynote speaker for the Friday event happened to be the wife of one of the partners at the architectural firm where I worked. Cindy was a prominent businesswoman who possessed a great sense of humor and wit. I had met her several times at various office functions, and she was also aware of the loss of my wife.

Her husband, Steve, happened to be at my desk after I bought the tickets, chatting about the project I was working on. I mentioned I was going to the event where Cindy would be speaking Friday night.

"Yeah, she told me she had something to go to and give some sort of speech," he said. "She's pretty much not looking forward to it. One of those obligations she has to do all the time. I'll tell her you'll be there. She'll be happy to see a friendly face. Are you going alone?"

"No," I said with a pause. "I'll have a date."

He smiled kindly and approvingly. "I'll definitely tell her to be looking for you."

****

Friday evening arrived, and I was so looking forward to seeing Caliana.

She was going to give me a little time to mingle and campaign alone before meeting me there. It was the usual crowd of local businesspeople, all talking up this or that. I knew most of the political types, but that was about all. When

I got our seating assignment, I discovered, much to my surprise, we were seated at the head table with the host for the evening and the various speakers, including Cindy.

Caliana texted she had arrived, so I went to the parking garage to meet her. She looked even more elegant and gorgeous than ever in a layered, black chiffon, partially see-through cocktail dress that said *Wow!* from head to toe.

"You look incredibly sexy in that dress," I said.

"Why thank you," she offered with a demurring smile.

How lucky am I to be with her tonight, I thought.

Without missing a beat, and as though she had heard my private thoughts, she said, "How lucky am I to be with you tonight, Turner, but I'm a little nervous. These are all your people."

I leaned in close and grabbed her hand. "Caliana, once they get a look at you in that dress, they'll all be *your* people, and you'll be introducing me!"

From then on, for the rest of the night, we never let go of each other.

We walked into the scrum of the cocktail-party crowd, and I saw Cindy. I introduced her to Caliana, and Caliana was duly impressed that I knew her. She knew who Cindy was and how important she was but had never had the occasion to meet her.

I sarcastically said to Cindy, "I know from Steve how much you're looking forward to speaking tonight."

She rolled her eyes, smirked, and tossed out a witty retort under her breath so as not to be overheard. We all laughed and then parted until dinner.

After a few more cocktail conversations, we were called to our seats with a ding-dong-ding of the dinner chime. We walked into the room of twenty large tables, elegantly adorned for the evening. Caliana and I walked through them all to the front and stopped at the head table where Cindy was seated and waiting for us. Caliana tugged at my hand and moved her body in to touch mine.

"Now I'm even more impressed," she whispered.

The dinner was the usual sort of too-long-an-event, meaning after an hour, it wasn't much fun. Sitting directly opposite Caliana and me, Cindy looked bored as one of the political speakers droned on. At that moment, I picked up my iPhone, got her attention, and mouthed for her to smile as I took her picture. I smirked at her and said I was going to send it to Steve to show him what *fun* she was having tonight.

Sensing a challenge, she pulled out *her* iPhone and, with an even slyer grin, took our picture. She pointed to her phone then mouthed, "I'm going to send this to Steve so he can see *you two* together. Ha!"

Score that one for Cindy. But she also sent the picture to me, and I showed it to Caliana. She positively beamed, then pulled my hand and arm closer to her body to embrace.

I thought this—now our *third* date—had possibly launched us into a real future together.

****

We both had crazy schedules to navigate the next week, and we struggled to find time to meet. After emailing back and forth, we finally decided to meet at a local upscale mall that Sunday afternoon to do some window shopping and just be together.

We met around four o'clock and spent the next two hours together in bliss. I learned about the clothes she liked, and she learned I could pick out things that looked great on her; she was shocked.

We flirted, held hands, continued serious conversations, and looked at each other constantly as we slow-walked through the mall and the stores. Being together here felt much more personal and intimate, which was part of my idea for suggesting it.

But our time together was much too short. We texted soon after to find another time to meet. In a moment of decisiveness, I decided right then that I wanted and needed to kiss Caliana; I just couldn't hold back anymore. For me, it was the way I knew to let a woman know how I felt, how wonderful she made me feel, and how much she meant to me. I also love kissing, and it was killing me not to be able to, given my feelings for her. I knew it could be fatal to our still-young relationship, but I was ready to step this up and hoped she would be too.

The Boys were supportive but worried.

We're with you. She's a marvelous woman, said Little Turner, *but this is all or nothing.*

Later that week, the scheduling gods looked kindly upon us and brought an unexpected snowstorm. The freaky storm closed schools for a few days and happily opened a window of opportunity in our work schedules for lunch together.

Ten inches of snow had been plowed off the streets the day before, so the winter-wonderland feeling was still there with the sun shining brightly and the crystal-blue sky looking gorgeous. It was all feeling magical and memorable.

For the first time, she asked me to pick her up at her home instead of meeting somewhere, and I took it as a good sign. Not totally dense or with my head in the clouds, I also realized it could've meant she simply didn't like driving on snowy roads, but I went with the former explanation since it better fit my plan for the day.

Once in the car, we greeted each other with the now wonderfully familiar embrace and kiss on each other's cheeks, then we headed out for lunch not far away.

But all I could think of the whole time was that I hoped she finally felt comfortable enough with me, and we had come far enough along, where a kiss would be welcome. I knew I was supposed to wait until she gave a signal, but I was at the breaking point. I had decided if the answer from her was no, then it was time to go our separate ways. I just didn't know what more she needed from me or how to proceed from where we were.

Back to her place after lunch, I pulled into her driveway and turned off the engine. We turned to each other in our seats and hugged once again. As I gave her the usual kiss on her cheek, I lingered a bit before moving my lips toward hers and—excitedly, I thought—felt hers moving toward mine. But just as our lips touched, she abruptly stopped and pulled back. As I leaned back to look at her face, she gazed intently at me, but I couldn't read her. I hoped perhaps we might try again, but she instead thanked me for lunch, got out of the car, and walked to her front door without me.

The Boys shouted as soon as she started to get out of the car, *Noooo! Take it back! Tell her you're sorry!*

But it was too late. There were no take-backs allowed on this one, and I didn't want any take-backs; I simply wanted Caliana to go forward with me. If she wasn't good with my actions and expression of how wonderful I thought she was and how incredible she made me feel, then she was not good with *me*, and it needed to end, as painful as it was.

Over the next week, I sent a couple of friendly emails to see if I could prompt a response, but there was none. I knew she was traveling, so I tried to reason she was too busy to respond. Finally, when I knew she was back in the country, I emailed her.

EMAIL SENT: Lunch?

Caliana,

Are you back in the groove of being back? I am off a few days next week and wanted to see if you would be up for lunch Monday or Tuesday. Would be nice to see you.

Turner

EMAIL RECEIVED: Lunch?

Hi Turner,

Sorry for the delay in replying! It's been crazy catching up with old and new business! I would love to have lunch with you but I am very busy with work. I will take a raincheck on this one. I hope all is well with you and the boys.

Best,

Caliana

It was a raincheck that would never be used.

YEAR TWO

The One-Year One

CHAPTER 7

Heart Twiddles

GIVEN THE SILENCE AFTER CALIANA'S last email, I heard loud and clear that we were done, and I unpaused the button for new matches on eHarmony.

A flood of new women came pouring in like a torrent of water from a perpetual cistern. The hibernation of winter was ending in Washington, D.C., spring was in the air, and the desire of men and women to seek and meet was ramping up.

In only a few days, I had thirty new matches to go with ones from the previous month left hanging during my time with Caliana. I fell back to the shotgun approach, discarding those who were clearly no and tossing out *winks* and *smiles* to others like grass seed on a lawn.

I lined up first and second dates like boxcars on a train. Becoming a semi-professional scheduling juggler, weaving women and dates together at different levels of progression, was clearly a skill-set acquisition for online dating, as well as mastering the art of being able to put on a fresh new face when meeting someone only hours after having met another.

First meetings always included a conversation about dating. You had to fess-up—or fudge—about what you'd been doing, for how long, and how often you went out, all the while trying to be clear that "this time" was different and special.

The latter, of course, was so much bullshit. If you began to master this particular art of bullshit, then you were well on your way to becoming numb to the feelings of others and thoughtless in the ways you treated them. While never mastering this particular skill set during my time on Venus, I nevertheless found myself applying its principles from time to time.

Among the new matches was one I hesitated on day after day. She had six photos of herself on her dating profile, all attractive, but it seemed to me that no more than two looked like they were of the same woman; it was odd. I had been through enough by now to suspect anything remotely suspicious, so I kept her in limbo for a week, unable to decide what to do with her. But then she initiated a first round of pre-communication questions, and I began to slow-walk my way through them.

It so happened my cousin Wendy was back in Washington, and I was anxious to see her. I wanted to get her take on Caliana and have fun with her going through the large batch of new women. She came over to my house, and once again with wine in hand, we settled in to chat about Turner's dating life.

Wendy's take on Caliana and her strict rules for kissing was that it was a cultural thing and doomed from the start. However, she was glad I had gotten "the hots" for someone—all good, in her opinion.

From there, we turned our attention to winnowing down the wide assortment of dating profiles, and just as before, she was quick and cutthroat as she went through the photos.

"No."

"No."

"No."

"Good grief no!"

"Hmmm ... maybe."

"Ah ... who's this?" she asked.

She zeroed in on the woman with the seemingly different pictures. I explained she had been a match for a week or so, but the differences in her pictures made me hesitant. I told Wendy she had already reached out to me, and we were in the Q&A phase, but I didn't know what to do with her.

"*What* differences?" she said. "I don't see any differences. I *like* her. What's her story? What's her name?"

Her name was Emily; she was fifty years old, divorced, and had two children.

Wendy read through Emily's profile and, just as before with the Washington diplomat she picked out, declared, "I like her. I like her a lot! You need to get in touch with her ASAP!"

"Really?" I asked. "Why?"

"I-IIIII j-uussst like her!" said Wendy.

"You don't think the pictures are odd?"

"*Nooo!* She's great!"

And with that, Wendy snapped the iPad shut, handed it back, and drank the last of her wine. "My job is done here. Don't blow it!"

I responded with a mix of skepticism and gratitude.

First communications with any match were pretty routine and repetitive by now. Emily was number twenty-five during my time on Venus, and her messages were fairly ordinary and appropriately cautious. But, in a moment of I'm-not-sure-what, she let her guard down, and it changed the conversation.

"I'd just like to find a great guy," she wrote. "Might that be you? You seem really nice."

With these few simple words, she revealed a bit of her heart, some of her longing, possibly some regrets and heartbreak, and made me feel good, all at the same time.

I returned her kind words, and we moved our conversation to the real world.

Her second email to me was a link, without comment, to a story about a WWII wife who waited sixty-eight years to find out the fate of her missing-in-action husband. It was a story about bureaucratic incompetence, but more importantly, it was a story about enduring love. The widowed wife never moved on and never remarried, saying only that she was "married to Billie all of my life."

The message from Emily was clear; true love is something special and enduring, and she wanted that kind of love … and it gave me pause.

The sentiment of true and enduring love touched my heart, and deep down, I wanted that too, but … *wow* … that's some pretty heavy love stuff to put out there in a second email.

In our next emails, we began to share the details of our lives and approved Google searches on each other. She found a lot about me because of my run for Congress, but she had more to fill in about herself.

With our email conversations going well, I suggested we talk on the phone. She excitedly said yes, and then we ran into what would be a perpetual problem—scheduling. Her schedule was seemingly more difficult than mine, but we finally settled on a call for the next Sunday at noon.

On the call, I got the whole story about her marriage, divorce, and her recent breakup with her longtime boyfriend. The behavior of her ex-husband was abhorrent, and the ex-boyfriend had taken advantage of her financially. She hesitated several times while sharing the details, expressing concern about disclosing some of the choices she had made and now regretted. For too long, she had accepted a cycle of explanations and apologies from both. In retribution, she made decisions as payback that were ultimately not in her best interests and had to be undone with yet more consequences.

The complexity of it all was more than a little uncomfortable to hear, and I wondered what I might be getting myself into. She explained the details in a straightforward way, acknowledging her regrets and missteps alike, but still, I found the whole download of information a bit unnerving.

As The Boys and I were pondering all she had shared, she quickly pivoted the conversation.

"Turner, I don't want to be wasting time."

"You mean with men?"

"Yes, with *you* men!"

"Do you want to get married again?" I asked.

"Yes. Do you?"

"Right now, given where I am, still re-emerging into life? … No."

"Do you rule out changing your mind in the future?" she asked.

"I know enough about life to know that nothing can ever be ruled out, so sure, it's possible I could change my mind, but right now it's a no. I need to be clear and honest about that, and I don't want to waste time being in a relationship with the wrong woman. I can be on my own, but I would love to find a woman who I'm crazy about."

Our cards were now on the table. We paused for a few moments to process what each other had said.

We shifted back to lighter conversation, and she told me she was a manager in the finance office of a major local hospital. She was able to work from home more often than not, and the added flexibility allowed her to better balance work and full-time parenting. She was heavily involved in her community and church and lived about forty-five minutes away. The distance was a bit of a concern, but I figured we'd see how it went, especially since nothing had gone *anywhere* with *anyone* in the last ten months.

She was incredibly kind and thoughtful after I told her the story of my wife's passing from heart failure. She expressed an empathy that was remarkably accurate in understanding the pain and difficulty for me, my boys, and my extended family. I had told the story now twenty or more times, but Emily was spot on in her understanding. Her expressions of sorrow were comforting and supportive, and her kindness began to ease my concerns about her past history.

As we spoke, I told Emily that one of my two children had special needs—something I told almost every woman I met—but I realized Emily was the first person I felt comfortable enough with to share the details, including my regular trips to Massachusetts to visit him and oversee his ongoing education and care.

Switching to my high school junior at home, I told Emily that I shared with him the general information of my dating life, but he had never met anyone I had gone out with; he would only meet someone who had the potential for a long-term relationship. She said her kids were being nosy about her getting back out into the dating scene, including checking emails and texts on her phone behind her back, but she was trying to be careful.

By the time our ninety-minute call came to an end, I knew I liked Emily, and the feeling seemed to be mutual. Wendy had done it yet again; she picked out a great woman, one who was fun, laughed easily, and was silly in a sexy way. She also worked hard, took her parenting responsibilities very seriously, was understanding, and knew what hard knocks and tough times in life could be like. In short, she seemed to get *it*—that elusive something we all think everyone else should get but rarely does. And she seemed to like me.

We agreed we should meet, but in trying to find a date and time, the scheduling gremlins kept getting in the way, as did, oddly enough, her ex-boyfriend.

EMAIL RECEIVED: Dates for Meeting

> ... so yeah, that Saturday night is out. Seeing a friend that night at an event (okay, so it's my ex-boyfriend—have to be honest). It is the only night I can do this, and I promised, so I have to go ...

This was my first experience with any sort of ex in the picture, and it gave me pause.

The Boys were concerned, too, and as usual, Darrell got right to the point. *I don't know about this, Turner. I think this could be some slippery shit we're stepping into.*

As she provided more details, I found myself impressed by the kindness of her gesture to the ex-boyfriend, but what else was I to think? Because she was busy every Friday night for a while, had her kids every other weekend, and I had Saturday parenting obligations sprinkled in, it was looking like it would be a month or more before we could ever meet. *If she's okay with it, I can be, too,* I thought, that is, until her email the next day.

EMAIL RECEIVED: Dates for Meeting

> Good morning. Well, this is frustrating. Can't even meet the guy I am interested in! Guess I will have to keep all of those other eHarmony inquiries going, sighhh. . .
>
> Will let you know when I am done on Friday . . . unless I have a date! :-)
>
> Emily

Although it was not without a sense of humor and well-done teasing, The Boys were less than amused, and I was a bit irked as well. But there was something about her that kept drawing me in.

We began talking regularly on the phone after our kids had gone to bed, often late into the night. After each call, I found myself looking forward to the next; Emily was becoming something special. But I had no idea how she felt about me until our fourth phone call when she said something totally out of the blue.

"Turner, I just love talking to you. You're so sure, so calm, so thoughtful, *and* you make me laugh. *And* ... I love hearing your voice."

In that instant, my heart skipped a beat ... then it began to flutter.

"It's going to be hard hanging up tonight," I said.

"I'm glad to hear you say that," she said softly. "Every night talking to you has been hard for me."

The pause that followed wasn't silence; it was the beginning of two hearts connecting.

That night, I couldn't sleep. Her words played over and over in my mind. Determined to figure out a cute and unique way to express beyond words how she was making me feel, I turned on the bedside light, grabbed my laptop, and studied the keyboard. I began to look for a symbol, a combination of letters or numbers, *anything* I could use in writing to express what I was feeling.

And then I found it.

It was an obscure key, one I hadn't used since math in college, but it seemed perfect. It's called a tilde, squiggly, or twiddle (~). But now, it was a symbol of my growing affection for Emily and how she was making my heart flutter.

I shared it and what it meant in a text to her the next day, and her response made my heart flutter even faster.

Wow! The Boys exclaimed.

With the unequivocal exchange of pitter-pattering heart symbols, they knew their Turner had been hooked. But their Turner *still* had to be landed, meaning Emily and I had to meet.

Over the ensuing weeks, our texts became over-the-top flirtatious and then some.

I was home in the middle of the week on one of my son's spring break days, and we had already exchanged some sixty-five text messages by early afternoon. I was about to take a midday shower when she casually texted.

EMILY: Think of me when you are in the shower. XOX
~~~~~~~~~~~~

… so of course, I did.

It was an exciting bit of thinking; The Boys can attest to that.

After four weeks, we finally found a narrow sliver of time when we could meet. She apologized that it wouldn't be a "date-date," but she could stop by my house in between obligations she had not too far away; she would only have about ninety minutes.

"We can at least finally meet," she said.

CHAPTER 8

Complicated

FIVE WEEKS AFTER WE FIRST connected online, Emily and I were going to meet. There was a new sense of anxiety and pressure, and we talked about it in our texts, emails, and phone calls. We laughed about it, and we worried about it too. Then I had an idea, one I thought would fit her and us perfectly, so I proposed it in a text.

> **ME:** Instead of any pressure or worrying about a first-date kiss after we meet, why don't we kiss at the beginning, before we say a single word. Just come in, kiss, and we'll go from there! You can say Yuck! and goodbye, or more, please! What do you think?

> **EMILY:** YES!!!

In the days, hours, and minutes leading up to her arrival, I thought about how I'd like it all to go, how it might go, and how I hoped it wouldn't go. With my son out of the house for the day, I was watching for her car from his bedroom window. She was pulling in the driveway when I went to the front door and opened it ever so slightly. She got out of her car, looked around, then saw me peeking through the door. A smirky, shy, then sly smile came to her face, and she strode determinedly up the steps—I was smitten before she walked in the door.

Before I could even close the door, we kissed, locked lips, and kept kissing. I wrapped my arms around her, and she wrapped hers around me. We pulled each other close, then closer still. After one of the most passionate kisses and embraces I could remember, I tilted my head back slightly.

"It's you … you're real," I whispered.

"I am," she whispered back. "More please."

I pushed her back, pressed her into the wall, and we kissed even more passionately.

Now with Turner hooked and landed, all The Boys could say was, *Don't stop! Don't stop!*

We went downstairs to the family room, curled up on the sofa, and made out like two lovestruck teenagers for ninety minutes. We talked, but not much. We had been talking, texting, and emailing for five weeks. Who needed to talk now? I had found out all I needed to know: she was strikingly pretty, disarmingly fun and silly, and totally hot.

Finally, we stopped kissing, held each other in silence, reveled in the moment, and took it all in. The ninety minutes went by much too fast, and we reluctantly parted ways. But we were now of one mind.

****

I was up crazy early the next morning for a business trip to Miami; to say my mind flipped back and forth between Emily and the work at hand was an understatement. It was a wonderful surprise when I checked my email that evening on the bumpy cab ride back to the Miami airport. She had sent an email with a link to a music video for *Ho Hey,* and I played it as I made my way through the streets of Miami. We emailed back and forth before I boarded the plane.

EMAIL RECEIVED: Just Have to Send this to You

I LOVE this song.

EMAIL SENT: Just Have to Send this to You

Do we belong in each other's hearts … just like in the song?

EMAIL RECEIVED: Just Have to Send this to You

The words are:

You belong to me; I belong to you; you're my sweetheart

I hope so. Time will tell!

EMAIL SENT: Just Have to Send this to You

Time will tell indeed, but a "reserved" sign is being placed on my heart right now.

EMAIL RECEIVED: Just Have to Send this to You

You say the sweetest things!

It was now clear I needed to let my son at home know what was going on, so one night at dinner, I brought up Emily. I showed him her picture, told him about her, and asked for his thoughts. This could be the first woman in our lives since his mom died, and I was nervous at what might be going through his mind. It had to be weird for him.

My son and I have a special relationship for many reasons, I suppose. I always allowed and even encouraged sarcastic and snarky comebacks directed at me as long as they were not hurtful—some verbal roughhousing as it were. It allowed him to be on a level playing field with me and to have some amount of control in our father-son relationship, which I knew was important in a teenage world where control can be hard to come by. I always made sure he got from me as good as he gave, but on this evening, he dished it out and put my concerns at ease.

"Ehh … whatever" was his first response. But then he found his footing.

"You're both kind of … ah … you know … old. What exactly does she see in you anyway?"

"I can't imagine," I said, "but it's not like I'm a total loser you know."

"No, not a *total* loser … although you did lose your hair," he remarked. "So, are you going to have a g-i-r-l-f-r-i-e-n-d, Dad?"

"I might. It's why I've been doing all this dating stuff for the past year. And, need I remind you, you've been trying to get a girlfriend too."

"Daaad's got a girlfriend … Daaad's got a girlfriend," he sang melodically and mockingly. "Hey … maybe she can give me some inside tips on getting a girlfriend too."

"I'm sure she could."

"Hmmm … okay. Can I be excused?" were his final words on the matter.

That was too easy, I thought. *I guess we'll be dealing with this as we go along.*

Emily and I were desperate to see each other, and despite another difficult and frustrating scheduling exercise, we were able to find time for a date—our first date—the next Saturday.

She said she wanted to get a first, small glimpse of my life. I told her about the country club I belonged to, and she asked if I would take her there. I knew she would fall in love with it—it is such a beautiful and special place for me and our family—but first we had to make a few "parent-dating" decisions.

Since she lived further out, she would drive to me, and we would go together. My son would be home, but I thought it premature for an introduction. She agreed, so meeting at my house was out. An elementary school was nearby, so we decided to meet there.

Upon meeting on a bright, early-May day, she hopped into my minivan and we locked lips for a make-out session before driving to the club. We strolled the grounds for a bit, got a couple of drinks, then walked over to comfortable seats facing the golf course and snuggled two chairs together as best we could. I started telling her more about my family's history at the club, and we talked about this, that, and then nothing at all. What mattered was that we were together now, and she was getting a firsthand glimpse of my life. I was so happy she was with me, and she was so content that her smile never left her face.

As we sat, I put my hand on her bare arm and began to lightly stroke her skin with my fingertips. I went from her hand, down the inside of her arm, then to the inside of her elbow, where her skin was the softest and most tender. She tilted her head back, then down, then turned to me and locked her gaze on me. A different smile then came to her face.

"That … really … turns me on," she said under her breath, looking deep into my eyes.

Then she bit her lip, and her gaze turned more suggestive.

"Well … it seems to me that's only a good thing," I said, moving my head close to hers, mirroring her suggestive gaze, stroking her arm even more lightly, and making her grin become a grimace of restraint.

Then, a mischievous, sly, challenging, smirky smile that I was quickly learning to love came to her face.

"This is going to get complicated … fast!" she said.

"Really?" I said in my best and always-ready Southern accent. "I'm a pretty simple, small-town, Southern boy. I'm not sure I know how to do 'complicated.'"

She smirked more emphatically and with more determination.

"Yeah, well … you small-town boys are the most dangerous, my mama said. You had lots of time out there in the country on summer nights with nothing much else to do other than to get *complicated* with those Southern girls."

I turned my hands out and raised my left eyebrow in a "What? … Me?" innocence-claiming gesture. She glared at me more deeply with her sly grin. My heart beat fast and skipped beats all at once.

Time stood still in that moment. We reached for each other's hands and entwined our fingers. As we did, she looked at me with a smile of unsuppressed joy, vulnerability, and wanting.

The rest of the afternoon and evening, we never broke our touch. It was all we could do to keep from jumping on top of each other right then and there. I told her the club had lots of rules, but none I was familiar with about close-contact making out, although there were some general guidelines about decorum.

After six hours at the club, we headed back to the school and the darkened parking lot. After I pulled in beside her car and turned off the engine, we turned and locked ourselves together. But it wasn't the most comfortable position.

"Well … there's a third-row seat back there," I jokingly said. "I'm not sure this is what they had in mind when they designed it, but it's pretty versatile."

She looked at me like, *You have to be kidding?*

"Is this what you do with all your dates?" she asked incredulously.

"Well, actually … no. All my dates up until now have been total duds, so you're the first. It was just a suggestion. But given my son's at home … it's all I can think of. I know it's pretty unromantic. Sorry," I said sincerely.

Undaunted, she made her way to the back. "Get your butt back here."

I did as I was told, and we went horizontal on the seat … which was uncomfortable, too, so we popped back up and locked arms, lips, and tongues. My hands went under her blouse and slipped off her bra. After a few minutes, I slipped it back into place on her.

"This would not be good if the cops came by," she said, laughing.

"Yeah, I can see it now in the local paper," I said. "Parents caught in compromising position in elementary school parking lot on Saturday night."

We both laughed.

"Then," I continued, "they would drive me home, ring the doorbell, and my son would come to the door. 'Ahem … son … is this your father?' the police would say. 'I think you need to have a frank conversation with him … Have a good night young man. Sorry to have bothered you.'"

****

I told Emily the story of how my cousin Wendy picked her out from among forty or so other women. She loved the story and hoped "if we stayed together" (funny how that phrase began to creep into her conversations), they could meet.

I wanted Wendy to meet Emily too. I had fallen hard for her, but I also wanted validation from Wendy. This would be a huge deal for my family, friends, and everyone who knew me. I wanted to tread carefully, very carefully, and really be sure.

I had been keeping Wendy up to date on how things were going, and she was positively giddy every time we talked; we spoke on the phone a few days after my club date with Emily.

"Sounds like you really like her?" she said.

"I do. You did some real good pickin' there, Wendy," I said, pulling up my Southern accent again. "She's something else. Although I can't yet say she's the one. Right now, it's all hyper-intoxicating infatuation, of course, and pretty darn great, but I'm wondering if it's all going too fast."

I then filled her in on Emily's marital and relationship history.

"Okay … sure, that's a bit complicated," Wendy said, "but at this stage of life we're all a bit complicated. Just look at me … and you."

"Hey, wait a minute," I said sharply. "My complications aren't the result of any decisions I made. They're because of events and circumstances thrust upon me."

"Yes … well, that's true, dear. I'm sorry. That wasn't fair of me."

"So," I paused. "Should I be doing this if I'm not sure about her?"

Emily had easily won over my heart, but my head and heart were not in sync. The situation with her exes had continued to linger in my mind, as she often brought them up. Resolving our scheduling conflicts had been surprisingly difficult and contentious, and Emily had no qualms about putting all the blame on me, totally unfairly, I thought. But Wendy quickly cast aside my hesitations.

"Oh good grief! Like I said before about what's-her-name, you're not agreeing to marry her, for goodness' sake. If you like her and you have the hots for each other, then go for it! You don't have to make any promises to her, nor her to you. You just met her … ennnn-joooyyy it! Okay? Do you need to hear it from me again?"

When I met with Abby on Monday morning, she was less concerned about Emily's history than I would have expected, but she was still pretty surprised.

"Well," she thought for a moment. "I would say if you enjoy being with her, then keep seeing her. Your eyes are open, but you've found someone you truly like, more than any of the others. How many has it been now?" she asked.

"She's number twenty-five," I said, caught in the spotlight of her gaze.

Except for the relationship history, Abby liked Emily and downplayed my not being one hundred percent sure.

"No one is ever one hundred percent sure. Give me a break! I'd love to meet her," Abby said.

"You will," I responded. "You will."

But the scheduling gremlins quickly got back to work keeping us apart. Meeting Wendy and Abby right now seemed out of the question, and finding other times to get together in May was close to impossible—frustratingly so.

But on an upcoming Friday night my son would be away on a school trip. I mentioned to Emily that my house would be empty that night, not knowing how she would respond.

"Oh, okay, well … my kids will be with their father starting at five that night," she said, thinking out loud, "so-o-o-o I'm free."

Then, with a playful look on her face and a couple of raised eyebrows thrown in, she said, "I could do a sleepover … if you invited me, but it would need to be a clothes-on arrangement in bed."

Even in pajamas, our Friday night together was pretty darn nice. Our heavy make-out session went well into the morning hours.

The next morning was all smiles, kisses, and happy talk, but as I walked her to the door to say goodbye, she turned to me with a thoughtful expression.

"I really enjoyed last night, and we can do it again, but as things stand right now, if you're all hot and bothered and need more, you should look elsewhere right now until I'm ready."

"You mean … we can date? … But if I need sex, I should call Trixie or Tiffany and have it with them?" I said, awkwardly trying to repeat what I thought I'd just heard.

"Yes! Exactly!" she said, smiling with a self-satisfied expression.

"Okay," I said, trying to buy time to figure out a comeback. "I think there's an app for that … let's see …"

I pulled out my iPhone and went to the app store. I began to mockingly type in "Sex … when … your girlfriend … says … no … Ah, here it is!"

She lunged for my iPhone but with a different smirk on her face, one that said *Darn you!*

I was perfectly fine with where she stood on the issue of sex, but the zinger about being free to go find it elsewhere as we continued dating and having sleepovers felt more like a taunt than the fun little joke I thought she intended. It made me feel the same way I did when her frustration at our not being able to meet led her to write that she would "just have to keep the other eHarmony inquiries going"—I didn't appreciate it, and the humor got lost. I was finding I couldn't sort out the mixed signals she was sending. Too often, I was left scratching my head not knowing what was in hers.

During the rest of May, we were able to meet only once a week on weekday nights—a dinner here, drinks there. We progressed the relationship with lots of phone calls, texts, and emails, and it felt like we were slowly becoming closer. That made it all the more frustrating when the three-day Memorial Day weekend came, and she was totally unavailable. That, in turn, made what happened at dinner the next week even more surprising.

"You know," Emily began, "I'm tied up both Friday and Saturday night again this weekend, but … I could come over Sunday afternoon and we could …" she paused with a wink-wink and a mischievous smile on her face.

"That would be great. What do you …" I said, then paused. "Oh, you want to … get t-o-g-e-t-h-e-r?" I said, hesitating again, unsure if I was reading her correctly.

"Yes, that's what I mean," she said with an adoring smile that changed into a more serious expression. "I want you to know I don't come to this decision lightly. As my faith has grown, sex means more to me and represents more. But Turner, I really really like you. I think you're an amazing father and an incredible man."

As I felt my heart beating, I reached for her hands across the table.

As we gazed intently and tenderly at each other, Darrell and Charles remained silent. Little Turner, however, spoke the same words I was thinking.

It's time.

"If you're up for it," I said, "I think it's time for you to meet my son and for him to meet you. I don't do this lightly either; it's a really really big deal for me, you know that. You'd be the first, and I don't know how he might react. What do you think?"

A sweet smile came to her face, then an exaggerated look of real and mock trepidation.

"Oh, wow," she said.

I felt no such mock trepidation; it was all real. This was a moment I was never quite sure would happen.

Emily and my son met a few days later on Saturday afternoon at my club's pool. With all the build-up and anxiety, it was over in the blink of an eye. My son came out of the pool when she arrived, said "hi" as he was dripping wet, then immediately jumped back in. Later, we all enjoyed a nice and leisurely dinner together. All things considered, it went well.

Of course, we playfully teased each other the whole time, too—she looking totally hot in her bikini— knowing full well that the next day we would be taking things between the sheets—so Trixie and Tiffany would never need to be called.

CHAPTER 9

More Complicated

A WEEK LATER, AFTER OUR time between the sheets at my house, we were at Emily's home on a Saturday night. While making dinner, she tossed out a comment ever so casually.

"So ... can I cancel my eHarmony account now? Are we good? Because I've got four guys on hold," she said, pointing to her laptop on the counter.

What?! The Boys shouted.

I was taken aback—and then some. I had suspended my account after our first date at the club and assumed she had too.

"Oh?" I said. "I stopped eHarmony more than a month ago, but you've been hedging with guys waiting in the wings?"

Ahem, Turner ole boy, said Charles, carefully wading in. *This is the old 'female-jealousy ploy' to reel you into 'commitment-land'.*

"Well, we couldn't ever meet!" she said with exasperation.

"Wait! Was that my fault? We both had parenting conflicts we couldn't change, but I've been available all of May except for two days the entire month. You've had lots of parenting and personal obligations that I haven't criticized, so I don't quite see how this all gets put on me."

"I want to see you more!"

"I do, too, but what's the deal with telling me like this? 'I've got four guys on hold, Turner. What should I do with them?' How does this work exactly in your mind?"

She pursed her lips, stuck up her nose, and turned to the stove.

"Let's see them," I said.

She walked over to her laptop, pushed a button, and her eHarmony screen popped up.

"You can look at them, but I'm not going to show you," she said.

Partly to continue the *discussion* we were having and curious about the other guys, I looked.

To my eyes, all four were better looking than me, which was a bummer. But then I had to laugh because they all used the line "I like long walks on the beach."

Ha! Darrell shouted. *That's just a panty-dropping line for gullible women! Ha ha!*

It was interesting to see their profiles, but it was time for a decision from her on this.

"Handsome fellows," I said. "Maybe they're hungry and would like some dinner. Why don't you invite them over, and I'll go home?" I made a move to leave.

Mad that whatever she had planned was going off the rails, she grabbed me, squeezed me, and kissed me. "I'm sorry," she said.

Dinner that night was nice, and the overnight make-up sex was, too, but I was left wondering how much the mindset of online dating had changed the fundamental nature of dating itself and the relationships that came from them.

Was the digital-dating world all about always having one iron in the fire and another ready to go, just in case? I hadn't been in a new relationship in twenty-four years. I felt positively old-fashioned, naive, and a bit like a chump. The question of whether I needed to—or should—change my views and values about dating was one that lingered from that point forward. But the reality was that my views had already changed over the last year; I just didn't realize how much.

****

With the eHarmony bullpen of men seemingly behind us, Emily began to introduce me to some of her friends in June. An evening Nationals baseball game with a group from her office was especially nice. But as much as we tried to move our burgeoning relationship forward, we kept hitting more scheduling bumps, and they rarely went well.

When Emily was otherwise busy on weekends, I occasionally tried to plan something with friends. One particular silent-treatment-inducing incident occurred when I went to another baseball game with family friends a few days after we had gone to the one with her coworkers. Her brief email the Saturday morning of my game telegraphed, in no uncertain terms, once again, her hurt and unhappiness.

EMAIL RECEIVED: Ball Game

> Good morning. I have a lot of thoughts and emotions running around in my heart and my head right now ... I understand your desire to go with them. Have a great time.
>
> Emily

Emily and I couldn't be together, but my plan to spend time with some of my dearest friends—ones who had supported my sons and me tremendously during the last few years—was somehow wrong, really wrong, in her mind.

For sure, there were no heart-fluttering symbols in our emails that morning. Instead, I imagined a symbol popping up on my phone that represented the middle finger, such was the tension.

So ... why are you doing this? The Boys asked, taking the opportunity to chime in. *Having a girlfriend, that is? Isn't it great, really great, to have a woman in your life?*

During the ballgame, I purposely didn't text Emily, even though I wanted to. She, however, sent a short text early in the game.

> **EMILY:** Hoping you're having fun with your friends.

It was a perfunctory text, and she was trying to reach out, but I didn't respond. She texted again an hour later.

> **EMILY:** Are you ignoring me?

ME: Yes, I am. I don't want to say anything unkind. I want to just enjoy the game and the company of my friends. I'll text you when I'm back home later.

Emily was busy the entire weekend, and the silence between us hung heavy in the air until we spoke on the phone Sunday night. She agreed I did nothing wrong in going out with friends and apologized for making me feel guilty; she just wanted so much to be with me.

Even as we got past this episode, it was the second time something like this had come up—hurtful for both of us and with me on the receiving end of "your-girlfriend-is-not-important" accusations. It was still mostly her schedule, plus the distance between us, that was limiting our ability to get together, but I was getting all the heat. It made me wonder how this was all going to work—*if* it would work—and perhaps she was thinking the same thing. She used the "if-we're-still-together" comment more now in conversations when we spoke. She later admitted to saying it just to get under my skin, and it worked.

****

If this had been a step back in our relationship, then the next few weeks, I hoped, would include big steps forward. Emily and my mother-in-law, Mary, would meet over dinner at Mary's house, and she would meet more of my family over July Fourth.

At Mary's house, the scene was odd, I had to admit—bringing a woman to meet the mother of my late wife—but it was a measure of how close and important Mary was to me. The dinner went marvelously well, and Emily got to see firsthand the incredible woman I had described to her.

On the Fourth of July, Emily met more of my in-laws at the club. She saw how close they were to me and, quite simply, that they were my family. Emily was received so warmly by them that she positively gushed. She beamed a happy smile and was now encouraged about our evolving relationship.

Right after this, we thought it was time for me to meet her two kids. Emily thought long and hard about how to pull this off. Her kids' favorite cousin was to be in town, and Emily thought that might be a good time for it to take place—safety in numbers as it were.

My office in Georgetown overlooked a big park on the waterfront, so she arranged a weekday outing for the four of them to see the sights and shop. She would text me to come down for a short, casual hello when they got to the park.

When we met just after lunch that day, I did my best not to be "mom's boyfriend" but just a nice, not-creepy guy. I didn't try to be their pal or anything like that; I would've crashed and burned.

Emily's niece was warm, chatty, and curious about her Aunt Emily's new boyfriend; she seemed to like me.

Emily's eleven-year-old daughter was like my son when he met Emily for the first time. "Hi … okay. Can we get some ice cream now?"

But her thirteen-year-old son was … let's just say less than thrilled … and leave it at that. I looked at Emily, but she was helpless to make anything happen that wasn't going to. At least the ice had been broken, and that was the important thing since they would be seeing me around more often.

****

Emily had purchased tickets for us to go to Wolf Trap to see Harry Connick Jr. in concert in early July. We were both big fans.

I planned to introduce Emily to more friends of mine that evening, a husband-and-wife couple who were keen to meet her. The wife had struck out in several attempts to set me up with a few of her friends a year earlier. My not being Catholic proved an insurmountable obstacle, it turned out.

To make the evening more special, I arranged to drive a cool set of wheels. Nine months earlier, a friend and fellow car enthusiast had acquired a classic 1969 Jaguar XKE roadster, one of the most beautiful cars ever made. I was at his home the day it was delivered, and he generously offered to let me take it for a spin. He and his wife had been very kind to my boys and me the previous couple of years, and he extended an offer for me to use the car if ever I had "a really hot date."

Enter a really hot date.

Emily came to the house in a halter top sundress, and I suggested we leave early because old English cars can be a challenge to drive. I couldn't be sure how well I would do with the Jag. It had already cut out on me a few times just getting it home.

Hundreds of people stared as we drove among the line of cars inching bumper-to-bumper toward the Wolf Trap entrance; Emily soaked it all in with a big smile. We parked with difficulty—try making tight parking maneuvers in a car with a hood a mile long—then went to a picnic area where we met my friends. Emily was her usual sweet, funny, gregarious self and easily won them over. Being with Emily while Harry Connick Jr. sang about love was positively magical on a summer evening. When it was over, Emily and I reluctantly walked back to the car for the drive home. It was then that Emily gave new meaning to the phrase "top-down" driving.

Driving back, Emily said the warm breeze blowing through her hair and dress made her feel liberated. Quick on the uptake, I explained a new rule of the road for the night in the convertible. "If the top is down on the car, then your top has to be down, too, babe."

"I *really* like you calling me 'babe,'" she said with an adoring smile and eyes full of emotion.

Then, her expression changed to her sly, smirky smile, whereupon she untied her halter top and dropped it to expose her breasts.

"Ha! You can look but can't touch," she said, laughing in victory.

In our frequent little games of one-upmanship, it was now my turn to gain the upper hand, and I did so by literally keeping my hands to myself. She expected me to be frustrated in being forced to look but not touch or to have my hands swatted away if I reached over, but I didn't.

She looked at me first with a smug and cute "gotcha" grin, but then as I only casually looked at her and focused on driving, her expression changed to frustration. "How can you sit there and not touch me?"

"I want to big time, but you told me not to."

"Oh! … You're infuriating. Touch 'em already, and hurry up before someone sees us!"

****

In June, I told Emily that I'd love to get away with her for a weekend in July if we could make our schedules work. She melted at the idea of time together with no clock, no obligations, and total "us" time for almost three days. We decided to go to Annapolis for a long weekend, and I made all the arrangements. It felt like we were riding a crescendo in our relationship, growing closer and closer during the last month.

Our weekend in Annapolis was more than I could have hoped for—totally wonderful—and made me feel like our relationship was now on the verge of becoming a journey together.

And then ...

Five days after our return, on a Friday, I was driving to the airport for a weekend trip to Boston to see my son. Even with weekly Skype calls to see and talk to him, I didn't like going more than two months without visiting him in person and spending time together, and it was now getting close to three months since my last visit. The next day, Emily was flying out with her kids for their annual two-week vacation at her parents' summer home in Michigan.

Driving to the airport, I called to chat with Emily, hear her voice, and wish her a great vacation. I knew we would be in touch constantly, but I was going to miss her.

She was oddly polite and rather quiet at first, then finally, she launched into what was on her mind.

"Turner, I'm so frustrated we aren't spending more time together!"

"What?"

"I'm just so frustrated."

"Frustrated that you have to be away for two weeks?"

"No!!!!" You're not getting it!!!"

"Wait a minute. I'm not getting what?"

Silence ... and more silence ...

"What is it that I'm not getting?" I asked again, slowly but calm with tension.

"Turner!" she exclaimed in frustration.

"Seems to me," I began cautiously, "we just had a great month of July. You met some of my family—the most important people in my life. We spent a lot of wonderful time together, not to mention the three-day weekend we just had, which I'm still on a high from, and you're saying you're frustrated that we're not spending enough time together?"

"Yes!" she said emphatically.

I was stunned and at a loss to understand, but I was trying.

"Look … I thought … I thought we'd both been doing pretty well in getting our schedules to work, especially with you having the kids every other weekend and your ex who keeps putting them back on you when it's *his* weekend to have them. Are you mad at *me*?"

"Yes … no …" she couldn't figure out what to say, and then she did. "Turner? … Are we a couple?"

"What?! Are we a couple?!"

Oh boy! shouted The Boys. *You're on your own, pal, good luck … We're outta here. Bye!* "Those little chicken fuckers," I mumbled to myself.

"I'm lost here, Emily, really lost. What's going on?"

"I want to know if we're a couple," she said emphatically.

I went silent. I needed time to process all of this.

Driving under the overpass of the Memorial Bridge that connected Arlington National Cemetery to the Lincoln Memorial on the other side of the Potomac, I struggled to think of what to say.

After quite a bit of silence on the phone, I finally spoke. "Emily, we just met three months ago. We've seen each other about once a week when our schedules worked and less when they didn't. It's hard to see you even when they do work because we live forty-five minutes apart … I can't just hop over to your house, even though I would love to see you every day. I've been doing the best I can, and I thought you were too. I like you very, very much. I canceled my eHarmony account right after we met, I liked you so much, but then found out weeks later that you were still checking out guys online. I've introduced you to my family, something I've not done with any woman *ever!* I took us away last weekend for three days that I'm still lost in bliss about … but now … with this … I don't know WHAT we are …

"Are we a couple after just knowing each other for three months? No … I don't think so. We're *dating*, Emily … we're dating and still getting to know one another. I thought it was going well and getting better, but with this … with this, I feel like I've been smacked upside the head, and I'm feeling foolish for thinking all the thoughts I was thinking about us and a future together. So I'm lost right now listening to you, really lost, quite frankly."

Silenced ensued on both ends as I drove into National Airport.

I don't need this … and I don't want this … no way, no how, I thought.

"I have a plane to catch," I said, "and you have packing for two weeks to do. We'll catch up with each other later."

We said quiet goodbyes and ended the call.

"What the hell was that?!" I shouted in the car.

The Boys peeked their heads out from their hiding places and sat silently … like they were afraid I would take their heads off if they so much as blinked.

They were right.

I was seething on the flight to Boston, just seething.

I obviously can't do what's expected of me. All I can do is be kind, thoughtful, loving, and there for her, I told myself.

… but we're just too far away from each other. This isn't going to work, I decided.

In Massachusetts, I took my son down to the family house in Cape Cod for the day to visit with other relatives who were there and sent Emily a few photos. I put away the *issues* we were dealing with for the time being, and Emily seemed content to do the same. I sent her two photos of the house on the water's edge that weekend, adding "XXOO" at the end, and she reciprocated. Over the next two weeks, she sent twenty emails with notes of daily activities and photos of her at the lake house in Michigan.

Toward the end of her two weeks away, she emailed me about calendar dates for having dinner with some friends. Her email included a forwarding of the entire email string of their back-and-forth as they tried to find a date in September. I imagined her sending the email string was her way of giving me a soft introduction to her friends *and* indicating that our current issues were just bumps in the road to be gotten past. The email conversation had begun right after the Fourth of July holiday.

Four emails into the string was a particularly noteworthy comment to her friends. "… and you can meet Turner too if things are still … *plugging along,*" she wrote.

When I made note of that to Emily, she wrote back.

EMAIL RECEIVED: Dinner

> Was wondering if you might see that. Hmmmmm … Do you think we might hang on 'til then? Dinner will be the 21st :-)

Recalling our time in July as I was riding the *crescendo in our relationship,* I now knew she was firmly in the if-we-are-still-together mode and talking to her friends about it that way too.

This had *chump* written all over it, as far as I was concerned.

The Boys amusingly recited in a Gregorian-chant-like way, *Chu-u-u-u-m-m-m-m-mp ... Chu-u-u-m-m-m-m-mp ... Chu-u-u-m-m-m-m-mp ...*

After she returned from her two weeks away, we met at one of "our places," a park halfway between where we each lived. Seemingly without taking a breath, she picked right back up where our phone call had ended.

"We're not together enough, and that's a problem," she said sharply before softening. "I want to be with you, Turner."

"I want to be with you, too, Emily, but I don't know what more to do other than what we've been doing. I thought we'd been managing it all pretty well the last few months, given all our responsibilities. I enjoy every minute I'm with you."

I thought that last comment might elicit a smile or a "me too" response, but no.

"It's the sex, isn't it? You're just in this for the sex!" she huffily said.

"No! Absolutely not ... it is NOT about the sex!" I shot back.

"Sex! Sex! Sex!" she smugly spit out.

Hmmm ... we've heard that before, haven't we? The Boys said, thinking back to our French encounter at the International Monetary Fund cafeteria.

I then went through what I'd said on the phone two weeks earlier, and she went back to the "couple" thing again.

"Are we a couple?"

"When you say that, what do you mean by it? Are we in a permanent committed relationship? If that's what you mean, it seems I was more committed to this relationship than you two months ago. It wasn't me who had four guys teed up on eHarmony."

"That's low!"

"It's true! I'm just stating facts."

She then passed on that line of attack and went to another.

"I want to know you're in this for me and not just another notch in your belt."

"You really think I'm just in this for the sex?! After introducing you to my family and everything else?!"

143

"Well, I don't know. You tell me. If it's not about the sex, then what's it about?"

"What's it about?! It's because I find you incredibly attractive, sexy, smart, fun, a great parent who I respect. Someone who understands that life can be hard, and it's what's inside you that pulls you through the tough times. That your spirituality is important to you, that you are involved in your community, and you have so many people who care about you and none more than me … and you make me feel wonderful and I love being with you … except right about now!"

With my last little dig, she stuck out her tongue.

The silence between us was deafening.

"Okay, if you think this is just about the sex …"

"I do!" she interjected.

"… then no more sex, we'll just see each other, and it's strictly dating."

The look in her eyes said it all. *Ha! Right! A man and his cock! That'll last all of two seconds,* she was saying with her smug expression.

"Yeah, right," she uttered contemptuously.

Then with decisiveness and derisiveness in her voice—and confident of victory—she said, "Fine. We'll just date. But no sex, Turner. None!"

****

We had a date scheduled for the next evening on a Saturday night, and it started like a date with your sister might feel—the sister who doesn't like you.

Emily established strict defensive physical and verbal boundaries and was ready to go on offense at a moment's notice. As the evening wore on, it became a little more friendly, but loose hand-holding was as far as it went. When I took her home, she asked if I was going to stay over.

"Really? Ahem … I hadn't planned on it, but … I can if you want me to," I said.

"Well, only if you want to," she said.

Oh good grief, The Boys piped in. *Stay already!*

After a long pause, I said, "I'll stay."

With each of us in grandma and grandpa pajamas, she established an invisible line in the bed. I think to her surprise, I stayed well on my side of it. The next morning, I could tell she was somewhat hurt at the state of affairs.

Two days later, we had a rare date during the week. When I arrived at her door, I rang the doorbell and waited outside instead of just going in. Opening the door, she gave me a cordial but reserved hug and a peck of a kiss on the lips. We were remotely polite with each other the entire evening. At the end of our date, I offered a simple peck of a kiss back. She then lingered for a moment, seemingly wanting more. Obvious cracks were starting to show in her wall of determination, but since it was a weeknight, there was no staying over, and I went home.

Four days later, we had tickets to see *The Book of Mormon* and met for dinner before the show. I arrived first, got our table, and waited, facing the entrance where she would come in. When she arrived and turned the corner, she certainly wasn't wearing grandma clothes. She looked positively ravishing in a draped, short black dress with a dropped, exposed back. She bounced and jiggled her way to me with a determined smile on her face. As I stood to greet her, she offered her cheek for me to kiss.

Okay, I thought. *For someone with a moratorium on sex, she's dressing, walking, and bouncing like either, 'Let's have sex' or 'I want you to think about the sex you're not going to get, buster!'*

It was clearly "game on" tonight.

I'm going to make him crumple in the presence of my hotness, she had to be thinking.

So, happy to play along, I said, "You look totally hot!"

She then flashed a mischievous and smug mission-accomplished smile.

She said a mother next door remarked that she looked "saucy" as she was leaving the house.

"Yes, 'saucy' ... spicy saucy," I said, giving her a slow look up and down.

She was loving every minute of taunting me. This was payback time, and she was darn good at it too. She was giving me full doses of jiggling boobs, glimpses of bare breasts when she bent over, intentional glimpses up her dress when she crossed her legs, and bedroom eyes turned up to full wattage. She was here tonight to take no prisoners in this game of sexual one-upmanship, and the score right now was Emily one thousand and Turner zip!

After dinner, we walked across the street to the Kennedy Center. As is often the case in hot Washington, the theater was too cold inside from the cranked-up air conditioning, especially for someone in a saucy little black dress.

I gave her the seat on the aisle, and I went one in.

"It's chilly in here," I said. "Let me give you my coat to drape over your legs and lap. You'll freeze otherwise." I also wanted to cover up her intentionally overexposed legs and hiked-up dress to shut down her game.

Taking my coat off, I started to drape it over her legs, but just before I did, a thought popped into my head. Putting my coat on her lap, I slipped my right hand underneath and put it on her bare leg just below her short dress line.

"That might help keep you warm too," I said as I gently touched the inside of her thighs. "Don't want 'Miss Saucy' to get chilly tonight."

She tried to hold back a smile, but her facial expression gave away a grudging acknowledgment of, *Well, aren't you the clever one, Mr. Grant.*

The lights were dim and would be darker still when the play began, so no one would notice what was going on. It simply looked like my hand was on her lap.

"You plan on leaving that there for the whole show?" she asked.

"I certainly don't have to," I said. "I was just trying to be a thoughtful gentleman by keeping you warm because it's so cold in here tonight."

I lightly touched her between her legs at mid-thigh, then moved up until she grimaced a tight smile with her clenched teeth and closed lips. She was about to lose her ability to sit still in the seat, so I teasingly moved my hand back toward her knees.

"You know I can stop you if I want to," she said.

"Of course, you can. Just say 'stop.'"

She gave me a sideways glare from her eyes, a smile of, *I accept your challenge,* then turned and locked her gaze toward the stage, feigning ignoring me. Over almost three hours, I moved my hand and fingers gently over her bare thighs and up her dress, then glanced over to see a smile of determination on her face that I could easily read.

You'll never break me … but don't stop trying.

She was pretty amazing at being able to sit statue-still as I tried to turn her on at unexpected moments with 2,300 people in the sold-out opera house.

As applause thundered during the curtain call, Emily gave me a look that said, *How long are we going to keep up this charade?*

I looked back at her with a relaxed smile and an expression of, *I can outlast you because I told you, it's not 'about the sex.' It's about you.*

In our long walk down to the car, we decided we both hated the play but enjoyed going to the theater.

"Maybe we should buy a Kennedy Center subscription for the upcoming season—if we're still together," she casually offered, "and request they crank up the air conditioning!"

I then took her home, but since her kids were there with a sitter for the night, I didn't linger.

The next Friday night was my last in town before a week of travel for college visits with my son. I went to Emily's house after work, and she pulled no punches. It was clear she wanted the evening to end in the bedroom, and I happily gave in. After an hour in bed, she reclined back, like Kate Winslet in the nude scene from *Titanic*.

Wearing nothing but a self-satisfying grin, she said, "So ... does this mean we're back together again?"

With so many confusing messages from her in the last few weeks, I took the words "back together again" to mean we were "okay again" and good to go as though the whole thing had never happened. Regardless of her meaning, I thought she had made her bigger point quite clear:

It *was* about the sex ... for her.

CHAPTER 10

The "I Love You" Thing

WE WERE NOW "GOOD," AS she said, but only as good as planning for no more than a few months out. Doubts about our relationship didn't disappear, but we cast them aside and moved forward, enjoying our time together and generally becoming the couple she wanted us to be. For the most part, we leapfrogged from weekend to weekend with only rare chances to see each other during the week, but it all felt really good—actually really great. We better understood each other's hopes, dreams, longings, fears, buttons not to be pushed, and everything else that comes with an evolving, deep relationship.

I took Emily to a political event at the home of Virginia's future governor and gave her a taste of hobnobbing, political style. I introduced her to more of my friends and family, including Abby and Wendy.

Abby and Emily were close in age, so they bonded quickly over shared life experiences, divorces, and pretty intense good-natured ribbing of me. Wendy and Emily bonded instantly as well, and I became the target of their more mischievous tag-team teasing and verbal zingers. Wendy was so taken with Emily that she arranged a lunch for her to meet the matriarch of my large in-law family, who was also Wendy's mother.

The matriarch was a grand dame of Georgetown and had warmly embraced my joining the family twenty-four years earlier. She brought me into the social circle of old Washington at countless dinner parties, private clubs, and foreign embassies around the city. For lunch that Thursday, it was just the three of us in the sunroom of her home of sixty years. Emily was kind, conversational, and lighthearted, understanding how to make a ninety-six-year-old woman feel comfortable amidst the confusion and forgetfulness that can swirl in one's mind at that age. However, in a moment of clarity or confusion—we were never quite sure which—the matriarch held Emily's hand on the sofa and said in the most intentional, kind, and heartfelt voice, "So you like our dear Turner, sweetheart? You seem so sweet and good for him. He's been through so much, you know, but he's been strong for his boys and us. He's so dear to us. He so much deserves happiness and someone like you, so sweet, so sweet you seem. And you're okay with … you'll be able to … you can help him … with his problems?"

Sitting across from Emily when the matriarch uttered those words, I raised my eyebrows in a half-cocked way. *What did she just say? My problems?*

Ha! You just got thrown under the bus by a ninety-six-year-old woman, The Boys roared with laughter.

A half-suppressed smile came to Emily's face that said, *I've got you now, buster!* And she did.

As we walked to my car after the three-course lunch, Emily said in the most condescending baby voice possible, "Can I help w'iddle Turner with his w'iddle pw-oblems …" then broke into raucous laughter.

All I could do was roll with the subject of "Turner's problems."

Fortunately, Emily not only passed this particular family introduction, she aced it.

****

Several weeks into September, with our kids back in school, the two of us were thrown into our prime-time-parenting routines once again. The time between seeing each other on weekends felt painfully long. There were also still weekends when we didn't see each other at all, whether it was for my trips to Massachusetts, her weekend business trips, or her community work. We exchanged notes often during these endless times apart, expressing our feelings for each other and how much we wanted to be together. To say we both had raw feelings of wanting was an understatement.

Early fall is always a time of being inundated with clothing catalogs in the mail. Flipping through a few of them, I thought about finding and buying something for Emily for no particular reason other than I wanted to. In the Bloomingdale's catalog, I saw a dress I instantly knew would look great on her and might even be perfect for a wedding she had told me about.

Two of her friends were getting married the Saturday of Thanksgiving weekend, doing a Brady-Bunch-type merge of their families. She told me about it back in the summer and hoped I could go with her, "if we were still together," of course.

She already knew I was the rare man who liked to shop—it's really about appreciating good design, no matter what it is—and I wanted to find her a dress that was unique, elegant, and special. After several weeks of catalog shopping and mulling over this particular dress, I showed it to her at my house one evening.

"What do you think? Is this something you'd like? I know it's not something you'd normally buy for yourself, but I thought it might be great for the wedding in November," I said, not sure what she might say.

She looked at it long and hard ... then looked at me ... then looked at the catalog again. I had underestimated how she might react.

"You found this, for me? ... You want to buy this, for me? So I can wear it to the wedding? ... With you?"

"Yeah ... I thought you'd look terrific in it."

Emily looked at me again, but now with emotion-filled eyes that expressed how touched she was. She then slid off her bar chair where we were sitting at the breakfast counter, draped her arms over my shoulders, and melted into me. I could feel the wetness of her tears on the side of my face.

"So I guess you kind of like it?" I said.

"Oh, Turner, you're unbelievable. But this is so much money," she said with alarm in her voice.

"It's fine," I said. "It'll be worth every penny to see you in it."

While she was there and we were on the subject of what to wear for the wedding, I thought I'd show her something else, but I *really* wasn't sure how *this* might go over.

I had told her about some of my wife's jewelry I helped design. There was a pair of earrings I thought would go particularly well with the dress and, given how she cut her hair, would look great on her. They were white gold, diamond, and pearl, and very contemporary in design. I asked if she would like to see them, and she said yes.

"I don't know if this is creepy or odd to suggest since they were a gift to my wife, but since there is a lot of *me* in them, I wondered if you might be interested in wearing them to the wedding with the dress?"

She looked at them intently for a few moments.

"They're beautiful," she said. "Oh my gosh, they're gorgeous!"

She walked over to the mirror and quickly put one on, then the other. She turned her head this way and that way, looking at them and—I thought—admiring them, but I wasn't sure.

"Are you sure you wouldn't mind, and it wouldn't be too weird for you to see me wearing them?" she asked.

"No, I'd love for you to wear them. It would make me smile every time I look at you."

Wearing a smile herself, Emily turned back to the mirror and continued swiveling her head back and forth. Then she turned to me, gave me a serious, adoring, emotional look, then melted once again into my arms.

****

The "I love you" came unexpectedly, totally out of the blue, and right in the middle of sex one night. I'd always assumed it would be more movie-like romantic, along the lines of what I had experienced before, but ... nope.

"I love you, Turner-r-r-r!" she said, strained and out loud.

While the lovemaking continued unabated, The Boys stopped cold, and for the first time in a long time, they argued.

Whoa! Whoa! Whoa! ... Hold on there, Kemosabe! Charles exclaimed. *She said it! She said, "I love you!"*

But wait a minute, Charles continued anxiously. *Is she in love-love with our boy Turner, or just loving the moment with our boy?*

Then Darrell piped in. *She's having fun, half out of her mind, and who the fuck cares? Just go with it, bros!*

Then Little Turner's quiet voice emerged, forcing me—the real Turner—to go on autopilot for the rest of the evening while the various conversations played out (yes, men may not be able to "fake it," but we have an autopilot mode for times like this).

Is this just an in-the-moment thing, like Charles was saying, Little Turner wondered, *or is she expecting that from us too?*

With all three conversations from The Boys talking over one another, I pretty much cut to the chase.

I'm not ready for this! I said to The Boys. *Not even close. Last I heard, we were still in the "if-we-are-still-together" dating mode.*

This was big—momentous—and not something to let go of. So the next morning, I brought it up. "So … about what you said last night."

"What?" she said. "Oh! … the 'I love you' thing?"

"Well, yeah. The 'I love you' thing. I was awake half the night thinking about it. I wasn't sure what you meant by it since you kind of … shouted it out—blurted it out, really—in the heat of the moment."

She then offered a smile of mild satisfaction at the suspense.

"Hmmmm … I guess it *was* a bit in the moment … but I do love you, Turner, and I love making love to you too," she said with a sly smile and a double eyebrow raise.

"Ah … okay … but somewhere in there was an actual 'I love you'?"

"Yes, there was," she said with a vaguely implied certainty-ishness.

"Okay … then I guess I have to tell you, that saying 'I love you' is a big, big deal for me, and I'm not sure I'm there yet. It's something I'd give a lot of thought to before saying it. You know guys and the 'I love you' thing? Well, it would be everything for me to say that."

She looked at me again with a smile of calm satisfaction, quite content to let me squirm.

Finally, she said, "I understand, Turner. I didn't say it expecting to get the same back. I know you give a lot of thought to everything you say, and you really mean what you say. That's okay. When you do say it, I know you'll mean it, and it will mean the world to me."

The Boys mulled this over a bit, then Charles spoke up. *Well, Boys, I think we're in some sort of I-love-you limbo here. She's in control, and we're on the clock. Turner old boy, you're the one who's got to figure this out. And by the way, let us know when you do.* Charles quickly extracted himself and The Boys from the matter entirely.

****

In October, Emily decided to host a large party that would bring together many of her friends, along with people from work and her various community activities—almost fifty people—to meet the new "couple."

She began to prep me since I would be the focus of her closest friends as the new guy in her life. They all personally knew her ex, who had departed the scene less than a year before, and Emily was concerned the scrutiny could be intense. As the party drew near, she told me, with some trepidation, there was a possibility her ex-boyfriend might be there too.

"How's that?" was my not-so-happy question.

She explained he was not invited, but that one of her close male friends who she had to invite—he was gay so there was nothing between them—was an instigator of sorts. He might bring the ex to the party just to make mischief.

"He loves to stir the pot," Emily said with exasperation.

"Then tell him not to stir the pot," I said.

Her timid response showed me how she could be a pushover, as she had complained about when her ex-husband asked her to take the kids when it was his weekend to have them.

"Well, that's just great," I said. "Maybe I should skip the party."

She frowned, gave me a reassuring look, then a kiss like a mom might give her baby to soothe a boo-boo.

With little else to do, I prepared myself.

The night of the party came, and the guests poured in quickly. Emily certainly had a wide circle of friends and acquaintances who all seemed to genuinely care for her. As the party moved into the night, I got countless looks and silent gazes.

"Hmmmm ... so that's him."

Her ex didn't show up, but mutual friends did. Emily said a report about me would get back to her ex pretty quickly.

As the evening progressed, things were seemingly going along fine and without any visible drama, but I realized at some point that I was totally bored and uninterested in her friends and the other people I was meeting.

What was it? I was the Washington cocktail-party veteran and usually enjoyed these sorts of things, but this was r-e-a-l-l-y boring.

I had experienced this feeling several times in the past few months at dinners where I met various friends of Emily's. I confessed to Abby during date debriefings, that as Emily's friends talked about their work, families, and everyday lives, it seemed I had absolutely nothing in common with them and I felt oddly unsettled. Abby expressed concerns about problems ahead.

I smiled my way through mind-numbing conversations, but my fake smile eventually made my face hurt. Many of them worked in the government—its own world to be sure—but others worked in the private sector like Emily and me. Yet I remained uninterested and, frankly, didn't want to be there.

This started me on a soul-searching journey. Had my newly altered filters of life in the aftermath of my wife's death become too fine to a fault? Could I not enjoy and appreciate people, life, and regular stuff anymore? Worse still, was I somehow broken from my experience? Or perhaps I was now some sort of I-know-life-like-you-all-don't kind of snob.

It was a soul-searching exercise that went on for the rest of my time on Venus. I was fully back in life, but it seemed like I was still set apart too.

What was going on?

A few days later, I learned that while I was bored and soul-searching at the party, quite a bit was going on.

An hour into the evening, Emily had said to me, "Okay, you're off the hook for having to meet anyone else. You can relax. Let me catch some people, and you can stay here safely with my friends." When she reappeared thirty minutes later, she wore a happy smile and was positively giddy.

But as Emily now anxiously and nervously recounted, when she was off mingling with her guests, a friend of hers started hitting on her. He was apparently unaware that a new guy was in the picture—that would be me—and that I was there. News of this had spread to mutual friends outside of the party, including Emily's ex-boyfriend, as did various interpretations of what happened next. The gist of it was that not only did Emily not dissuade the friend from making a pass, but she also enjoyed and encouraged it.

Emily then shared with me a Facebook Messenger dialogue she had with her ex-boyfriend on the matter. In the messages, the ex said he had a problem with her being hit on by another man while I—her current boyfriend—was in the same room. Emily then told her ex that she didn't owe him an explanation of her love life.

From there, in an apparent act of standing up for truth and justice—or more likely payback to Emily for breaking up with him—the ex-boyfriend intimated that what happened might find its way to me. Emily was now trying to get ahead of it.

In the process of confessing all of this, Emily muddied the waters by first saying that something had happened at the party that fell under the heading of "too much information," but if I wanted to know, she would tell me. Somehow it then became "my fault" for asking about something I didn't even know happened.

EMAIL RECEIVED: The Facebook Exchange :-)

> Turner, you were the one who was pressing me tonight to tell you all about it!! Now it's too much information? A lot of senseless drama and I had no plans to tell you ... but you asked. Sighhhh.

Emily dismissed it all as her ex trying to ruin our relationship and that I "was falling for it." I had no way of knowing anything beyond what she told me. I wondered if this was part of the middle-aged-dating normal I would have to get used to or just the *normal* in dating Emily.

I concluded the latter, and the doubts about our relationship that had taken a back seat the month before returned.

****

The emails came three weeks later.

EMAIL RECEIVED: Thanksgiving Plans

> Turner, we really need to talk. When do you have time?

EMAIL RECEIVED: Thanksgiving Plans

> Today and tomorrow there won't be time or place for a serious conversation, and frankly, I don't even want to talk on the phone. Maybe we can find time before you leave town Thursday?
>
> ... I had a fabulous time Saturday with you. I loved every minute with you—I am happy when I am with you. Emily

EMAIL RECEIVED: Thanksgiving Plans

> Oops, I meant to have said ... LOVE, Emily.

EMAIL RECEIVED: Thanksgiving Plans

> It is not WHERE I am at or where you are, it is about how we feel about each other, isn't it? Sleeping with you without a connection is just horribly empty to me.

EMAIL RECEIVED: Thanksgiving Plans

> I had reservations in the beginning of having sex too early and this is why. I have learned that for me, it needs to be an expression of how I feel and the next step in an already deep and committed relationship. I used to feel much different about it, but with what I have been through and my faith, sex is much more precious and due respect ... Emily XO

EMAIL RECEIVED: Thanksgiving Plans

> I can't wait to snuggle with you next to your pretty fireplace on Saturday.
>
> Emily ~~~~~~

So, what happened?

I confess, I was both dumbfounded and not surprised at all. I cast a wide net trying to figure it out, including the continuation of my soul-searching.

My take on what happened goes like this.

Her "I love you" of seven weeks earlier, followed by my feelings about the "incident" at the party, had amplified the different paths we were on. She had become more invested in us as a couple with a future together and wanted actions and words to indicate I was in the same place.

I was *not* in the same place.

My doubts about us not only hadn't abated, they had grown since the party.

Looking back over my calendar at the eight Friday and Saturday night opportunities to be together since her party, four had "No Emily" notations written on them when she wasn't available. She came in once to have lunch with me in Georgetown during the week, but otherwise, we didn't see each other from Sundays to Thursdays.

That put a lot of pressure on the four evenings we *did* spend together, and the "I-love-you" clock was ticking loudly.

On Saturday nights, when she had her kids for the weekend, she always arranged sleepovers for them at friends' houses, and I stayed over. The evenings and nights were certainly wonderful, but the next mornings were a different matter.

I preferred not to have my son wake up at home Sunday mornings with me still out on my date from the night before. I also needed to be home in time to get ready for church at nine o'clock. Given that we lived forty-five minutes apart, that meant an early wake-up, with me leaving no later than seven in the morning.

This *never* went over well.

"I don't understand what your hang-up is," she said often and unhappily. "Why can't you stay another hour in bed, let your son wake up on his own, get his own breakfast, then pick him up and go straight to church?"

"I just don't feel comfortable with that," I always responded. "In fact, I would feel very uncomfortable with that."

I remembered the look of hurt on her face, along with the verbal and emotional silence, as we kissed and I left on the most recent Sunday morning. So when the "Turner, we really have to talk" email came the next day, it was no surprise.

I think she thought my leaving at seven was too easy for me, perhaps because I was always diligent about leaving on time (I actually had to rush to drive home—once getting a speeding ticket). In her mind, my wanting to be home with my son when he woke up instead of lingering in bed with her equaled "sleeping with (me) without a connection ... and (feeling) horribly empty." And now it wasn't only Sunday mornings that she was going on about, but our entire relationship was being painted with this one big brush dipped in "horribly empty" paint.

The way she framed the whole thing took my soul-searching deeper— perhaps something *was* wrong with me. Perhaps I *was* somehow broken from all that happened with the death of my wife and her battle with depression that preceded it. Maybe I *was* set apart from everyone else now, and my "filters of life" *were* closed too tight. Quoting from one of my email responses to Emily, "Maybe I'm not cut out for this anymore."

Expressing and confessing these sentiments seemed to have the effect of turning Emily around. She began to offer support for me and our relationship. It felt like she had rushed back to defend me against myself and wanted nothing more than "to snuggle with you next to your pretty fireplace on Saturday."

I felt positively whipsawed by the back-and-forth emotions of the week.

The Boys asked—some more strongly than others—why we shouldn't call this and move on. I tried explaining—to them and myself—that I thought Emily and I had a connection that rose above the bumpy relationship roller coaster we had been on. Even the best relationships require work, and it was work I was still willing to put in. However, the soul-searching that had started and the doubts I had about myself were only the beginning of a struggle for me to understand and reconcile the past, present, and what I continually felt was an unknown and scary future. The hard lesson I was learning about this *seeking my future* business was that it was no walk in the park. Exactly halfway through my time on Venus at this point, it was a difficult-to-navigate path in some very dark woods. Getting out of those dark woods would take more time and require difficult decisions.

CHAPTER 11

Right on Schedule

EMILY WAS READY TO BURST with excitement at the upcoming wedding of two of her best friends.

Originally just hoping to have a date, she now was going to a wedding with many of her friends on the arm of her boyfriend of seven months, wearing an elegant dress picked out and bought for her by said-boyfriend, wearing diamond, pearl, and gold earrings from the same said-boyfriend, and transported in what would be—for almost anyone—a Cinderella-elegant, head-turning white carriage: a new Mercedes SL sports car I had taken delivery of that very morning. Then at the reception, she would be dancing with "Mr. He-Dances-So-Well," which she was looking forward to probably most of all.

Emily's jaw dropped at the sight of the car when I arrived at her house. When I opened the door and took her hand to help her settle down into it, she beamed. But looking at her, she positively took my breath away; she was enchantingly beautiful in her new dress, sparkling earrings, and exuberant smile.

Arriving at the church, her smile was undiminished as I offered my hand again to help her out of the car. She looked around to see if anyone might catch a glimpse of her getting out, but as usual, we were on "Emily time," which meant we barely made it there before the wedding started, and everyone was already comfortably seated inside.

As we entered the church, it felt like it was as much *her* day as it was the bride's. She positively glowed in unrestrained happiness as we walked down the center aisle to our seats.

The wedding was lovely and happy guests clogged the ballroom entrance as we made our way inside a nearby country club for the reception. Emily grabbed a glass of sparkling wine from a waiter's tray, but I took a glass of sparkling water. She looked at me a little funny, but I said I didn't want alcohol on an empty stomach, knowing the party would go long into the night.

We found our table with three other couples already in their seats. Two of the couples knew Emily, and the wives stared at her dress and the sparkling earrings. Emily began to swivel her head as she had done in the mirror months before so her friends could better see the earrings.

"These are them," Emily said to a friend on my right.

Emily took one off, handed it to me, and I passed it to her friend. She "*oohed*" and "*aahed*" over it, glared at me, then passed it back with a grin of either envy or skepticism, I wasn't sure which.

A waiter came around with the usual white and red wines in hand. As he asked which I preferred, I realized my stomach felt a bit off, so I thought I'd better stick with sparkling water.

"Neither for me, thank you," I said to the waiter. "Could I get a club soda with lime?"

With my few words, Emily looked at me, shocked and crushed.

"What's wrong?" she said, looking hurt. "You don't want to have fun tonight?"

"What? Because of the wine?"

"Yes, because of the wine. Why don't you want to have fun tonight?" she demanded to know even more hurtfully. I was ruining her Cinderella evening.

"I don't need alcohol to have fun, and besides, my stomach feels a little off. I'm going to take it easy on food and drink tonight. That's all," I said, trying to reassure her. "We'll have a wonderful evening, I promise."

My words did little to bring her out of her now-terrible mood.

She turned her gaze down to her food with a *how-could-he-do-this-to-me* look on her face.

I was more than annoyed at her reaction. It felt like I was back in college when most everyone thought getting drunk was the way to have fun. I was the rare person who wasn't much of a drinker, but I loved to lead the group of frat brothers who brought the aluminum bass fishing boat into the frat house living room for parties and fill it with ice and beer.

I might not have liked to get drunk, but everything we did was hilarious and, yeah, fun!

Just when there seemed to be little I could do to make things better, the band started playing and saved me.

As is often the case, it was an orchestra-type band that played old standards the first half of the evening—my favorites to dance to—then cranked it up with more contemporary tunes as the night wore on. I put out my hand to ask her to dance in a gesture of reconciliation. Emily offered a small smile and walked with me to the dance floor.

It was empty of anyone else—first songs always are—and we began to swing dance. We had practiced a little, and I reassured her I would give her a strong lead so she would know what to do. Her face lit up a little more, and her pouting evaporated as I led her through the first few spins. She saw a few heads turn toward us to watch, and then her full-beaming smile returned.

While I enjoy swing dancing, foxtrot, waltz, and tango, without a doubt, the most fun I have is doing my own unique, close-body schmooze. It's a kind of free dancing that is improvisational. If tango is vertical sex, then schmooze is its slow-dance cousin.

When the first slow song was played, the dance floor became packed, so I took Emily off to one side.

"Just follow me. You'll feel from my body what to do," I said, "but this'll be a little different from anything you've ever done before."

With our bodies in full contact, I began to dance slowly, and then quickly, and then slowly again. I then brought us to a momentary but full stop. From there, I took her into a fast spin as we tightly embraced. To finish what I call my "Fred and Ginger" move, I slowly brought us down to a slow spin, then to a sensual, embracing pause, holding us firmly together.

Then, as she waited and wondered what would happen next, I did a quick *Dirty Dancing* move—a fast little dip-and-grind with my leg coming up firmly between hers.

"What was THAT?!" she asked, gasping and unable to contain a laughing smile.

"It's me dancing with the woman I'm crazy about."

"Well, if you do that again, it'll be crazy all right ... crazy with me coming right here on the dance floor," she said breathlessly.

"Works for me," I said, bringing her back upright, ready to drop her again into the little dip-and-grind.

"No! Don't you dare!" she said, gripping me tightly and keeping me from moving her down. "Where did you learn to do that?!"

"Do you remember the movie *Dirty Dancing*?"

"Yeah," she said warily.

"Well, one night years ago, when I was dancing in Boston, we had a two-hour *Dirty Dancing* lesson. It was one hell of a class. You could make friends real fast if you wanted to."

Her mouth dropped open with a look of shock, and said, "You're unbelievable, Turner Grant!"

As we came off the dance floor, a woman quickly moved toward us.

"I wanted to tell you both how much I loved watching you dance. You two are great. I wish someone would dance with me like that."

Emily laughed. "It's like that line from *When Harry Met Sally,* 'I'll have what she's having.'"

The evening went marvelously well and was *fun* after all. Emily couldn't stop smiling the whole way home. Her kids were there with a babysitter, and both of mine awaited me at home, so I kissed her goodnight and left. I was feeling better, too, just as buoyant as she was, even without any wine.

The next day, Sunday, was a fly-day for me, an up-and-back to Boston to take my son with special needs back to his school after Thanksgiving. It was a routine I could do in my sleep, flying up on a one o'clock shuttle in the afternoon and arriving at two thirty. A staff member would come to the airport to meet us and take my son back to school, and then I would grab an early dinner and take the five thirty back to Washington.

All was well until the moment I signed the check for dinner. I realized in an instant my stomach was not a happy camper, and I might be in trouble. Boarding the plane, I glanced at my watch. Based on how I was feeling, how long did I think I could go before getting sick?

I was not going to make it.

Luckily, I was in the next-to-last row in an aisle seat. Fifteen minutes into the flight, I got up and told the flight attendant I was going to be sick. She quickly gave me a bag, and I went into the lavatory and threw up. Back in my seat, the flight attendants rushed to mid-plane twice where two other passengers had gotten sick but had not made it to a lavatory.

"Okay, what's going on tonight?" one of the flight attendants said as she walked past me. "Is this the upchuck express or something?"

Looking at my watch again, I tried to figure out how long it would be until the next convulsion would have me doubled over again. Luckily, I made it to the ground and into the airport terminal, but I knew I couldn't make it home. I found an unoccupied family restroom, opened the door, and quickly locked it.

I was in there for thirty minutes, waiting in misery to throw up again. I called Emily to tell her what had happened.

"Oh gee, sweetheart, I guess your tummy really *was* off last night. I'm *really* sorry … and here I was thinking you were being a killjoy and didn't want to have fun," she said.

"How could you *possibly* think that, Emily?" I said with surprise, astonishment, and annoyance.

"I don't know. I just did. I'm *so so* sorry, baby … I'm r-e-a-l-l-y sorry."

****

As December came around, Emily and I tried to put all the drama of the fall and the wedding behind us. We focused on being together as much as possible, doing things that would solidify our relationship and move it forward.

It was a nicely busy month with family gatherings, office parties, and Christmas shows. I met her parents when they visited between Christmas and New Year's, and we planned another weekend getaway in January.

Even though our time together was still mostly on weekends, with all the activities, constant emails, texts, and phone calls, there seemed to be no concern from Emily that we weren't spending enough time together. Our correspondence was full of heart twiddles (~~~~) once again.

Our three-day weekend getaway in January was momentous on two fronts. I was finally able to tell her I *was* falling in love with her, and after staying in bed all morning making love on the last day, Emily shared with me where she was too.

"I want more sex," she whispered ever so softly in my ear. "I want us to pick a time and day each week for you to come to my house. It doesn't have to be the same day each week but obviously before the kids get home from school. That's what I want from my lover boy!"

"You mean for me to leave the office in the middle of the day, come to you, have sex, and then go back to work?"

"Yes, exactly!" she said.

The Boys pounced. *But it's not about the sex!*

Outwardly, I smiled.

Inwardly, I freaked out.

The pressure for me at work had dramatically increased in the New Year. Several senior people had recently left the firm, and some of their projects had been dumped on me, along with their teams, to manage. Some had deadlines looming just weeks away.

"Emily, I can't do that right now. I told you what's happening at work. My gosh, I feel guilt and pressure just going to the bathroom a couple of times a day. It would take me an hour to get to your house from Georgetown, an hour back, and an hour together in between. I can't pull something like that off."

"I don't see the problem. It's not that much time," she declared.

"It's three hours away in the middle of pressure-packed ten- and twelve-hour days. There's just no way!"

Of course, that was the wrong answer. She had the option to work from home and could hop in and out of bed at the drop of a hat. Our magical getaway weekend ended on a decidedly unmagical note.

Over the next few weeks, Emily sent several emails with links to information she thought might be helpful in letting me know where she was and where she thought I was not.

EMAIL RECEIVED: 7 Reasons You Might Be Afraid of Love

Good article for Turner to read!!

EMAIL RECEIVED: Is Love the Greatest Pain of All? This Man Seems to Think So

I like this poetic short film and relate to it. Maybe this explains why it is hard when our time together ends.

In mid-March, Emily forwarded the entire email string from the year before, when we first communicated after meeting on eHarmony.

EMAIL RECEIVED: This and That

> One year ago today, you suggested we talk on the phone
> ~~~~~~~~~~~~~~~~

While I spent a lot of time thinking about Emily, my mind was also on my son at home. With acceptance letters in and decisions made, he was all set to leave for college in the fall, and I found myself walking through the house and beginning to think, "What now?" and "What if?"

For the longest time and in so many ways, Emily and I kept getting stuck on how to work around the physical distance between us. It was a constant and glaring issue, and not just because of the sex. Because the distance was so great, it seemed to me there could be no gradual merge of the two of us—it would have to be an all-in move for us to go forward.

What if Emily and her family moved in with me? I began to consider.

Then more questions followed.

Would they even want to move in here?

How could I make all this work if they did?

What if they said no?

Is this the life and future I want?

I thought about which of her children might get which room and which might serve as Emily's home office. I started doing this mental "what-if" exercise almost daily, thinking through every possible scenario, every possible problem, and a solution to each.

I often thought about all this while standing in the hallway with our family picture wall. In the nearly year and a half since meeting Marilyn, I had replaced some photos of my late wife with pictures of my sons.

Guess these last ones will have to go too, I thought. The next day, I reluctantly took them down and replaced them with current family photos. But it didn't feel right.

With all the possible changes afoot, I found myself thinking about the previous four years since my wife had passed away.

In the year we lost her, one son went off to school in Massachusetts and my other began high school. At the time, looking four years ahead was nothing less than daunting. It was full of anxiety, fears, and unknowns.

Would we make it?

Could we make it?

How would we do it?

What would we be like when we got there?

And now ... we were there, almost four years later.

He's really going to college, I said to myself. *We all made it; we actually made it.*

But there were so many mixed emotions as I stood in front of the wall of photos. I felt sad that my wife wasn't here to see her grown boys, then pride pushed some of the sadness away. I thought about my high school son's accomplishments and my life as a parent, focused and driven by his school schedule and needs, and doing all I could do to shape him into a fine young man. I thought of my son with special needs and how far he had come, able to experience and give so much joy. He was on his way to having a good and happy life.

And then it hit me. *I don't want to do this anymore,* a voice in my head said, and it wasn't The Boys.

It was my voice, loud and clear. *I'm exhausted, spent, and done with having my life driven by the daily, weekly, monthly, and yearly schedules of kids and schools from here to Massachusetts. I've done it, and I don't want to do it anymore.*

Ahem ... what about Emily and her children? The Boys now spoke warily.

Yeah ... right. What about *Emily and her children?* I thought.

The next day at the office, I told Abby what had happened the day before, including the realization that I didn't want to be in the business of parenting kids on a daily basis anymore.

"But where does that leave Emily and her kids?" she asked.

"Not with me," I responded with sadness.

"Oh my! You have to tell her," Abby said ominously but with certainty. "You have to!"

"I know, but I'm not sure if my feelings are set about this or fleeting and just in the moment. It washed over me as I stood there in the hallway thinking about it all. It caught me totally off guard."

"Oh, this is huge! You have to be sure, but if you are, you have to tell her," Abby said.

"I know, I know! She made it clear she doesn't want to be wasting her time, and now I may be doing just that."

Then I shared with Abby what else had been swirling in my head the last few weeks, all seemingly triggered by the realization that my high school son would be leaving for college and my life was about to change dramatically.

When my wife passed away, I took five months off work to deal with the transition forced upon us. I thought at the time I had done everything I needed to do, but now I realized that, while I had done a lot in those five months, there were things I had simply frozen in place for the sake of continuity and stability. The reality hit me that I needed to deal with these things before I could move on with my life.

Then there was Mary. At ninety-two, her health was beginning to fail even more than it had before. She had made a pact with herself that she would hang on long enough to see her grandson graduate high school and leave for college.

"If I can just hang on," she said, "I want to see your son and my grandson graduate and leave home to begin his next chapter. Life for me will then be complete."

I promised to be there for her, and she gave me her medical power of attorney to make any necessary decisions when the time came.

"It's coming this year," I told Abby. "I just know it, and I'll need time for her; I promised her, and I'm going to keep my promise."

Then I went back to my sons. "And I want to finish their childhoods with us all together this summer, someplace special. Bermuda or Cape Cod, maybe," I wondered out loud.

We had relatives in Bermuda and, along with Cape Cod, they were the two most special places we enjoyed as a family year after year while the boys were growing up. Both were magical places for us. But this last proposition would be difficult given the state of affairs at the firm. Abby asked how I was planning to finish my children's childhoods, given our overtime-packed workweeks.

"Well, that gets me to the last two things," I said. "My health is terrible. I'm aging faster than the years on the calendar say I should. Sleep is five hours a night, at best. I mean, I have to go down to the parking garage after lunch to take twenty-minute naps in the back of the minivan to get through each day. It's pathetic, and I feel guilty even doing that. The work at this fucking place is killing me. I hate this damn place!

"Each morning, I walk in and say to myself out loud, 'I hate this place, I hate this place, I hate. This. Place!' I mean, I literally do that every morning as I come off the elevator."

"Yeah." Abby sighed. "It's pretty awful here. But what are you going to do about it?"

The partners at the firm had taken full advantage of the Great Recession to squeeze every ounce of blood and life out of the remaining employees, and everyone had been miserable for years. Now, with the economy gradually coming back, employees, senior staff, and even principals were beginning to jump ship. Morale was plummeting, and the projects being dumped on me came with meager, demoralized staff.

Mary knew all too well about my unhappiness at work, and she sympathetically listened to several years of my complaining. One night over dinner, while I was going on about it again, I blurted out in utter frustration, "I hate that place. I'm done ... burned out ... toast. And now I have all these things I need to do," I said. "I just want to quit."

Without missing a beat, Mary said, "I think you *should* quit ... if you can."

"I can," I told her. "I can."

When I was in graduate school at Harvard, I made friends with a few guys at the business school who kindled a passion in me for business and investing. I had honed my investing skills over the years and knew I could comfortably do something else or walk away from work all together if I wanted to.

Looking at Abby now, she was impatiently waiting for me to answer her question.

"I'm going to quit," I said. "I'm just going to leave. I'm not going to get a job anywhere else; I'm just going to quit and do what I need to do for my family and me."

"You can't do that," she said, trying to pull me back from what she thought was a ledge I was about to jump from.

"Yes, I can," I said.

"No, you can't."

"Yes ... I can," I said slowly and definitively.

Not only was I about to quit my job, I was about to leave architecture for good—Mr. "First in Class" thirty-five years before in college; Mr. "Graduated with Distinction" from Harvard; and Art Vandelay! I was done with them all.

Abby looked at her watch.

"You have to be somewhere?" I asked.

"No, just double-checking to see if your midlife crisis is arriving on time. Let's see, you bought the fancy sports car, you're going to break up with your girlfriend, and you're going to quit your job."

She laughed. "Yep! Your midlife crisis has arrived right on schedule!"

Abby's laugh that day was the last I heard for quite some time.

CHAPTER 12

The Past to Be Forgotten

THE POPULAR BILLY GOAT TRAIL goes along the Potomac River and the C&O Canal in Maryland, just outside Washington, D.C. I've never been much of a hiker. I suppose it's because I grew up in the country where a tree was a tree and a river was a river—all unexciting to me. I prefer walking and exploring cities and towns in the footsteps of architectural history.

"Can we go home now?" was my usual response after ten minutes of hiking.

But on this weekend in early April, I made sure to leave home at the crack of dawn to get one of the scarce parking spots near the trail entrance. I had a lot on my mind, and it was time to make some decisions.

It was a nice, cool but sunny morning on the trail, and the leaves on the trees had not yet burst forth. Even from thirty yards away, I could see the white rapids of the river and hear its rushing current.

My career and my relationship—what should I do about each?

Both had consumed my thoughts for the previous six weeks. But now, for someone for whom a ten-minute hike could get boring quickly, the two hours of scampering over rocks and walking narrow trails went by way too fast.

I called Emily later that day and told her I had gone on a long hike to do some thinking. She said she wished she could have been with me and could know what was going through my mind. She knew about the work issues and the long list of things now needing to be done four years after my wife's passing. She also knew my feelings about my children as college loomed for my son, as well as my concerns for Mary, but likewise, she seemed to know something was up about us. I wouldn't be pressed into the details of what I was thinking because, once again, she was unavailable to get together that weekend. But the hike along the trail that morning had clarified both.

First, I would quit my job.

Second, I would tell Emily I didn't know how to move forward in a future together, given my feelings of not wanting my life to revolve around children. After all I had been through and accomplished with my sons, I was ready to be done with that phase of life.

I scheduled a meeting for Monday afternoon with the partner who had hired me eight years earlier, and Emily asked if we could have dinner two evenings later on Wednesday.

It would be one hell of a week.

****

Mine was the dream of many—it was a take-this-job-and-shove-it moment.

When I sat down with the partner in the conference room, I immediately got to the point. "I'm not happy here at the firm, and I'm leaving. But you should know, I'm not quitting to go to work for another firm like everyone else, I'm just leaving."

I first explained the personal issues that needed my time and attention in the next six months. The partner immediately offered a reduced workweek to help me deal with everything. I rejected his offer and then went into the litany of issues that made working there intolerable. Second, I told him I wasn't giving him two weeks' notice and bailing like everyone else. I would work until my current projects were wrapped up, even the ones dumped on me because of the departure of others.

When I emphasized that I was quitting work altogether with no plans to go anywhere else, he wistfully lamented, "I wish I could just quit and walk away."

After meeting for an hour, I left the conference room and walked back to my desk; Abby was waiting. The smile that broke out on my face said it all.

"Damn you! You told them! You're leaving me! How could you? Congratulations! I hate you!" she said, smiling and offering a big hug.

"Thank you, sweetie," I said. "I'll savor this moment, at least for tonight. Then Wednesday night will be Emily's turn, and that's going to hurt—a lot."

****

Emily's request to go out for dinner was the worst idea I could imagine, and several possible scenarios ran through my mind.

If the conversation started right up, we might never get to ordering dinner, and she would walk out on me. Or, we'd have two cold and uneaten dinners in front of us when the reality of what I was telling her sunk in. Or there was a possibility she would throw her dinner at me and walk out the door.

Despite my best efforts to act normal when I picked her up, she immediately knew something was amiss.

"Turner, what's wrong?"

"You know I've had so many things churning in my mind lately, and I want to share them with you tonight, but I'd rather wait until we're at the restaurant, if that's okay," I responded.

She looked at me with fear and foreboding all over her face. The restaurant was near her home, so we got there quickly. We sat down, ordered, and then I began.

"Emily, during my long hike, I tried to sort out a lot of different things, most of which you already know about."

I then took her through the story of how I began thinking about how to move our relationship forward, of me getting to "I love you," and of asking her and her kids to move in with me.

As I continued, she began to get a hopeful expression, as though my bombshell news wasn't going to be bad after all but perhaps the opposite.

"I thought about who might like which room, where your office might go … and then I started thinking about the last four years. How everything in my life has been driven by my children … and then it hit me."

"What hit you?" she asked.

"That I don't want to be in the parenting business anymore."

"What?" she asked, looking confused.

"It hit me like a two-by-four as I was standing in the hallway and looking at the photo wall. I don't want my life being driven by the responsibilities and schedules of parenting school-age children anymore."

"You mean mine?"

"I mean anyone's."

"You mean *mine*!" she said, frozen and unmoving.

Then, she made a pivot in the conversation.

"You *hate* my children?"

"No, your children are wonderful," I tried to say with affection. "I just don't want to be in a parenting role anymore once my son goes off to college. I realized how hard and all-consuming the last four years have been for me and … I'm done with that, and I don't want to do it again … for anyone."

She then looked at me hard. "You *hate* my kids is what I hear you telling me!"

"No, I DON'T hate your kids."

"Then what?!" she said, now demanding answers I struggled to give.

"Look …" I said, desperately trying to explain. "I *had* fallen in love with you and wanted to figure out how we could move forward. The distance between us has been such a problem, and I wanted to solve it. It seemed to me the only way to do that was to merge our two lives together. But then, in the process, it hit me that being in a parenting role was really something I didn't want anymore."

Silence hung in the air.

"Why didn't … why didn't you tell me this at the beginning, Turner? Where's all this coming from?"

"I didn't *know* in the beginning. Like I said, it just hit me as I thought about how to move us forward. Then I told Abby at work, and she said I had to tell you—you needed to know, but I needed to be sure. That was six weeks ago, but now, I'm sure. You said you didn't want any man wasting your time, and it seemed to me I might be doing just that."

More silence, and then hurt washed over her face.

"Well *thank goodness* for Abby, then," she said, finally dropping the fork she had been holding in midair over her plate.

It was then I felt the bond that had held us together for the last year begin to slip.

"Is this your way of breaking up with me? Is this what it's all about?" she demanded to know.

"No!" I said emphatically. "I didn't come here with some excuse to break up with you, but I confess I don't know how we move forward."

"And you thought it would be a great idea to take me out for dinner to tell me all of this and break my heart?" she said.

Wasn't our idea, said Darrell.

Shut up, Darrell! said Little Turner.

"No! There was no good place to do this. I'm so sorry, Emily. I'm so, so sorry. I didn't see this coming. Really, I didn't … I was looking for just the

173

opposite. This is not what I wanted." My voice was growing more desperate in an attempt not to inflict more pain and hurt.

I was breaking her heart as sure as we were sitting here in the half-empty restaurant.

Our conversation for the next twenty minutes rehashed everything over and over, but with the same sad outcome.

Our dinners were not touched.

"Can we please leave?" she asked.

We drove in silence back to her house, holding hands all the way. Parked in the driveway, I turned toward her, and she toward me. I leaned in to give her the most comforting hug I could, but she leaned in for a kiss, a kiss with everything she could muster. I felt both her passion and her desperation as she tried to pull me back from what I was doing.

My heart and my soul were crumbling, even as I resolutely held to my conviction of what needed to be done. I had to be honest with her. Isn't that what women said they wanted from men? But breaking up with Emily seemed cruel, so cruel.

We then pulled apart. She suggested I take time and space to figure out *my problems,* saying the family matriarch had been right to label them that way. I should take all the time I needed. She said she needed time to process it all too. She didn't want us to stop communicating, however. She wanted us to share our thoughts and feelings as much as possible.

Emily then asked if I wanted to start dating again and see other women. I told her that was the last thing I wanted to do and that none of this had anything to do with wanting to see other women.

"I find it hard to even imagine wanting to date again, quite frankly," I said. "This is too hard; I can't hurt people like this."

As we looked at each other in the darkened car, illuminated only by her porch light, I saw both resignation on her face and hope that this would not be the end.

While it didn't seem like the end, it did feel like the beginning of the end.

****

For the rest of April and May, Emily and I emailed and texted. It wasn't daily, but enough to keep up with the goings-on of each other. We didn't talk on the phone.

I still saw no way forward together, but I was trying to be as gentle and kind as possible. I was inflicting enough hurt as it was, and I harbored hopes of salvaging a friendship. But by stringing it out instead of just ending it, my attempt to be kind was, as she made clear, just the opposite.

"You're so cruel," were her exact words.

My job at the architectural firm finished up the first week of June. My focus then turned to my son's high school graduation. In a text to Emily, I shared some of the emotions I was feeling about this major milestone in life. Her frustration and anger lashed out in a text, blasting me for making my son's moment somehow all about me. I thought it was vicious, and I responded by telling her, "… maybe it's time for you to move on."

She later emailed an apology, then asked if I could accompany her to a meeting where she had a legal matter to deal with. This gave me hope that, perhaps, a friendship was possible.

In the summer, she let me know she had begun dating again, and I confessed I had gone out a few times too. I told her I had wanted to end the dates as soon as they had begun because it seemed there was no purpose to it anymore. I had fallen in love with a wonderful woman, yet I had failed in making a future with her. It seemed the whole effort to find love was futile, so why bother at all?

She seized upon my confession to unleash what would be a summer-long barrage of fury expressed in handwritten letters and emails, marking the final demise of our relationship.

VARIOUS EMAILS RECEIVED:

> … I really don't think you even know what a normal, healthy man-woman relationship looks like.
>
> … You were always very inconsiderate; you whined and complained too much about your job; you did not take a sincere interest in my friends and family. You also talked about your wife's family way way too much—very tiring to listen to.
>
> … The ghost of your wife was everywhere. How can any woman compete with a ghost?

... The fact of the matter is, Turner, you fell in love with me, probably more than you ever have been. But you were not ready for it, were afraid, and backpedaled using my children— something you knew I could not or would not change—first and foremost as the reason. The moment you mentioned them being an issue, I should have walked. That was such betrayal and one of the most unloving things anyone could have ever said or done to another person, especially with the love I have to give.

... If you would have been willing to actually talk like a grown-up ...

... It seems you can hurt other's feelings but can't take getting your own feelings hurt.

... I hope you are okay sorting through your "problems."

... You used me.

EMAIL SENT: (No subject)

Emily,

How does one end a relationship when one realizes it is not the right one? That was my task/burden/choice/obligation. It seemed to me there was no good way to do it, but I can tell you I gave it my absolute best in trying to minimize the hurt, but I suppose that's not possible. Breaking a heart is breaking a heart.

I regret very little. I found you, found someone I wanted to be with, to get to know deeply, to expose my vulnerabilities to, laugh, love, and so much more. I regret that when I realized we had gone as far as we could go, ending it caused so much pain.

I wish I could have found a better and decent way to do it.

That's all; I have no more words to offer. We both know how hard life is day-in and day-out. In the end, I wanted nothing more than to still be your friend, to be there to support you, and keep a part of the great connection we had.

I tried. I failed. I'm sorry.

Turner

****

After several months of no correspondence, we exchanged emails in late October and early November. Emily's feelings toward me seemed to have thawed, at least a bit.

A few weeks later, in December, when I was out Christmas shopping, I bought her and her children a gift and delivered it to her doorstep. She wasn't home at the time, but she texted an hour later, lamenting that she missed being able to see me. She thanked me with tremendous kindness in her words.

An event came up the next spring she was to be a part of, and she invited me to attend. It was great to see her, and she looked very happy. When we finally had a chance to say hello and chat, I got a polite, lean-in, shoulder-tapping hug. I then knew for sure she was okay and had moved on.

That next Christmas, a year and a half after we broke up, she posted on Facebook that she was engaged.

I was not surprised.

I pieced together a timeline from the comments on her post and figured out she had met him the year before around the time I was dropping off my Christmas present.

In the end, she had gotten what she was looking for: a man she loved and who loved her the way she wanted and needed, and the marriage she so wanted. A week after I congratulated her on their engagement, she unfriended me on Facebook. She had found her future, and I was her past to be forgotten.

I never saw or heard from Emily again.

YEAR THREE

The Far Side of Venus

CHAPTER 13

Enigma – Part I

IT WAS PRETTY EASY TO sum up how I felt in the months after breaking up with Emily—I felt like shit.

Here was someone who was wonderful, who loved me, whom I loved, yet we had no future together. It made absolutely no sense, except that I *did* have problems.

Her scorching emails of May and June—that would continue through the entire summer—left me battered and bruised from head to toe and from ego to heart.

I was angry, too, at the world in general and at the whole notion of dating, women, and relationships. But as jaded as I was with a good-sized chip on my shoulder, I began the tentative steps of getting back out into the dating world. Presumably, it was because I cared about finding someone special and falling in love, but I told myself that I didn't, and I wouldn't care anymore. When I began my journey on Venus, I felt I had to first prove myself to the women I met and ensure that my heart was in it before they had to prove themselves to me. My attitude now was reversed—I would meet new women with skepticism that had to be allayed before vesting my heart into any situation.

My subscription to eHarmony had long ago run out, but Abby had been using the free dating sites, and I *damn* sure wasn't going to pay for this stuff anymore. I put together an OkCupid profile and answered their unique set of questions.

The algorithm gods on eHarmony work more like a matchmaker, and they won't show you anyone they don't think will make the cut. But OkCupid doesn't make matches per se, rather, they show you everyone who meets your filtering criteria—age, race, religion, distance, income, and so forth—along with a *percentage of compatibility number*. You'll get one profile that shows a 67 percent match, another that shows a 96 percent match, and then it's up to you to decide what to do next.

After signing up, I only had to answer a few questions before being shown women's profiles. But then, after seeing several profiles, they asked me to read and answer a lot of specific (but optional) multiple-choice questions. The more questions I answered, the more data they had for calculating a more reliable *percentage of compatibility number,* or so the thinking went.

The questions were about dating, lifestyle, religion, ethics, sex, and more. Once I answered enough questions, OkCupid sorted women into categories of seemingly higher compatibility with my particular interests in mind. They offered a "likes travel" group of matches, a "likes sports and fitness" group, a "likes art" group, and so on. The option to add a personal answer to any given multiple-choice question allowed me to give a specific response or qualify my answer. Anyone looking at my profile could see my answers to a particular question, as long as they had answered it too.

The detailed questions they asked about sex started easily enough, but then they got pretty darn personal pretty darn fast. I felt like a voyeur reading answers of the most intimate nature from women whose pictures were right in front of me. I was amazed people would reveal this kind of information to perfect strangers, but they did, and … so did I, at least to some extent.

> *Would you need to sleep with someone before you considered marrying them?*
> *Regardless of future plans, what's more interesting to you right now, sex or love?*
> *Would you consider sleeping with someone on the first date?*
> *How many dates before you would consider having sex?*
> *Are you open to trying new things in bed?*
> *How do you think your sex drive compares to what is typical for other people your age?*
> *Are you kinky?*
> *How much communication is ideal during sex?*
> *Do you like the lights on or off during sex?*

Do you find the idea of shaving a partner's pubic hair exciting?
Would you allow your partner to kiss you after having performed
oral sex on you?

The questions go on and on, but you get the idea.

With my now couldn't-care-less attitude, I opened up the dating distance to one hundred miles, throwing out dating-darts like crazy in all directions. There were rapid-fire meetings of new women, one after another. I went through them like potato chips and unabashedly used the Mercedes roadster to attract them and anything they cared to offer.

Okay, who is it today? Who am I going to meet, pretend to like, and then ghost? I thought.

The Boys were freaking out. This wasn't Turner. This was some sort of Dr. Jekyll and Mr. Hyde thing going on. They were worried, and so was I.

I was hurting, floundering, and wallowing in self-pity. But oddly enough, my couldn't-care-less and cavalier attitude seemed to have the *opposite* effect on women from what I had imagined; they were seemingly *more* interested in me, not *less*.

****

I saw Ava's picture on OkCupid the last week in June. It was a photo of a woman walking on a beach on a windy day with mansions in the background. It looked like the grand old mansions in Palm Beach, although her profile said she lived in Richmond. It was an evocative artsy-type photo, very sophisticated, and very alluring.

According to OkCupid, we were a 96 percent match.

I sent her a note, more off-the-cuff than carefully written, and she responded back within an hour. With no hesitation, she suggested a phone call for later that day.

She's fast, thought The Boys.

That evening, we had an interesting, hour-long phone conversation. I was more gregarious than usual with my new attitude, and that seemed to set the pace for a lively, if not businesslike, conversation. I told her I loved the photo of her—it seemed more like a work of art. She proceeded to tell me about the unnamed but famous photographer who took it.

She also talked about her work—a lot, sort of. She was the head of client relations for a private investment company, although it was a bit unclear what she actually did other than attend parties and benefit galas. She worked and traveled on the East Coast, West Coast, and in Europe. She was moving back permanently from Palm Beach—or as permanently as something like this could be for her—to Richmond, where she was from.

Just like when she mentioned the photographer who took her picture, she did a lot of name-withheld name-dropping, a conversational art form I was less familiar with. In Washington, name-dropping requires a name to actually be dropped to have an impact. But Ava did it with the explicit intent of letting me know she dealt with people so important and rich, they had to remain anonymous.

She offered little personal information about herself, even as she interrogated me pretty thoroughly. By the end of the call, however, I was curious enough to want to meet her, even if it meant driving an hour and a half to Richmond.

But I didn't even have to ask.

"Let's have dinner," she said. "How about next weekend after I finish moving my Palm Beach furniture into storage? I'll be out of pocket until Saturday, so how about Sunday evening? I know the perfect place. You'll love the food and the building. It's an old brick industrial mill building that was marvelously redeveloped by an architect friend of mine. I know the owner there too. It's probably too late to get reservations, so I'll just give him a call. I'll get back to you on a time if that's okay."

"Sure," I said, "that sounds great."

Okay-y. She's different, I thought.

The Boys agreed, but they thought it was a total waste of time. *Isn't this a wee bit out of the way?* asked Charles. *It all feels sort of … desperate.*

But I thought we needed to shake things up. *We need to get away from here and break free from everything we've been doing.*

Ava sent me a friend request on Facebook, and I finally learned her last name. I Googled her and found she had absolutely no presence on the internet—zip! Such a situation in the digital age could only be done by trying really hard not to be found, but she had done it. I did find obituaries for what might be relatives, but even those were minimal, cryptic, and intentionally private by the information they didn't give out.

We emailed a bit during the week, but it was more about logistics. Even as I expressed happy expectations for meeting her, she was more measured as she wrote about her move back to Richmond, the contacts she had made in the last year, and the need to keep in touch with them, lest her business suffer.

Finally, in her last brief email the day before we were to meet, she wrote, more perfunctory than enthusiastically:

EMAIL RECEIVED: (No Subject)

Look forward to meeting you. Smiles –A

****

The Sunday summer afternoon drive felt strange and out of the ordinary. In the last few years, I had traveled frequently to the suburbs of Richmond for board meetings but never downtown. Even with navigation, finding my way around was confusing. The restaurant was deep in the heart of Richmond and surrounded by some pretty sketchy areas. But when I finally arrived—early, of course—I found an upscale residential and retail development among numerous nineteenth-century industrial buildings.

It was a busy and popular place, living up to Ava's hip description. I told the hostess I was meeting someone for dinner and would wait at the bar. I was a good fifteen minutes early, so I ordered a drink, settled in, and occupied myself by catching up with the news on my phone.

A few minutes later, I was caught by surprise when I felt a woman's presence just inches from me. With the first glimpse out of the corner of my eye, I saw that two large breasts had arrived—a couple of steps ahead of the rest of her—and were actually hovering right in front of me.

Her breasts said hello, and then I was greeted from behind them. "Turner? Hi. You're here!" she said, somewhat surprised.

So are yours! The Boys offered in a quick retort, with Darrell hooting and hollering about her hooters.

She was slender and fashionably dressed. She had on a white fishnet top layered over a white, snug, crew-neck tank top, with white jeans and white stiletto heels. She gave nary a hint of a smile but instead offered an intense stare with her piercing eyes. She wasn't a natural beauty—remarkably unremarkable, actually—but she exuded confidence and had style in spades, which made her intensely attractive.

She put out her hand to shake, but she was so close I had to do a contorted reach-around maneuver with my right hand to avoid her breasts.

If I so much as turned an inch, I'd be in her bra.

She said she had already talked to her owner-friend, and our table was ready.

Sitting at the table and looking across at each other, Ava started speaking quickly and a bit nervously about the food and the restaurant, all the while staring in such a way that I knew she was doing a full appraisal of me. I tried to focus on the conversation and less on the scan her eyes were doing, but it was just so obvious.

She then asked how my drive was and if I had any trouble finding the place. I decided right then we needed to get off this businesslike small talk. I channeled my inner Darrell, conjuring up once again my most charming Southern accent.

"Well, it was fine … but ya know, I've never driven an hour and a half before to meet a *girl*."

She stopped cold and stared at me; the reluctant hint of a smile came to her face. She then coughed up an involuntary laugh, like a drink of water going down the wrong way.

"That's actually very sweet … what you just said … and the way you said it," she said softly.

"Well, I really don't want you to worry," I said. "If I'm a lousy dinner date, you'll be able to get rid of me soon enough. I'll drive back to where I came from, and you'll never have to see me again."

She then began to relax and engage in a more personal way. But even as our conversation flowed, it was pretty clear that her default way of talking was in this direct, semi-emotionless, businesslike manner.

I dove right in, asking the usual questions about what she did, life in Richmond, and her family. For the next thirty minutes, she gave a curated history of herself, and it was nothing less than jaw-dropping. She was an heiress whose job brought her into contact with others across the country in the top 1 percent of the top 1 percent.

The no-name name-dropping from our phone call the week before was now done *with* names, and some of them were very familiar. No matter which of the dozen or so people she talked about at any given time, she usually followed it with some variation of "… and they made millions in just a few years—they are one of my best friends."

It didn't take long for me to figure out I had no business being with Ava. Everything for her seemed to be about money. For me, it was about family. I needed to have dinner and just go home. But she finally grew weary of talking about her rich friends and began to ask a few things about me.

She knew the basics—Southern boy, architect, Harvard grad, stay-at-home dad, congressional candidate, widowed, and so on. Anytime I said something about myself in answer to one of her questions, however, she would invariably detour back to one of her friends and their millions before circling back to me and asking another question. Finally, she came around to my run for Congress and asked why I ran.

It wasn't an answer I had to think about twice. Immediately, I felt a bit of emotion welling up inside.

"I'm a special needs parent. And I've learned over the years that sometimes you have to fight for what's right, and it's hard. But I've also learned sometimes you have to fight against what's wrong, and that's even harder. And if you care and if you can, you have to get involved because there are so many who care and can't. And if you care and if you can and you don't get involved, then what's right will never be done, and what's wrong will never change."

Then, in a whisper, I said, "That's why I ran for Congress, Ava."

As I spoke, she became motionless, and a stunned look of silence enveloped her. After a few more seconds passed, slowly, and in a measured tone of restrained emotion, she spoke. "You sound just like my father, Turner. He was a great man. He did great things. What you said … it's exactly what he would've said."

She just looked at me … transfixed and mesmerized. Then, she grabbed her purse and began to fumble to find her phone.

"I want to show you something," she said, flipping through photos with her thumb on the screen.

She then showed me a photo of the two of them together. It was another artistically done photo, a striking and powerful image. She slowly pulled her phone back, and her eyes lingered on it for a moment.

"I miss him so much."

From then on, she spoke less about her rich friends and more about regular things. It was rather enjoyable.

Finally, it felt like it was time to wind things down. Looking at my watch, I was astonished to see it was nine o'clock, and we had been talking for almost three hours.

She was truly an interesting and fascinating person. She had an incredibly charmed but private life that she was kind enough to share with me over dinner. But I wasn't the guy for her, it seemed to me, and there wasn't much in the way of chemistry that I felt either. We did have a great meeting of the minds on several topics, and I would've enjoyed another dinner conversation with her, but this was a textbook one-and-done date.

She offered me a tour of the building—the architect had done a really nice job of creating a very special place. She knew by now that I was a design snob like her and I wasn't easily impressed, and she seemed pleased to have been able to wow me with her choice of venue.

Going outside to the parking lot, we walked mostly in silence as she stayed a step in front of me. I made note of the gorgeous evening to try and get her to say *something*, when, near her car, she abruptly turned around.

"You wanna take a walk?"

I was surprised because all the signals I was getting—not the least of which was her silence—was that the evening was over.

"Sure. That'd be great. Let's check out the other buildings."

It was a summer evening when the last aura of twilight magically lingers in the sky. We started a long, slow walk, first along the main road beside a large residential development, a combination of new construction woven into old brick mill buildings. From there, we went into a residential mews, sort of a J-shaped roadway path, and then retraced our steps. It was nicer being with her now as we walked because she let her guard down and we talked randomly about regular stuff—not the people she knew who made millions, not her posh travels, nor the rarefied air in which she lived. We were nicely alone, and our walk together was the best part of the evening.

Finally, we arrived back at the spot where she had made her pivot thirty minutes before. I gestured to give her a polite hug goodnight but then decided a kiss on her cheek might be welcome before parting ways.

She reciprocated as expected, but when I went to release her and pull away, she held tightly. In an instant, she slid her lips from my cheek to my lips, lunged her tongue into my mouth, and started half-sucking the life out of me. I had just exhaled when she locked on, and I struggled momentarily to catch a breath, almost gasping. She then pulled her right leg up, curled it around my waist, and pulled me tight. She not only had me in a lip lock, she had me in a half-crotch lock too.

Once the surprise of what was happening settled in, I happily settled in, too, and the vertical make-out session went into high gear.

The Boys started cheering and chanting like cheerleaders at a football game, urging on the offense to score.

Here we go, Tur-ner, here-we-go! Clap clap. Here we go, Tur-ner, here-we-go! Clap clap.

She was having a hard time keeping her balance on the one stiletto-heeled shoe, so she put both her arms around my neck, pulled herself up, and swung her other leg around my waist. She now had me in a full leg-wrapping crotch clutch.

As she struggled to hang on to my neck and keep herself off the ground, her arms weakened and she finally let go, sliding back down to the pavement.

"Let's go find someplace to sit down," she said with an almost frantic look on her face.

Across the street we went, looking for a bench or anything to sit on, but there was nothing. We ventured into the courtyard of an upscale condo building and then into a large, arched building pass-through with steps going down to the main lobby. Seeing nothing else to sit on, we sat down on the top step, twisted toward each other, and resumed the intense make-out session. But it was awkward and uncomfortable for both of us.

Expressionless and without a word, she let go and stood up. I thought she was going to say something like, "This isn't working at all," and be done with it, but that's not what she had in mind.

With a clear look of determination on her face, she pushed me down onto the stone pavement, picked up her left stilettoed foot, aimed it, and put it down right between my legs. As she stepped in, she shifted all her weight to that foot. From there, in a singular motion, she dropped down onto my thigh with her crotch and locked her lips back onto mine while going full prone on top of me. She then began to furiously hump my leg with all her weight bearing on her crotch while thrusting her tongue down my throat. She reached one hand behind, clutching and pulling me in as tight as she could to grind even harder. Her other hand pulled my head ever tighter into her furiously hungry lips.

I can only describe it as a full-body attack while simultaneously being waterboarded with wet lips and a tongue.

In the first few seconds, I couldn't figure out what the hell was going on. But then, as I got my bearings, my hands grabbed her body, and I began to explore her. I pulled her closer and ever tighter, then went on to find out what the limits were on this grinding tryst.

There were no limits—anything I wanted to do was fair game. She audibly, with moans and groans, let me know she wanted more of everything I was doing.

Then a series of thoughts flashed through my mind.

One, it looks like I'm assaulting this woman. I could easily be arrested and thrown in jail, even though she's the one on top and the one who jumped me.

Two, whoever's monitoring the security cameras for the condo complex is getting quite a show.

And three, her large breasts pressing me down and bulging out every which way? They were big fake boobs—weaponized breasts—and she knew how to use them.

It was a buzz saw of passion and horniness on the steps in the glow of the condo lobby lights.

Party on, Garth! Party on, Wayne! The Boys shouted, mimicking the lines from *Wayne's World*.

I don't know how long this continued, but at some point, it got way out of control. I felt less like I was getting lucky and more like I was pushing my luck.

I momentarily freed my lips from hers and said, between kisses and gasps for air, "Okay … you either need to take me home … or send me home … because this is becoming … painfully uncomfortable … in more ways than one."

"I can't take you home yet," she said, continuing her humping and grinding. "I don't know you well enough. I have to feel safe with you … and trust you first."

"Safe? I think … it's safe … to say … we're not safe … out here … doing this."

And with that, she went into overdrive, a crescendo of frenetic humping and moaning in what I could only conclude was her coming to a final orgasm.

Then she stopped.

She lay there, limp on me, kissing me gently but not saying a word at first.

Then she said, "Sorry about the jeans. It might have been easier for you if I'd worn a dress, but then again, we probably would've gotten into some serious trouble."

After a few minutes, she silently got off—her face expressionless—extended her hand and helped me up. We walked in silence back to the parking lot in the dark, quiet night. In the middle of the road, she stopped, grabbed me, and kissed me again.

Pulling back but with her arms still around me, she looked into my eyes and spoke in a confessional voice. "I'm attracted to you."

"Yeah … I sort of noticed."

She giggled.

As we set foot in the parking lot, she turned to me and we locked lips yet again. She then pulled away, looked toward the back of the restaurant, and led me to a dark corner. She put her back to the wall and pulled me in. I noticed her nipples were protruding from under her clothes like missile tips.

"They're attracted to you, too, and wanted to say hello," she said.

I pinched them with my fingers.

We kissed again, and she pulled me in closer still. She started to shimmy her back up the wall, then came down with all her weight on her crotch and my thigh between her legs.

A few moments later, she relaxed her body and released her tight grip.

"I think I should probably go now," she said breathlessly.

I looked at my watch and was stunned to see it was after midnight—another three hours had passed since dinner.

As I closed the door to her car, she rolled down her window; I leaned in for another long kiss and ran my hand up and down the entire front of her body.

"Call me," she said. "Let me know you got home okay."

I was only twenty minutes outside the city when the phone rang.

"So how are you doing?" she asked.

"Well … thinking about you, *a lot!*"

"Good! You surprised me tonight, you know?" she said.

"That makes two of us," I said, and she giggled.

"Call me tomorrow. I'd like to see you again," she said.

"But you said you don't trust me."

"Not *yet,* I said. It takes *time* for me to trust. Do you want to see me again?"

"Yes."

After pausing, perhaps to think, she simply said, "Goodnight, Turner."

****

The next day, I heard nothing from Ava.

Given the night before and her unexpected call on the way home, I was a little surprised. Then I realized it could have been nothing more than a one-and-done fun date as far as she was concerned. Right before I went to bed, I emailed her, asking if she might like to get together in Richmond on Saturday in two weeks, perhaps to play some tennis or "other activities."

I ended the email with "a penny for your thoughts."

A minimal response came the next day.

EMAIL RECEIVED: Seeing You Again

Sounds perfect.

Over the next two weeks, her infrequent communication never went beyond the necessary date-night logistics. I had no idea where she lived, and she didn't want me to know. She forgot about my playing tennis idea and totally ignored my suggestive comment about "other activities." A few days before our date, she texted an agenda for the evening. She would meet me in the city, and we would go from there.

AVA: There are some art galleries I'd like to show you I think you might enjoy. They're not in a part of town most people know about, but I know most of the gallery owners personally. Then we can have dinner nearby on the riverfront. I

> know the restaurant owner
> too and will make sure we
> get a good table. See you
> then.

Her texts were like her in-person spoken conversation—businesslike and with little emotion or affect.

It all felt a bit odd.

The anticipation of seeing her again was more curiosity than anything else. It was a dating expedition into the unknown.

She gave me the address of a gallery in an older part of Richmond. It was in a historic neighborhood with some very nice older buildings scattered about.

When we met at the art gallery, she offered an expression of recognition, a faint smile, and a hesitant quick peck of a kiss. It wasn't the welcome I expected given our mutual body explorations two weeks before.

She immediately launched into tour-guide small talk about the gallery. It wasn't until a few minutes later that she bothered to ask, "So how are you?"

"Been looking forward to seeing you again," I said, reaching for her hand.

At that moment, her expression changed from tour guide to date, and she gave my hand an affectionate squeeze … then she let it go before resuming her tour-guide duties.

I finally decided she was just incredibly nervous about meeting me again, so I worked to make her feel as relaxed as possible. After a nice hour or so of exploring galleries with pretty funky local art, we went to my van and drove to the riverfront.

It was another gorgeous, warm summer night, and it was especially nice near the water where the restaurant was. The hostess led us to a patio on the river side and sat us at the most private table with an unobstructed view of the water. Ava asked if the owner was in this evening.

"Yes, he is. I'll let him know you're here," the hostess said with deference before quickly departing.

Ava launched into her now-familiar narration of the restaurant, how fabulous it was, how well she knew the owner, and how much money he made.

I wondered if this bragging thing was what she needed to do to feel secure about herself. Was it to make sure she was always the most superior person

TO VENUS AND BACK

in the room? She's an heiress! What more did she need? Couldn't she see how unflattering it was?

To poke at her a bit, when talk turned to drink orders, I rolled out a story. With the waterside setting and warm air, I told her it felt like a Dark & Stormy drink night.

"What's that?" she asked. "I've never heard of it."

I went on to explain that a branch of the family I married into included the Goslings of Bermuda. They make, in my opinion, the best and smoothest rum in the world. The Dark & Stormy cocktail comes from Bermuda and can only correctly be made with Gosling's Black Seal Rum and ginger beer.

"Only high-end bars and those with specialized knowledge of cocktails usually carry Black Seal," I told her, "and it's the only thing to have when you're in Bermuda."

"I've never been," she said reluctantly, seemingly confessing to a rare deficit in her life.

She instantly became tight-lipped and went on the defensive. "I'm *sure* they have it here," she said.

After I made the request, our waiter went scurrying to the bar to ask, and Ava visibly held her breath. He returned with a disappointing, "I'm sorry, sir, no. We don't have Goslings."

Shortly after our cocktails were served—with my second choice of drink— and dinner ordered, the owner came over to say hello to Ava. They were doing gushy-gushy posh talk between them when I conveyed my disappointment about the restaurant not having Goslings.

"My family in Bermuda makes it," I told him.

Gushy-gushy posh talk went to gushy-gushy apology talk, and he promised they would have it by Monday.

"Your cocktail is on me, sir, along with my sincere apologies," he said.

Knowing looks of some sort were exchanged between them, and then he left.

"I'm sorry," Ava said.

"No worries."

Starting with the Bermuda branch of my in-laws, she began to ask more questions. Then a text arrived on my phone.

"Everything okay?" Ava asked as I glanced at the text.

"Yes, it's fine. A friend was asking how our date was going."

"Oh, who is he?"

"Actually, it's a she—one of my best friends."

The warm summer air suddenly became icy cold, and Ava's face went Mount Rushmore.

As she held still with her icy expression, I went on to explain my relationship and friendship with Abby, but her glare only intensified.

Silence continued between us until she finally spoke.

"You can't be just friends with a woman. You're so-o-o-o naïve," she said definitively and condescendingly.

"She's a super-wonderful friend, and you would enjoy meeting her," I offered as nonchalantly as possible. But her intense glare went unabated.

"Well, Ava, I have to tell you, I have a number of very dear female friends, and they're nothing more than friends. For my wedding, I had five female friends travel down from Boston to celebrate and dance with me, and my wife thought it was the most wonderful thing in the world. She even bragged to others about it. So if this is a problem, I *really* don't know what to say."

That began a thaw in her expression.

"I'm not skeptical of you; I'm skeptical of the women," she said quietly.

"There's nothing there, Ava. They're just wonderful, great friends."

"How many are we talking about?" she asked.

"Very good and dear friends? Well … four or five very close ones, then more acquaintances. They were friends of mine before my wife died, my wife knew them, and they've been incredible to the boys and me. Some of them are married, but not all. Abby is my very best friend, period, man or woman. I tell her everything, and she does the same with me."

Her eyes widened. "She knows about me? What did you tell her?!"

"Just that I met a woman named Ava in Richmond and filled her in on a few details. But I didn't … ahem … give her any specifics about our first date."

She gave a knowing smile, relaxed a bit, but skepticism remained on her face.

I actually *had* told Abby that Ava jumped me.

"Now you know what I have to deal with all the time with men!" Abby responded quickly.

Then I talked about Mary, Wendy, and all the other important women in my extended family, what they had done, and how much they meant to me. I spent a lot of time talking about Mary.

Then, in a big moment, I told her the truth about how my wife died. I had been thinking for a while that I needed to learn how to talk about this and be more comfortable—or less uncomfortable—getting it out there. Oddly, with Ava, I felt less hesitant than usual. I also thought my opening up about something so serious and personal might get her to put her guard down and finally open up herself. There was an interesting woman in there I wanted to get to know, but so far, it had been pretty much impossible.

"You're only the second woman I've met who I've told this to."

She looked at me with sad and concerned eyes. "I'm … so sorry, Turner. How awful … for everyone. I can't imagine."

I looked at her and then out to the river to avoid her stare. She gave me that *look*, the one I got on the rare occasion I shared the true story.

Could they see something in me that I didn't know? Did I have any visible cracks?

I always wondered.

The rest of dinner was pleasant. My revelation moved us past the Q&A phase of meeting one another and, dare I say, maybe even established some amount of trust.

The evening was still young and the skies a soft blue as we made our way out of the restaurant. Walking by the owner, he spoke out in a loud voice. "Make sure you come back Monday. We'll have that Black Seal Rum for you!"

We took a walk to a brick courtyard next to the restaurant. It was a yet-to-be-developed, old industrial zone and was pretty much dead.

We looked at each other.

"What now?"

"How about a kiss?" I said. "I think I remember you doing that pretty well two weeks ago."

She came in and gave the most unenthusiastic kiss imaginable.

"Okay, so maybe not," I said.

"Well, not here," she said. "We're out in the open. I'm not good at public displays of affection, just so you know."

With that remark, I realized she hadn't once reached out for my hand the entire afternoon or evening. When I had reached out for hers at the art gallery, she had immediately let it go.

"Well, do you want to go back into town and do something? Go back to your place?"

"No. Like I said before, it takes time before I can trust and have you come to my place."

"Ahem ... I hope this isn't too personal, but did something terrible happen to you in the past?" I asked.

"No, I'm just very cautious, and it takes me more time than most."

Then, in an awkward pivot of subjects, she blurted out, "I will only date monogamously. I don't do serial daters."

Caught off guard, I paused to consider her out-of-the-blue statement.

"Ah, yeah, that's perfectly fine," I said. "I hate the serial-dating treadmill. It's too easy to get on and then too hard to get off. But ... are we *dating*?"

Then, silence again, which by now I was learning was one of her many traits.

"Well, just thinking out loud," I said to fill the silence and sort out the moment. "Maybe I should give you a ride home and we can call it a night. We had a nice dinner, a nice evening, and that's great. We can let it go at that. What happened last time certainly doesn't have to happen again. That can simply be the you-remember-what-happened-the-first-night-we met thing we can both knowingly smile about when we're old and gray. I've got my vacation to Cape Cod with my sons for the next two weeks, so let me give you a ride home, and I'll see you when I get back."

"Well ... maybe," she said. "Why don't we go back to your van and figure it out?"

Back in the parking lot, the van was surrounded on both sides by cars parked too close to open the front doors. So I suggested we go in one of the middle sliding doors, then crawl up to the front. Going in, she took a glance back to the third-row seat. I immediately had flashbacks to Emily and our make-out session there on our second date over a year before.

No one ever thought of a family minivan as a make-out machine, but it sure seemed ready-made for it, I thought. (I would later learn that teenagers for the past two decades have known quite well the make-out potential of the family minivan, but it took my going to Venus to stumble across this fact.)

"Let's go back here," she said, making a turn for the third-row seat.

She immediately sat and put her back to the side of the van, extending her legs out the length of the seat. I fell into her arms to kiss her—or at least tried to—but once again, as it was on the steps, it was rather uncomfortable.

"Wait a minute," I said.

I broke our hold and pulled the shades up all around the dark glass to give us more privacy. Then I grabbed the seat-back release and reclined the seat.

"That's better," she said.

She spread apart her legs in her white jeans like it was an invitation to unzip them. As I began to, she stopped me.

"No, not here! There are people right outside the window," she said, hearing people getting into the car next to us.

"Well," I said, "except for going back to your place—which we can't do—I'm rather out of ideas."

Then she unbuttoned and opened her shirt to expose her large breasts in a sheer bra, and we went at it again for a few more minutes.

"This isn't working," she said, "but I have an idea. Let's drive to a park near my place … it'll be nice."

With her giving directions, we made our way from the riverfront to an affluent area in the middle of Richmond. She had me do a U-turn on a main avenue and pull to the curb.

"There's a park bench right there. Pull the van up to block the view of it from the street."

"But where's the park?" I said.

The bench was in the middle of a wide sidewalk in front of a high-rise apartment building facing the four-lane avenue. It looked like a bench used to wait for a bus.

"It's quiet here this time of night. No one will be here but us." Then out of the door she went in a flash.

I hesitated.

"Come on, it's perfectly fine," she said, standing by the bench, waiting for me.

I got out, walked over, and sat down. She climbed up on the bench and put her feet on either side of me. Then, as before, she dropped down and began a vigorous forward-facing grinding lap dance as we locked lips.

"Okay," I said between breaths. "I'm confused. You don't like public displays of affection, but public displays of horniness are okay?"

She exploded in laughter.

"That's the second time you've made me laugh like that! *Nobody* does that!" she said with a rare, full grin.

Then silently and without a word—as was her way—she pulled back, reached behind her shirt, and started fidgeting with something. From there, she began to twist and wrestle with herself under her shirt until—in the way only a woman can do—she pulled her bra out from under her shirt.

"There. You can get at them better now," she said.

I reached my hands under her shirt to feel her large, bare, generously enhanced breasts. We then resumed our lip-lock kissing. She continued her lap dance as we sat under a tree with the streetlight filtering through the leaves. She seemed not to have a care in the world, but I couldn't get out of my mind that the cops were sure to arrive at any moment to put a spotlight on us.

Hey, you two, what's going on there? Are you okay, ma'am? was how it played out in my mind. It's always the guy's fault, so, yeah … what did she have to worry about?

But she knew her neighborhood well. Over the next forty-five minutes, few cars passed us and no one walked by.

Now getting late, she asked me to drive her home. She kissed me goodbye and wished me well on my vacation.

"Be in touch. Next time I'll let you pick me up here, and I'll show you inside. I have some fabulous pieces of furniture and art I think you'll like. I'm starting to feel more comfortable with you now."

What an enigma, said Charles, *a fascinating enigma.*

She seems to live in the moment, added Little Turner, *not always such a bad thing; I'm just sayin'.*

I'd been living in the shadow of my past while searching for a glimpse of light into my future; was that a vise squeezing out the present? Was that what Little Turner was saying? Was this one of my "problems?"

****

It had been over two weeks since the park bench in Richmond, and we now greeted each other on a sidewalk in Washington. As she came in close for a kiss and reached for my hand, the first hint of real affection came to Ava's face.

It was a Wednesday evening, and Ava had come up to have dinner with me at the club. She arranged some business in town for the day and was staying with friends in D.C. for the night.

She had walked across her friends' perfectly manicured lawn to meet me on the other side of a tall hedgerow. After our kiss, she led me back across the lawn and inside the splendid and well-appointed home. I was introduced to her friends, and we chatted for a few minutes. We belonged to the same club and tried to find members we both might know but came up empty.

As we prepared to leave, Ava paused, taking note of the Mercedes roadster.

"Nice car! No third-row seat, but … it has a nice long hood. It has possibilities," she said, slowly running her hand along the length of the hood and grinning slyly.

Inside the car, a lip-locking kiss was immediate, but it was difficult with the large console between us in the low-slung car. She then asked if we could put the top down on the drive to the club. With her hair flying in the wind, off we went for the ten-minute drive.

She had been there many times before, so no tour was needed. We went to the terrace overlooking the golf course, where I had dined before with Joyce and Emily on delightful summer evenings like tonight.

Conversation was mostly about life in the present, which included a fair amount of upcoming travel. She would be off to London and perhaps Italy. She'd need to go to San Francisco in late August or September, then maybe a stop in Aspen on the way back. A trip to New York and a zip down to Palm Beach would be needed too. Client meetings, board meetings, and seasonal parties were par for the course for her this time of year.

My travel plans were decidedly different.

The following week would be a family gathering to give my college-bound son a memorable send-off. Then I would drive him to freshmen orientation via my childhood home and a visit with Grandma. I would then stay most of the week to help move him in and buy anything he needed. Then back up to my mother's home for a few days before the drive to Washington. This nine-day journey to take my son into the next chapter of his life and me into empty nesterhood was sure to be emotional in ways I couldn't possibly imagine.

After that, I had four days to gather myself before flying to Massachusetts to bring my other son home for his end-of-summer break. He loves trains, so I had promised we would take the Amtrak Acela for an all-day journey from Boston to Washington.

Doctors' appointments, fall clothes shopping, a trip to the zoo, and visits with friends and family would fill our week at home. We would then hit the road on Labor Day to drive back to Massachusetts, where I would spend a few days making sure he was all set for the fall. My reward after this would be three days with dear friends at their seaside home in Boothbay Harbor, Maine. They kindly offered me some peaceful R&R, food aplenty, gorgeous sunset views from their porch on the rocky shore, and gentle conversations about what was next for me and my life.

The final legs of my travel would be the long drive home from Maine, a day to regroup, then back to Richmond for two days of board meetings. I wondered out loud if we might be able to meet on one or both evenings.

All in all, it would be 4,000-miles of driving, from the Florida Gulf Coast up to Maine, over five weeks in my aging minivan.

My long-winded and detailed itinerary elicited a yawn and silent stare from Ava. She had no children of her own, so this milestone of looming empty nesterhood was something she could only relate to from a distance. Or not relate to, as the case may be.

With dinner over and conversation seemingly exhausted, we walked over to the bench by the golf course in the twilight—the same one I sat on with Joyce for several hours on our first date. At one point, Ava turned herself sideways, put her legs over my lap, and leaned in for a quiet, cuddling embrace. Around ten, after the club closed down, she asked me to take her back to her friends' house, where she'd be spending the night.

The sky was dark when I pulled into the driveway, but the area was well illuminated by streetlights. I got out of the car and went around to help her out. She was wearing a short white skirt with white leggings underneath. As she unfolded her legs and swung them out, she made no attempt to hide the view up her skirt, even exaggerating the splitting apart of her legs.

"Nothing left to the imagination there," she said.

"Well, actually, there is. You're not exactly naked. You're wrapped up like a mummy."

When I closed her door, she leaned against the car, pulled up one of her legs, and hooked it over my arm as if it were a ballet bar. With one leg hiked up and her legging-covered crotch spread wide, heated cavorting commenced.

But it was yet another awkward and uncomfortably exposed scene by a street. We soon broke our hold and walked into the front yard.

The large house was dark inside. She had a key to let herself in, but she said we had to stay outside. We headed toward a gate in a tall wooden fence that screened the backyard from the street. Behind the fence was a pool with various lounge chairs set about.

"Let's see if we can get back here and not wake up anyone," she said. "I don't think there are any alarms."

Well, that's good to know, offered The Boys.

She tried the gate latch, but it wouldn't release. She then led me around the front to the other side of the darkened yard to see if there was another way in. In the process, we set off lights tied to motion detectors and, for the third time in three dates, the thought of cops arriving at any moment came to mind.

With no way into the back, we found a darkened corner of the front yard near some tall landscaping, and she draped one leg up and over my ballet-bar arm again.

"I wish I could get these darn leggings off," she said. "They're in the way."

"Then why did you wear them?"

"Because otherwise I would look like some sort of slut in this skimpy skirt at your fancy club," she said with a scowl.

After a momentary pause and glare, she calmly pulled my hand to her crotch and directed me in what she wanted me to do as she gyrated furiously. But exhaustion from standing up on one leg for so long finally did her in.

"Can you come down to Richmond Saturday?" she asked. "You can see my place, and we can go out for dinner and a movie … and I promise no more park benches."

****

The posh Richmond neighborhood was made up of large and mid-sized houses of various architectural styles that I guessed were from the early 1900s. The homes, sidewalks, lawns, landscaping, and everything else were perfectly kept and immaculate. Ava's home was an Italianate brick house with tastefully restrained details.

She came to the door in just a bra and white jeans, or so it seemed. She had on a see-through, orange gauze shirt that allowed a view of every detail underneath.

"Hi, wow!" I said.

"Hi and wow yourself," she said, coming in for a kiss.

I pulled back to have another look.

"I can see right through … nice bra. Why even bother with the top?"

"If you don't like it, I can change," she quipped back.

"Works for me, that is if you don't mind me looking and trying to figure out how I'm going to get that bra off you later."

"That was pretty much the plan … to keep you thinking about them. I know you like them," she said, giggling. "Do you want to come in, or are you just going to keep gawking?"

Two steps into the center hall foyer, my eyes gawked at something else entirely. The inside of her home was dazzling. It was furnished, not in typical cookie-cutter, Architectural Digest style, but with an incredible, curated ensemble of antique and classic modern furniture going back to the early part of the twentieth century. Art was everywhere, too, including some funky pieces I recognized from our art gallery browsing near the riverfront.

"Wow!" I said. "This is just amazing. It's stunning, Ava!"

"I thought you might like it," she said with a look of satisfaction.

She gestured for me to follow as we moved from room to room in what was clearly a much-practiced reveal of her home. Going from one piece of furniture to the next, I ran my hand along each, stopping to admire, then asking about its history.

"This is all I can fit in here at the moment. I have tons more in storage," she said.

"Can I go shopping in your storage unit?"

"Well … it's more like a mini-warehouse," she confessed.

"I believe it," I said. "I believe it."

After going through each room on the ground floor, we returned to the living room and I sat on the smartly upholstered sofa. She kicked off her shoes and mounted herself on my lap as she had on the park bench three weeks before.

"This feels familiar," I said. "But much better inside than outside on a park bench … or in a dark front yard … or on stone steps with *sex*-curity cameras looking at us."

She flung her head back, laughed, then stared at me with a self-satisfied look. From there, the familiar lip-locking, tongue-lunging kissing, and lap dancing commenced. We basically recreated our time on the park bench for the next thirty minutes.

Then she was startled.

"Oh! We missed our movie!"

"Bummer," I said, smiling. "I hope it wasn't one you were dying to see."

"It wasn't, but it could have been interesting being in a dark place with you. Guess we won't know … *tonight*," she said with sarcasm and mock disappointment.

"Haven't we been in enough dark places already?" I asked.

"I like the dark," she said, momentarily looking serious.

Then she quickly shifted gears.

"But I'd like to take you down near the theater anyway to show you another building done by my architect friend who did the restaurant where we first met. You'll like it, I think. Then we can catch some dinner nearby."

We walked outside toward the minivan for the drive over. When she saw it, she stopped and frowned.

"I wondered whether or not you'd drive the Mercedes. That's too bad."

"I wasn't exactly keen to be in a white Mercedes sports car while driving through the Richmond hood to get here."

"It's perfectly safe if you drive straight in. What a scaredy-cat."

"Fine, yes, I'm a scaredy-cat. Still want to go out with me?"

She smiled, walked over, put her leg up on my ballet-bar arm, and kissed me.

"All right then," I said and opened her door.

"It does have a nice third-row seat," she said, smiling. "It can be our Plan B for tonight."

A couple of miles away, we arrived in front of the Altria Theater in a bustling neighborhood of restaurants and stores. After parking, we walked a few blocks on our way to a newly opened building, designed by her architect friend, at the nearby university. It was a modern work of architecture with a fairly simplistic stacked-block aesthetic currently in fashion.

After exploring the building, we walked to dinner. Like the other restaurants Ava had taken me to, this one had a cool, hip ambiance and was packed. But she didn't know the owner, so like everyone else, we put our name on a list for a thirty-minute wait. We grabbed drinks and went to a small café table next to the front door.

It seemed like Ava had now come out of her protective shell, and being with her was very enjoyable. Smiles came to her more easily, and her conversation was less cautious than before.

Our name was finally called, and we were seated at a table near the bar, a fairly noisy area. We were halfway through dinner when I again mentioned the upcoming travels with my boys, including taking my son to start college.

"When my five weeks of travel are over and you see me again, I'll officially be an empty nester," I said, trying to remain upbeat. "I have no idea what it'll feel like. I'm a bit apprehensive, to say the least," I said, expressing my true feelings of worry.

I thought I might get a simple, polite reassurance from her. Let's be honest: this was no small thing looming ahead of me. Something like, "It'll be okay, you'll be fine," was all I really needed to hear.

Instead, she dropped her fork to her plate with the food she was about to eat. She looked at me and then went stone-cold silent.

Mount Rushmore all over again.

"What?" I asked.

She didn't so much as blink an eye.

"What is it?!" I asked again. "Is it about my being away for five weeks? I told you about this last time we had dinner."

The Boys, long happy and content to enjoy this weird crazy ride with Ava, piped in. *What the fuck just happened?*

More silence—intense silence—and a cold, cold stare from Ava.

All I could do at this point was stare back … in disbelief and utter confusion.

But then, as though a switch flipped, she raised her fork to her mouth to eat. After finishing chewing, she spoke. "I don't remember you telling me this."

"What? … You don't remember? I went through it in excruciating detail at the club the other night."

"Okay, I guess I forgot then," she said, with cool anger on her face.

From then until the end of dinner, the conversation was sparse, forced, and incredibly uncomfortable.

The Boys pretty much confirmed what I was thinking. *Okay, for whatever reason, this whole weird thing just got weirder. Why don't we get out of here and take her home? Nothing is more important than family. And if that's a problem for her, then it's a problem.*

We quickly left the restaurant and drove to her house. I pulled into the driveway and turned off the engine. I shifted in my seat to look at her, still baffled and clueless as to what this was about.

"Do you want to come in?" she asked, seemingly more out of courtesy than anything else.

Three hours ago, we missed our movie because we were about to take each other's clothes off, and now she was going through the motions of, "You want to come in?"

The question gave me pause. I knew I was about to say goodbye to Ava—probably forever. Dating the enigmatic Ava had been as much about curiosity as anything else. Now with her invitation to come in, it was nothing *but* curiosity.

"Sure," I said in a halfhearted response.

Once inside, she walked quickly toward the kitchen, leaving me standing alone in the foyer.

"Would you like some tea or coffee?" she asked.

"Sure. Tea please."

I felt awkward standing there, but I decided this was all on her now. I waited until she gave some clue or direction as to how this was going to go.

"You're welcome to go into the living room and sit down," she said from the kitchen.

I walked into the living room and sat in the middle of the sofa where, three hours before, she was happily grinding away on my lap.

She came in with a large silver tray with tea for two, put it on the coffee table, then sat in a chair next to the sofa about four feet away. I sat politely and quietly, drinking my tea in total silence. I wanted to make her feel as uncomfortable as she was making me, and it was working.

"We could watch a movie," she offered.

I had to laugh to myself at that one. "No, I don't think I want to do that … Maybe I should just go."

She looked at me, put her tea down, then came over and climbed onto my lap. She stared at me, arms limp and down by her side. Then, in a moment of decision, she put her arms around my neck and pulled herself in for a kiss. I put my hands on either side of the top of her legs but made no other move or gesture.

She kissed harder.

I moved my hands onto her sides but intentionally stayed clear of her breasts.

She pulled back from kissing and, looking directly into my eyes, said, "We can still do this if you want to."

"Really?" I replied. "You could've fooled me."

After staring at her for a few moments and with neither of us flinching, I moved my hands to her breasts and gently squeezed them. She then exploded like a windup doll finally being released.

"Let's go up to the bedroom," she said quickly, "but you have to promise that nothing will happen."

She jumped off the sofa, then took my hand and led me up the stairs.

We went into the darkened bedroom, and I started to look for a light to turn on; I could hardly see a thing.

"No lights!" she said. "I don't like lights. I prefer the dark."

"But I want to see you."

"But I don't want you to see me. I'm uncomfortable with that, but I'll make sure you know I'm here," she said, beginning to take off my clothes. "Besides, there's enough light coming in the window. You can see me well enough. And what you can't see, you can feel."

As our hands explored each other, standing naked in the dark, she pulled back from our embracing kiss, looked down, and reached between my legs.

"I'm going to make this a memorable night, and you *won't* soon forget me," she said.

And with that, she began to stroke me fast with her hand, but I grabbed her wrist and stopped her.

"No. *That's* not going to happen. You've been having your fun your way all this time, but I'll have mine my way. That's having *you* or *nothing* at all. No more teasing, not tonight."

She was startled by my seizing her wrist, but also, I think, from being told no. I don't think she heard that very often.

"But I'm not ready yet, and you promised nothing would happen," she protested.

"We're naked … in your bedroom … What am I missing?"

The Boys now jumped in, short and to the point. *It's time to end this little rodeo, Turner.*

She continued looking at me, not sure what I was going to do or what she was going to do. I let go of her wrist, picked her up, carried her to the bed, and laid her down. I crawled on top of her, my body on hers, and gave her a long kiss.

Then I pulled back. "I should go."

She stared at me in silence for a few moments. "You don't have to go!"

"If you're not totally comfortable with me here, then I shouldn't be here … I don't *want* to be here."

I got off her and the bed. She stayed, lying motionless in the dark, but continued looking at me.

"You can spend the night if you promise nothing will happen," she said again.

I could see the outline of her naked body in the dark. The streetlights from outside filtered in through the blinds, painting thin streaks of light up, over, and around the contours of her body.

"Like I said, I can't promise that."

Silence hung in the darkened bedroom. I walked to where my clothes were and began to dress.

"I'm really sorry I have to be away the next five weeks," I added.

She stayed silent.

Finally, without a word, she got out of bed and put on a robe. She walked out of the bedroom and went downstairs to the kitchen.

"Can I get you something before you go?" she said as I walked in a few minutes later.

"Thanks. No. I'm fine."

She walked me to the front door and I turned to give her a kiss, but she offered only her cheek.

"Maybe I'll see you around," she said, looking up at me, her eyes fixed on mine.

Now it was my turn to stare in silence. I tilted my head back slightly—a look upward in befuddled disbelief—before gazing down into her eyes. She seemed to be wondering what I was thinking—how could she not?

"I'm glad I met you, Ava. You're an amazing woman," I said after several moments.

I said it because I meant it, but also because I thought it might be unexpected and throw her off a bit—she hated to be thrown off balance or not in control.

She started to say something, then stopped herself, then tried again. I could see she was thinking and searching for words, but she struggled to speak.

It felt like the last grains of sand were slipping their way down the inside of an hourglass, so I cut to the chase. "Goodbye, Ava."

CHAPTER 14

Through the Looking Glass

You know the feeling you get sometimes? You want something *so-o-o* much that you throw everything you have into it? Then either gradually or suddenly, you realize it's *never* going to happen? Disappointment and failure wash over you, and you become *so* disillusioned when you finally figure out that what you were doing—what you thought was the right thing—was a path to nowhere or worse?

Okay.

Good.

Now you know how I felt about women and dating after Ava.

A lifetime of respect for the female gender was pretty much shattered after my odd and abrupt dismissal. I had been judged unworthy because I was being the father I needed and wanted to be.

And it wasn't just a judgment by the enigmatic Ava. I took it as a judgment by all women, the entire *Female Collective.*

"To hell with you all" was pretty much my sentiment.

Ditto! from The Boys.

"This dating thing is *shit,* total *shit,*" I mumbled to myself over and over.

With everything raw, hurting, and the smell of Ava still fresh on my clothes from the night before, I made the pivot to the coming milestone.

Empty nesterhood was here.

After an emotion-filled few weeks of getting one son off to college, I boarded a train with my other son on a sunny New England morning for the seven-hour trip from Boston to Washington. Settling into the quiet car of the

Amtrak Acela, he immediately fired up his electronics and tuned me out, so I opened my iPad.

I had suspended my OkCupid account after meeting Ava two months before, but the app was still there. With no small amount of resentment at myself for wanting to, I opened it up, reactivated the account, and stared at the screen.

There they were again—the smiling faces of countless women. Slowly, I began flipping through the matches that had accumulated during my time with Ava.

There were *lots* of women.

However, instead of the shotgun approach I used before to scatter and plant seeds everywhere, I found myself simply deleting them.

Why bother? What's the point? It's just more of the same, I thought.

But the pull of online dating was back.

Maybe, just maybe ...

Clicking through the matches, one suddenly caught my attention—a woman who lived in Paris.

That's odd. How's that even possible?

But curiosity got the better of me, and I began to read her profile.

Paris was different and exotic, and I wondered what women on the dating scene there might be like. The French are supposed to be the Olympic champions of romance and sex, but having already met two women from Paris, I knew they could be cold in temperament, judgmental, and totally lacking any sense of humor.

So I was pleasantly surprised when I read how beautifully, wittily, and passionately this woman wrote with lilting, romantic, and poetic prose.

She wrote about a man and woman passing each other on a Paris sidewalk, silently noticing one another and wondering if they should say hello. Then she wrote about a man and woman standing next to each other in a Paris Metro, becoming intoxicated with the faint scents of each other. In the process of reading this and the rest of her profile, I was positively drawn in. It was like my own version of *Through the Looking Glass.*

Wow! Why can't she be here?

The Boys heartily agreed.

It turned out she wasn't French at all but an American living in Paris. Her name was Dakota, and according to OkCupid, we were a 98 percent match.

There was only one picture of her, and it reminded me of the actress Jennifer Aniston from the TV show *Friends*. Reading her profile over and over, it was clear I had to reach out to her, even to faraway Paris; I just *had* to. I knew the odds of this going anywhere were slim to none, but there was the possibility of at least some witty or flirty back-and-forth correspondence that might soothe my bruised and fragile dating ego. Regardless of the outcome, I had to let this woman know she had absolutely drawn me in and that, in fact, I was an admirer.

But how to capture her attention?

After several drafts composed on the gently rocking train, I decided to go with something short and simple that referenced one of her wish-list items for men: "Fabulous prose, flawless grammar, and fitting metaphors, as well as having in your closet and feeling at ease in a tux will give you bonus points."

SENT VIA OkCupid:

> Hi, Dakota, fascinated by your profile. I must say, I have a question. Might there be extra bonus points for having a tux AND a white dinner jacket in my closet?
>
> All the Best -- Turner

Hopeful anticipation of a response left me tingling inside.

Two hours had passed since our departure from Boston's South Station. Her profile came up around Providence, Rhode Island, and we were now in Connecticut, nearing the New Haven station. As the train slowed, the red notification dot popped up on my iPad; Dakota had written back.

RECEIVED VIA OkCupid:

> Bonjour! Le monsieur se renseigne sur les points de bonus supplémentaires?
>
> The gentleman inquires about extra bonus points? Yes, extra bonus points may be awarded, but they still must be earned!

What other surprises are in your closet?

Hi and thank you, Turner, for writing – Dakota

She was bold, witty, and everything I had imagined. I quickly calculated the time difference and figured out we were six hours apart—one in the afternoon for me, seven in the evening for her.

After reading her response, I became anxious about what to say next. I had caught her attention, but *now* what? Writing was never my strong suit, and she was clearly a pro. I quickly went through several drafts for my next message to this beguiling woman, and off it went.

SENT VIA OkCupid:

Hi, Dakota, thanks for writing back.

FYI, I'm on a train from Boston, Massachusetts, to Washington, D.C., and I just happened to read your profile. I have to say thank you because my trip just became enormously more interesting than I thought possible only a few hours ago. Figuring out how to be granted 'extra bonus points' from a mystery woman in Paris has … well … diverted my attention and rather focused it too. More questions arise. What do I get with the extra bonus points vs. the regular run-of-the-mill points? Would these be French bonus points or American?

Regards from somewhere in Connecticut – Turner

She responded fifteen minutes later with humor, intelligence, and unhidden flirtation.

For the next five hours, we corresponded thousands of miles apart—me on a speeding train on the East Coast and she from a flat in Paris with a clear view of the Eiffel Tower. I alternated—as I came to learn she did too—between excited anticipation of another message arriving and nervous pressure in composing the next witty, flirtatious response.

In those hours, I learned she was originally from Illinois, was fifty-five years old, and worked for a company based in Paris with offices around the world. After working in Chicago following college, she pursued her dream of living in Paris with no idea what the future would hold. She spoke no French at the time but slowly began to carve out a life she loved. She married a European fellow and had several children. Now, twenty-five years later and divorced for several years, she was contemplating her future, much as I was.

The mystery of why we were matched was solved too.

Her company had made her an offer for an executive position in their Washington, D.C., office. Giving it serious consideration, she decided to see if there might be anyone of interest in the area. All the dating apps allow you to make any city in the world your home location, so she made hers Washington, D.C.

As my train was soon to arrive at Union Station, it was nearing midnight in Paris. She wondered if a phone call would be of interest the next evening, and we set a time of 11 p.m. for her and 5 p.m. for me. She had unlimited international calling, so she would call me.

When I got home that Sunday evening, everything Dakota was swirling in my head. *What happened today is why you go through this awful dating stuff*, I told myself. You just never know who might be around the corner.

First phone calls always made me nervous with any woman, but this time, it was nervous times ten or more. This was *really* going outside my comfort zone. Meeting a woman on the phone who's in France? It was either movie-like romantic or tabloid-magazine foolish.

The phone rang at five o'clock to the minute.

"Hi, Dakota."

"Hi, Turner."

We talked for two hours. The conversation began carefully and politely but ended with the two of us entering the zone where two people begin to shut out the rest of the world, focusing only on each other, intensely and intimately.

Before saying goodnight, she asked a question that caught me totally off guard. With it, she laid down a challenge, made my heart flutter, and sent my mind wondering.

"Are you the kind of man who likes to do surprising?"

Before going to bed, I sent a short email she would see in the morning. I took her suggestive question and made it my subject line—it was so marvelously adventurous and so subtly sexual, the way she had said it.

I struggled to sleep that night.

When she answered back the next morning, she first made note of our 98 percent match on OkCupid. She then went into a bit of small talk before casually proposing—as much as one can without appearing too eager—a trip to Washington at the end of the year to meet and celebrate New Year's Eve together. She explained she always came to the States at Christmas to visit her parents, and Washington would be an easy stopover on the way back to Paris.

EMAIL RECEIVED: Can I Do Surprising?

It would be a chance to see you in a tux (the white dinner jacket can wait for warmer days) and try out your ballroom dancing boast. Thoughts?

(xx) Dakota

EMAIL SENT: Can I Do Surprising?

Dakota,

An Xmas/New Year's Eve meeting/date/dancing cheek-to-cheek? I might get to first base? I like it, a lot …

(xx) Turner

P.S. Okay, Dakota, I just spoke with a very intriguing woman I have never met while she was in bed (with French lace sheets, I now know) at one in the morning Paris-time, and we could have talked forever … You may have evolved toward "French" ways, but I'm still very much an American fellow. I'm not ending the conversation we had last night and this particular correspondence of talk of New Year's Eve and such with air kisses (xx), I'm going for it!

Sign me

Turner XOX

Now before going any further, there's something *really* important you need to know.

During our phone call, Dakota asked if I was familiar with the movie *Out of Africa* with Robert Redford and Meryl Streep. It was an epic love story with Redford playing Denys Finch Hatton, an aristocratic English big-game hunter, and Streep as Baroness Karen Blixen. I had heard of it but never seen it. Dakota told me it was her favorite movie.

Its themes and plot, along with the name "Finch," would play a major and defining role in our relationship.

EMAIL RECEIVED: Can I Do Surprising?

Hi Finch Hatton,

C'est moi ... (Translation: It's me)

Delighted you like the idea of NY's eve in principle. I was actually on pins and needles waiting for you to answer, thinking—after the fact—I was being outrageously forward and all of the rest of it. But it seems there is something very special happening between us. I simply cannot believe how easy it was to talk with you yesterday evening—almost as if we had known each other forever. Sorry, getting carried away here—don't hesitate to rein me back in from time to time. :-)

I've never proposed or done anything like this before, but otherwise, it all seems very virtual and not very clever. We both seem to be rather real-world people who want to be in a serious relationship with someone we can see, hear, touch, and go places with together, yes? Make sense? Well, conversely, I don't want you to feel I am putting any pressure on you or getting ahead of ourselves. Maybe my biggest goal in bringing this up was to show you that I find you very interesting and do hope that we will actually meet ... being the hopeless romantics we are and all of that stuff.

Back to right now, I'm about to head to sleep because I need to catch up a bit as you might guess. I weathered the short night rather well, I must say, possibly due to the heady feelings of talking to a man I don't know in the middle of the night. I believe the last time I did something like that was about a decade or so ago—not a weekly occurrence, that is for sure!

So, Turner, and his "bases." You make me laugh. Haven't heard those words in forever. Well, look at you, going ahead and stealing a kiss, just like you said you wanted to in your profile. I like that clarity. And you see I kissed you back. I tend to do that sort of thing when someone gets my attention in the way that you have.

Utterly short-term thoughts—so, very early on you admitted you broke your rules, showed enthusiasm, "revealed" your identity, and now we have spoken. What about throwing caution to the wind and finding a moment to Skype this weekend?

And Turner says what now?

Dakota (sealed with a kiss)

EMAIL SENT: Can I Do Surprising?

My Dear Dakota,

Soooo much in your email, this could be c-o-m-p-l-i-c-a-t-e-d, Dakota! And to think you caught me on a train no less just a few days ago. ... How far we have come.

I like the idea of Skyping at some point soon, but what if we had dinner together for the Skype call? We could make roughly the same thing, with candles on our tables, and we could have a Skype dinner date.... Just a fun thought for a woman who has my rapt attention.

Let's see, you are about to get up as I am going to sleep (it's 11:52 pm my time).

Okay, I'm lying here in bed, under the covers, head on my pillows, laptop propped up on my lap, thinking about you, talking to you in my head as I type, thinking about you there with your head on YOUR pillows, and wishing you were here with me (there, I said it—no take-backs).

So Turner says this for now and more later.

Sealed with a very long Turner kiss XXOO

EMAIL RECEIVED: Can I Do Surprising??

Dear Turner,

So, here's the deal. When I started reading your email with the word c-o-m-p-l-i-c-a-t-e-d (wow, those hyphens take a while to insert between each letter), I thought, okay, he's come to his senses and will now write "you are such a nice and interesting person, but the distance is too much, so I wish you all the best in the years ahead." Thus, I'm sure you can imagine my relief when I got to the next paragraph.

I think a Skype dinner date is the most adorable idea I have ever heard. The. most. adorable. ever. Are you always this unbelievably charming? Oh my. I like it. A lot. And because I like it SO MUCH, my obvious reaction is to keep the meal choice simple, simple, simple to focus on what matters—seeing and spending time with you!

Hmm … so you wish I were there, with no take-backs, very good to know. Maybe I wish you were here? Well, not sitting next to me at my office, but umm … yes, I definitely wish you were here. Definitely no take-backs.

A very long Turner kiss … looking forward to finding out about those. I'm guessing there will be more than one. :-)

Dakota XOXO

P.S. I'm having the dickens of a time concentrating on my work. Wonder why? Or maybe I'll just accept that it feels wonderful? :-)

Dakota

That night, we talked again on the phone until close to two in the morning Paris time—although saying we "talked" doesn't come close to describing what happened. During our three-hour phone call, we bridged the ocean between us. We playfully, indulgently, and without hesitation began to explore each other personally, intellectually, and sexually. It was transformative.

Sometime during the night, she sent an email I wouldn't see until the next morning. But when I did, it confirmed that we were now together somewhere else. It wasn't Washington, and it wasn't Paris. For me at least, it was somewhere I had never been before.

EMAIL RECEIVED: suite à notre conversation d'hier …
(Translation: following our conversation yesterday)

I was in your dreams last night. Tell me I was not.

EMAIL SENT: suite à notre conversation d'hier ...

How could you not be ... but questions linger.

Black lace vs white lace?

Bustiers?

What we might say, how we might say it, how loud we might say it? Your ... ahem ... special wardrobe decisions when dining out together.

All day long vs all weekend long?

WhatEVER we might decide to do <u>together</u>?

Turner XXOXX

EMAIL RECEIVED: suite à notre conversation d'hier ...

Turner,

What a conversation! I could not sleep between 3-4 am with my mind turning over and over everything we discussed, what you shared, what I shared ... and I'm feeling a bit "dévoilée," which means literally "unveiled" or exposed. I truly hope it is all positive in your mind and not too left field. I can't believe we have discussed this already, particularly with the lingering debutante in me. She's feeling uncomfortable, though I make a big effort to keep her in check these days. :-)

Well, I think it started because you mentioned your "very private thoughts," so I started to ask questions, being an incurably curious girl and all. Secondly, as I was a bit taken aback by the questions on OKC, I wanted to make sure you weren't looking for a very different experience than that which feels right in my heart. From what I understand, it seems we both want something passionate but fairly mainstream, without ever becoming plain vanilla, is that right? :-)

Back to everyday life, I awakened with the thought, "Wow ... Turner is going through a massive transition right now!" I'm guessing, as a man, you have that quality of just "managing" things without too much song and dance. But you have just taken your youngest to college for the first time (huge) and another son is still with you for a few more days, with more family coming this weekend. You are not an empty nester yet but will be next week. That will take time to wrap your head around, let the dust settle, and see how you feel about the next part of your life. You have to walk through difficulty and pain to get to the other side, to find the "next" which is waiting for you on the horizon. I get it.

Because of the connection we have established, I am about to deactivate my profile. Men are still contacting me to meet, and I can't juggle balls like that emotionally. It's simply not who I am, and it's a bit overwhelming. I have no idea what could ever happen between us, but I want to find out more about who you are—your thoughts, your passion for architecture, your interest in public life, and anything else you wish to share. In addition, I love surprises.

Thinking of you, Dakota XXXOXXX

EMAIL SENT: suite à notre conversation d'hier ...

Dakota,

At this moment, I struggle to find the right words to describe you ... the depth and breadth of thoughts you have, the insight you appear to possess about me. How you are making me feel (in a myriad of ways), the sensual and erotic nature of our conversation last night (I don't think that was "plain vanilla" last night, Dakota, at least not American Vanilla, perhaps French Vanilla), that you go right after things you want to know, and how you do ALL of this in such a matter-of-fact way, in control, and with such ease ... I was so nervous last night, afraid I might make an unintended blunder because you have taken my feet right out from under me and I'm feeling a bit wobbly.

I totally missed the "uncomfortable debutante" (yes, if she IS still there inside you, I understand her discomfort at last night's conversation). That you are feeling "unveiled"? Yes, I would agree that you "exposed" yourself to me (as literally as one can do on the phone) but all positive and quite nice! After all, we would have made love last night if it weren't for that darn ocean between us.

Given all the enjoyable pleasures above, what is more striking is that you ARE getting me, the enormity of where I am in life at the moment, HOW I have been handling things, where my priorities are, and even a sense of where I've been. Since March, when I was only beginning to get clarity on what was coming at me and what I needed to do, I explained it to those close to me, who have known me so long, and they got it. But these are people who are the closest of the close and thus know all the "background" to me. Here you are, closing in on five days and two phone calls, and you get it NOW?! Well, that's taking and understanding me, what is most precious and important, and treating it with the utmost kindness and tenderness.

Go back to my profile, if you have not turned it off, and look again at the "six most important things" for me; "kindness" is on my list. I presume it is unusual for a man to be saying THAT is important for him. But it very much is important to me, and you are showing such kindness in that regard, Dakota. Some things are fleeting, but kindness stays and is remembered.

What is next? What is on the other side? Boy, those are questions I have been asking for the last four years. And now

I'm back on that ship, sailing toward the horizon. I still only see water for as far as I can see. I have no idea what is out there, which way the winds will take me, when I will arrive (if ever, but I pray and hope so), and where exactly I will arrive. How is it that you seem to understand this so well?

Sorry about your sleep last night. I try to picture you in bed, your face ... are your eyes open and annoyed they won't close, or closed and annoyed they won't help you fall asleep? I try to picture your hair on the pillow, you under the French lace sheets. Do you stare at the ceiling or bury your head in your pillow? Yes, I've been imagining those things, Dakota.

Because of our extended call last night, I did not have time to eat and went to my meeting rather hungry (in more ways than one, as YOU KNOW!). So, lest you think I'm the only one disrupting daily patterns of life, you have thrown me off as well.

I should get up and get the day going, but I'm finding it so delightful to be in bed writing to you, thinking of you, and wanting to be with you.

Thinking of you so very much,

Turner

EMAIL RECEIVED: suite à notre conversation d'hier ...

Dearest Turner,

You write so beautifully, it is lovely to behold and even more lovely to read and to savor. As in my epistles to you (I think we can no longer rightly use the word 'email' to describe with any facsimile to reality the depth of what we are sharing), there are many things which you have written which touch me, but one leapt off the page, so I'll start there—kindness.

Before I deactivated my profile this morning, I re-read your profile and the word kindness was one of the notions which struck me the most. Yes, I hadn't thought of it, but it may be a more unusual quality for a man to desire, which makes it all the more appealing, certainly to me and most likely to many other women. In addition to about 3,000 other things which

we seem to have in common, kindness is very high on my list too and even higher as I get older. What good is a handsome, smart, dashing, and funny man if he doesn't display kindness? And what will you be able to feel in your heart the day when he simply has too much pressure in every other area of his life to communicate well with you? None of those other qualities will matter at all. I guess within kindness are the notions of empathy and giving without expecting anything in return. I like to do little random acts of kindness any chance I get.

Ultimately, it's not that surprising if both of us deeply value kindness because we are creative people, willing to explore our emotions and sensitivity to see what we might be able to uncover and shape into something of interest.

Isn't that what we all want? To matter deeply? To have someone understand us? To be willing to admit very private things to at least one person in life? To also know, when we need the private place we don't share, that our partner respects it profoundly, not feeling threatened or insecure, knowing in our separateness, we have something more interesting to share with the other? Security but also surprise, the secret to sustaining and renewing desire in a couple.

Oops, I broke my earlier resolution today to write more concise notes to you! :-) I don't know exactly what to say at the end now—there are things which I would like to say, but I don't. You don't wobble alone, Sir; don't think I am always so in control. :-) In fact, it's when we let go of the illusion of control that nice things start to happen in life. And, of course, God made the world round so we couldn't see too far ahead.

Dakota XXXOXXX

I had a meeting the next night and was unable to talk to Dakota on the phone, but she left a voice message that I listened to before going to bed. I then sent an email response that she would see the next morning.

SENT EMAIL: suite à notre conversation d'hier …

Dakota,

You're so cute with your phone message. It IS hard to end an email, phone call, or phone message with each other, isn't it? It's even harder to stop thinking about you because thinking about you gives me a feeling of being close to you. As far away as we are from each other, I feel I can be amazingly close to you because of all we explored and "revealed/exposed" to each other in our last phone call. Things I now know about you, things I heard you say and talk about. I was especially happy to hear you say in your voice message tonight, "No take-backs," from our previous conversations.

I'm tired and sleepy so I will be brief. Nice dinner with my mother-in-law who lives nearby (one of the closest people in my life) and brother-in-law who is down from NY. I took him for an evening drive around the Capitol Mall in my convertible.

So 11 pm here and 5 am there. Did you have trouble sleeping this time? I hope not since you have a big weekend coming up. My apologies, sort of, for being such a distraction to you this week. I'm totally bewitched, bothered, and bewildered by you (I wish those were my words and not from a song, but I struggle to find the words to describe this at times).

Goodnight from here, where I am thinking of you so very, very much. You can't imagine how much I want to actually kiss your lips.

XXOXX

Turner

EMAIL RECEIVED: suite à notre conversation d'hier ...

Not such a bad email to wake up to, Finch :-) Doing my exercises, about to jump in the shower—and why aren't you here to jump in too? :-)

Dakota XOXO

Our emails to each other became lengthy, many, immersive, and ... well ... you get it. At any given moment, several emails strings were going at once across the Atlantic. Responses might lag or leapfrog another. One of us might be responding to an earlier email while at the same time, responding to the latest email, combining two responses into one, or splitting one email into three responses that could be several emails apart.

It was positively frantic at times!

EMAIL SENT: suite à notre conversation d'hier ...

Dakota,

A question. Is there a charge if I call your cell phone internationally, but you don't pick up? Yes, I'm up to something since you are a girl that "likes surprises."

Turner

EMAIL RECEIVED: suite à notre conversation d'hier …

Turner,

Trying to answer quickly as I love it when we communicate in real-time! I don't think there is a charge. What are you up to Mr. Mysterious?

Very sorry you didn't sleep well last night. The OBVIOUS reason is very obvious because I'm hardly sleeping at all either, nor am I that hungry. Hmm—these are signs of something.

Yes, I liked the lingering questions you had in your dreams, and you're right, you didn't hear much, if any, of the lingering debutante that night but … SHE was the one lecturing me at 3 am after our call when I couldn't sleep!!! :-) "Why did you say that? Why did you bring up this? What is going on? You don't know him! You are a nice girl, and nice girls don't talk about that!" and so on and so on. Well, I had a pretty long talk with her, reminding her I consider myself a nice girl AND I think about and do those things. As I said, I have to keep her in check every once in a while. :-)

I'm actually being productive, so must keep on in that vein, though I would much rather think about you, what it will be like to see you, touch you and … um … well, you know, and I know that you know, and you know that I know. Is that clear? I couldn't fall asleep last night and kept wondering what it would be like to have you in bed right next to me; I decided it would be the most natural thing in the world.

Dakota

Xxxxxxxxxxxxxxxx

EMAIL SENT: suite à notre conversation d'hier …

Dakota,

More "real time messages," I'm just out of the shower, and my robe is half on as I read your email and type. And yes … um … I know what you mean, and we both know what we are both thinking.

Turner XXXOXXX

EMAIL RECEIVED: suite à notre conversation d'hier …

You say your robe is half on; I would think of it definitely more as half off … perspective changes everything :-)

Wish I were with you right this very instant. :-) :-)

After catching our collective breaths—figuratively and literally—we decided a Skype call was needed ASAP and scheduled it for two days later on Sunday. Even with over one hundred emails in the last three days, we were both left terribly wanting.

She had grown children who would be in and out of the apartment that day because of a big event going on in the city. Assuming we'd be overheard, we decided to make this appear to be just a "Skype call with a friend."

We could hardly wait for Sunday evening to come, including The Boys. They wanted to know more about the "lingering debutante" who was lecturing Dakota at 3 a.m. *Sounds like we might have something in common,* they thought.

EMAIL SENT: suite à notre conversation d'hier …

My god, Dakota!!!! Most of my day so far has been devoted totally to you. Why can't I just be there to make love to you now?? :-)

EMAIL RECEIVED: suite à notre conversation d'hier ...

Wow, we really are both totally distracted, rather insane at our age, don't you think? Or lucky? I would call it lucky!

I'm not sure when or where we will be in bed together but we both like the idea. Think of ALL the people on the planet and everyone is hoping to meet someone special ... and very few people ever probably spend an entire day (and even fewer an entire weekend) in bed with someone whom they adore. "Well, nice work if you can get it and you can get it if you try." That's my song for the day; I believe it's Ella Fitzgerald. :-)

I'm going to come back to priorities, Finch. You have been devoting your entire day to me; I'm terribly flattered.

You haven't said anything about Finch. You do realize it's from Denys Finch Hatton in *Out of Africa,* played by Robert Redford, an actor I have always adored. Well, he really is getting WAY too old for me, so maybe one day you will take his place in my heart??? <3

Immersed in a flurry of heart-racing, often scorchingly erotic emails frantically exchanged, sometimes only seconds apart, I didn't understand why in the world *Finch* mattered. But I finally noticed and found myself mildly annoyed. Pet names that originate within a relationship and are said with affection are wonderful, but being called the name of someone I had no connection with, even a movie character, made me uncomfortable. By not responding when she mentioned his name, I hoped she'd just drop it.

Later on Saturday, we finally connected on WhatsApp. Being able to send text and voice messages back and forth in real time took our long-distance relationship to a higher level, if that were even possible.

We sent impulsively flirtatious messages of a very intimate nature (let your imagination run, and you'll have it) but also began to share personal fears and more tender emotions. Hearing each other's voices allowed us to sense many more layers and nuances, more than texting and emails could provide, although we still did a pretty good job in that department.

EMAIL SENT: The Woman in My Dreams

Try and make me blush.

Turner

EMAIL RECEIVED: The Woman in My Dreams

So that's your dare to mirror mine of a week ago, "can you do surprising?" Well huh, look at you, upping the ante!

I was upping the ante, but she *called* my dare and raised it tenfold.

Her long, detailed, and *very* descriptive email response made me blush in ways and colors I didn't know I could. She used her magnificent mind, intelligence, insight, and sensuality to create Cupid's arrows of powerful prose that could penetrate anything from any distance. She took feminine powers of sexuality into realms I had never known, and she did it *effortlessly* in some otherworldly way.

After reading her email several times, there wasn't much left for me to say.

EMAIL SENT: The Woman in My Dreams

I just want to unwrap you!

Turner

Her next quick-witted email reply kept a smile on my face the rest of the day. But as evening came, things turned more serious. Or rather, *I* became more serious about things.

In a long email, I shared private details about myself—*baggage*, as it were—I thought she needed to know. I honestly couldn't withhold certain things from her, given where we seemed to be going. She needed to know what she was getting herself into with me, and I needed to know she was okay with it.

I told her the true story of my wife's passing, along with some things from my past I hadn't shared with anyone but my wife. It wasn't only a measure of how hard I was falling for Dakota, it was a measure of how much I now trusted her.

I closed my true-confessions email by telling her that I felt like I was now "wa-yyy out on a limb." Then, in a huge moment of doubt, I sent one more email before going to bed.

EMAIL SENT: The Woman in My Dreams

Dakota,

Replaying all the correspondence, calls, and everything, I have one more question for you before I go to bed. Why me?

Turner

EMAIL RECEIVED: The Woman in My Dreams

My Dearest Turner,

Still in bed so typing on my tiny phone. I SO want to answer you in-depth (and you know I will).

I am simply writing to you now, letter by letter, just in case you have awakened in the night and are feeling vulnerable. We are no longer out on a limb because we are both on the same limb—the place where you share your fragility because you know the other person will honor it, nurture it and ultimately revel in it. From great complicity comes great creativity—feeling safe enough to be willing to take bold risks, good risks, noble risks, for things which matter, which ultimately lead us to a place of strength, forgiveness, hope, renewal, and joy.

And yes … in that place there is magical love-making too, a communion of souls, a meeting of minds, a giving of hearts, and of course, life wouldn't be complete without gorgeous, elegant lingerie … and someone to appreciate it. :-)

Is it Sunday night yet?

Dakota

EMAIL RECEIVED: Fitting Quote RE: Why Me?

"If you live the questions, life will move you to the answers."
–Deepak Chopra

Dear Turner,

Why you Turner? I know where you are going! You are going to that vulnerable place (and of course the twin of vulnerability is fragility), and maybe I'm going there a bit too right now. This is all scary stuff, but hey, I saw your profile, I was intrigued, we had all the basics in common, we wrote to each other, then it just all started to become magical, deep, exciting, wonderful, unexpected, rare, fun, and natural. I've thought about it, and if we lived in the same city, we would have gone out on dates for a while and then probably decided to get to know one another better ... in a way that includes breakfast the next day. But think about it, we have talked about and shared so much more than I ever have in the past in such a short period of time. I realized walking to work this morning that we are getting ultra-close to one another emotionally before making love, whereas often making love leads to emotional closeness and then sharing. Interesting, no?

I hope you aren't still feeling out on a limb, but remember, we don't do take-backs(!), and I'm so honored and moved by all that you have chosen to share with me. We have both been through a lot and have lived over half a century before meeting one another (whew, that sounds really long, doesn't it!) but now we have found each other and want to see what we can build together. Through everything in our respective pasts, we both still have a voice which says, "I want to be open to life and love," not such a small feat. There is so much I want to share with you too . . .

Dakota went on in her email to share some of those things—some pretty tough things. She also shared some of her future dreams and desires.

Most of us have things we keep inside and rarely speak about: difficult experiences, things that remain tender and fragile, things that make us afraid or uncertain. Sometimes, there are broken pieces in our hearts and souls, that— if we're able—we mend back together in some way and hope no one notices. Having revealed ourselves to each other so deeply and totally, Dakota and I found ourselves at a level of intimacy so profound that, for me, at least, it gave me pause over the responsibility I had been given.

Of course, Dakota was able to express everything so much better in words, far beyond my ability.

EMAIL RECEIVED: Fitting Quote RE: Why Me?

Turner,

Once we start to share the heavy stuff with one another, it lightens the load and allows us to imagine the future. Just know that I think you are so thoughtful and kind. Both are utterly wonderful and, in a way, new for me.

Thinking of you, Dakota XOXOX

CHAPTER 15

Finch

IN SIX DAYS AND SIX nights, Dakota and I went from being strangers to virtual lovers. No words can adequately express or convey the emotional immersion and transformation that took place.

It was total, and it was torrid.

We waxed poetic, riding the ever-increasing waves of intoxicating highs with thoughts of each other, fueled by each new message. With the kindred wanting and desire we found in each other, we willfully—even recklessly—upped the ante of our out-on-a-ledge soulful unmasking, elevated our dares to each other in sexual fantasy, connected and melded with intellectual transcendence, and traversed unexplored depths of intimacy. We touched and reveled in each other's virgin exultations that had never before been touched—ironic since we were 3,800 miles apart. In those six amazing days, our feet left the ground, removing ourselves from our everyday lives, and we were transported to another world.

In every second of every minute of every hour of every day, it was just Turner and Dakota.

Nothing else mattered.

But Abby had a different take.

"Yeah-hh, so-ooooo? Where do you see this going? Where could it *possibly* go?" Abby said cautiously and admonishingly at lunch that Saturday.

It was jarring and whiplash-inducing as she yanked me back down to earth from my otherworldly bliss.

During those first few days of emails and phone calls with Dakota, I told Abby what was going on—in much less explicit detail, of course—and shared with her how passionate and consuming it had become with my new American-French connection.

"I have absolutely no idea where it might go, but you're for sure the only one I can tell about it," I said. "It's pretty risky business I know, but I'm thinking … I might possibly go to Paris to meet her."

"I *knew* that was coming; I *just* knew it!" Abby shook her head. "I think this is *really* dangerous and not very well thought out. Just imagine what you'd be telling me if I told you I met a guy online, but he lived in Paris, and we were having torrid transatlantic communications—cybersex—and I might hop on a plane to go meet him?"

"I'd say you're *totally* crazy, and you've lost your mind!"

"EXACTLY!" she said.

"Yeah, maybe I've lost my mind, but it's not such a bad way to lose it," I demurred. "But I'm also letting you know because *someone* needs to know what I'm up to, just in case. I'm not *totally* off my rocker."

"Can we put that to a vote?" Abby shot back with a serious I'm-not-kidding look.

"Sure," I said. "All those who think Turner is off his rocker, raise your hand."

Abby raised both hands.

"You *can't* outvote me."

"Well, I can *still* say you're crazy."

"Yeah, that's fair," I said. "I need to know if I'm going off the deep end, but we are going to meet on a Skype call tomorrow night."

"Well, that should be telling," Abby said, now lowering her tone of voice. "Where are you Skyping from? The living room or the bedroom?" she said with a smart-ass smirk.

"It wouldn't really matter, quite frankly, according to Dakota," I said.

"Okay, sorry I asked, too much information. Nyna-nyna-nyna!" she said, putting her fingers in her ears.

"You're the one who said …"

"Yeah, yeah!" Abby said, now waving me off. "We're done talking about this for now, but *I want to know* what happens tomorrow night."

"Oh, you will," I said. "You will."

"Now *when* have I heard that before?"

The Boys had decidedly mixed opinions about all this transatlantic, transcendent, and *Out of Africa* stuff.

Darrell was just Darrell. He liked the sex talk. *Can you believe she said that?!* But all the other fancy talk was over his head and annoying.

If she wants to fuck, let's just get on a plane, go over there, and get on with it. I don't give a rat's ass about some shit that happened in an African movie twenty years ago. If she likes big-game hunters, heck, I'll show her my deer hunting rifle if that'll get her naked, but all of this Finch stuff is nuts! Don't like that shit.

Darrell's comments about Finch—if not very deft—were foretelling.

Charles was positively overwhelmed by Dakota—he was lost to intellectual lust. He rattled on endlessly about off-the-chart dopamine and neurotrophin levels. *Boldness, brains, beauty, and heart. She channels overwhelming feminine sensuality, all wrapped up in a bustier for us to take off! She's our girl!*

Little Turner was overwhelmed too … overwhelmed with *doubt.*

Doubt about what we were getting into.

Doubt about what this could ever be.

Doubt about what people would think if they found out what we were doing.

Doubt about living up to Dakota's expectations.

And *doubt* about Dakota living up to ours.

One thing Little Turner had *no* doubt about, however—we had to go to Paris. This declaration drew nods of agreement from The Boys.

We have to meet her.

****

After lunch with Abby, I texted Dakota about the possibility of coming to Paris. Four hours had now passed—it was late evening in Switzerland where she had gone for the weekend—and I was getting nervous waiting for a response.

Had I gone too far with this? I wondered.

Then, a chime rang on my phone—Dakota had texted.

"What took you so long?" was her simple response.

As I breathed a sigh of relief, I gasped for breath with excitement. Pushing aside Abby's comment of *What! Are you crazy?!* I set my sights on Paris to meet Dakota in three and a half weeks.

But there was something I needed to do and understand; I needed to watch the movie *Out of Africa*. I needed to know what this obsession with Finch was all about.

In the movie, Streep plays Baroness Karen Blixen, a wealthy Danish woman who marries and moves to Africa in the 1910s. There, she befriends Redford's character, Denys Finch Hatton, a British big-game hunter. After discovering rampant infidelity by her husband, Karen begins a torrid affair with Finch, and he moves in with her. While extraordinarily passionate, their relationship is marred by Finch's independent lifestyle, and he is often away. After refusing several marriage proposals, Karen reluctantly asks him to move out.

A plantation fire leads to financial ruin, and Karen is forced to leave Africa. She and Finch share one last emotional evening in the climactic scene of the movie, consumed by sadness at their impending separation, all the while still caring—even longing—for each other.

It's an awkward last evening together.

With music playing on a phonograph, they slow dance in the starry African night. Her face cannot hide her deep, passionate, and unquenchable love for Finch, nor can it hide the pain of knowing he will not or cannot love her back the same way. His face shows the gut-wrenching guilt he feels and the opposing forces of loving her and wanting her but not wanting, or being able, to give up his individualistic life.

There is collective desperation as they try to sear the memory of this moment in their minds. The feeling of foreboding is palpable with the coming sunrise and his morning departure.

Finch promises to return for her in three days to fly her on the beginning of her journey home to Denmark, but when he fails to return, she learns he was killed in a plane crash.

Even though Finch was never to be hers, his death is devastating. She will always carry a flame for him in her heart, for the most spectacular love—a rarefied love—she once knew and had in him.

As the movie ended and the credits rolled, I had the same thoughts most would—sadness at the tragedy but an awe-inspired desire to experience in real life the passionate love I saw on screen.

Guys don't always show or say they want that kind of love and passion, but I'll admit it; I do. However, as many who have made it to middle-age can tell you, the realities of life and love don't live up to cinematic storylines, except in fleeting moments.

What Dakota was in search of was something she was perfectly willing and capable of making happen, there was no doubt about that. It was a part of who she was—her sheer force of will and her womanly desires and abilities. But immersed in the heady feelings of passion and intimacy, and perhaps already falling in love, I felt my first moments of hesitation and worry.

It's a movie. How do I live up to that? Is she seeing me for me, wanting me for me, or am I the fantasy of Finch and Redford from a movie obsession?

When I told Abby about it, she expressed the same concerns. "Lots of people hold on to movie fantasies, but be careful; fantasies are not real for a reason. That's what makes them fantasies. I'm still not comfortable with this."

We'll see how it all plays out, I told myself, putting the movie and Finch away for the time being.

****

Sunday finally arrived, and our Skype call was only an hour away. It felt like a big-time first date—which it was—and I sweated every detail: what to wear, which room to do it in, and so on.

I took my laptop and moved it from room to room to see which would look best. I finally decided on the bar counter in the kitchen with the background of the family room and fireplace. Not wanting an up-nose view of my face on the laptop camera, I stacked large, heavy books on the counter and put my laptop on top.

"Perfect!" I said out loud. "Straight-on, good lighting, nice!"

Doo-dee-do ... doo-dee-do came the ring of the Skype call on my laptop ... and there she was.

We both just looked at each other for a moment at first.

"Hi," I said with a controlled smile.

"Hi," she said with a very wry and knowing grin.

I tugged at my shirt collar.

She flipped her hair back.

We gazed at each other, then began to talk in short sentences.

"How was your trip to Switzerland?"

"It was great. How's the weather there in Washington?"

"It's nice. How about there?"

"It's nice here too."

As we smiled and pretended to be *just friends*, her nineteen-year-old came through the apartment with a friend in tow, and Dakota introduced us. We made some small talk about the World Cup being played in France, and they moved on, none the wiser as to what was going on.

We kept the call to about fifteen minutes, but that was enough. We were both pulled in all the way now; this was the real deal. Before going to bed, I wrote to her, trying to express my overwhelming feelings of excitement and uninhibited intoxication for all things Dakota.

EMAIL SENT: Travels, Distance, and Stuck on You

Dakota Dear,

Just thought you might want to know, I'm so stuck on you!!! I wish I was with you there in bed, in the night, spooned up behind you for full-body contact, to smell your hair and all of you, your hand on mine, and my hand on your breast. We would be so close that to break apart would feel like love and life were being taken from us. Can you imagine what this would be like?

I want you soooooo much.

Turner X

EMAIL RECEIVED: Travels, Distance, and Stuck on You

Oh my, Turner, here I am in an open office space at 9:24 am reading your intimate email—let's see who can pull off a poker face now. :-) This is **so** beautiful, breathtakingly so (yes, I can imagine it, because I already have!) and rather similar to my thoughts as I was lying in bed last night.

Your woman in your dreams xxxoooxxxooo

The next morning, I worked out dates for my trip to Paris—flight times and other details—for what was looking like a five-day weekend. Soon after sending them to Dakota, she sent a list of possible destinations to choose from: Normandy, the Loire Valley, and the Champagne region. Normandy had long been high on my wish list of places to visit; I wanted to see where the Allied Forces changed the world with their beachhead landing in World War II. I also knew there were wonderful small towns in the area, quintessentially French and welcoming to Americans.

I told her my preference for Normandy and asked if we might be able to work in a visit to Mont Saint-Michel, too, another high-on-my-list place to visit. Mont Saint-Michel, the breathtaking island abbey and monastery, is a place of fascination for every architect, but I had never been during my two previous trips to France decades earlier. She loved the idea of adding Mont Saint-Michel and quickly began putting an itinerary together.

With the *who, what, where,* and *when* of my trip falling into place, all that was left to figure out was the last of the five Ws—*why.*

Why was I going to Paris on such short notice and for such a short trip?

People would want to know.

Generally speaking, I didn't think it would be questioned too much by family and friends that I was taking an out-of-the-blue trip just after becoming an empty nester. But flying across the Atlantic to meet a woman I had met online would have been an invitation to have my sanity and judgment questioned, as Abby had already done.

So I came up with a story that went like this.

A fellow board member from one of the organizations I served on told me he was off to Paris in late September to visit his sister. She had been living there for over twenty years and was recently divorced. Knowing I was open to opportunities, he extended an invitation to join him, meet his sister, and stay with him at her apartment in Paris. Everything would be taken care of. All I needed was a ticket, and we would be off for an extended weekend.

Dakota liked the story and thought it would do the trick.

Later that day, I told Mary about my plans. She didn't think twice about it. She was thrilled I was treating myself to this after everything I had been through the last four years. She also really liked the idea that I would be meeting this guy's sister.

It was looking like only nine days after meeting Dakota online, I was ready to book my flight on Air France to Paris. But then Mary called back and expressed a concern.

Over the summer, she had made it through her last stated goal in life—seeing her grandson graduate from high school and go off to college. It was truly a wonderful summer finishing the childhoods of my children, and I couldn't have done it without her.

Through sheer force of will, Mary maintained relatively good health and a positive outlook, but it seemed now she was beginning to let go. At ninety-two years old, she was a four-time breast cancer survivor, had survived two other cancers, had had hip replacement and hip-replacement-replacement surgery, and her eyesight was failing. With the beginning of forgetfulness, she said she was struggling to keep it all together.

"I'm worried about your going away and not being here since I'm starting to come apart," she said.

"Then I won't go, Mary. It's that simple," I replied. "I promised to be here for you. There's nothing complicated about that."

"I think it would make me feel more comfortable now that everything seems so uncertain. I'm not worried about dying. It's been a great life. I've told you that. It's just … well, you know. I want to exit gracefully without pain and have you in control of everything. Paris will always be there," she said.

"Yes, it will. It's settled. Don't even think about it anymore."

I was a bit worried about telling Dakota—especially with the still-fresh memory of Emily and the silent treatment she gave me for going to a baseball game with friends, even while she was busy all weekend.

But this was a no-brainer—family first. Period.

I need not have worried. Dakota was wonderfully understanding and didn't show any of the disappointment I knew she felt. She knew very well how important Mary was to me. Our time to meet would come.

Then, a few days later, Mary said she wanted to talk on the phone.

"I've changed my mind," she said. "I want you to go to France. I'll be okay until you get back. You know how much Ed [her late husband] and I loved France. It was our most favorite place in the whole world. We probably made twenty or more trips there. So I'll say it's okay for you to go as long as you promise me one thing—you have to take lots of pictures and show me every one!" She made the matter final with a loving laugh.

"That's a deal! But are you sure?"

"Yes, I'm sure. Go have fun in France for a few days then come back, and we'll celebrate your birthday at The Inn at Little Washington—my treat."

The Inn at Little Washington is an amazing, outrageously expensive, Michelin three-star French restaurant in Virginia, about ninety minutes outside of Washington, D.C. It would be an evening and dinner to remember.

I let Dakota know immediately that my trip was back on, and she quickly went back into high gear to plan. In short order, she offered a suggested travel itinerary.

First, upon my early arrival in Paris on a Thursday morning, she would pick me up, and we would go back to her place. She pondered out loud if perhaps I would be *up to the task* of making love to her first before taking a nap together—spooned up naked as I had described in my email—or if I would need to take a nap first to rest after my overnight flight.

"Asked, dared, and you'll get my answer when I get there. Remember, no take-backs!"

"Good," she responded. "Perhaps I should go lingerie shopping after work one day this week to buy a nice little outfit to welcome you in ... before you take it off. After our nap together, we can walk about Paris for the day and have dinner back at my place. The next day, we can head out of the city to Normandy, but I want to suggest a side trip to Monet's Giverny. Have you ever been?"

"No, but I know about it from art history class in college. That would be incredible to see," I said.

"Great! We can spend a few hours there before getting to our overnight accommodations near Normandy. Saturday will be exploring Normandy, then Sunday will be exploring Bayeux. The great Bayeux Tapestry is there, and you have to see it. After, we'll drive to near Mont Saint-Michel, spend the night, then tour it on Monday. In the afternoon, we'll drive back to Paris and spend your last night at my place," she wrapped up.

"How's that, Finch?"

Ouch! I thought. *How did Finch get back into the picture?*

For just a moment, I had a pit in my stomach. I was finding that whenever she called me Finch, it felt like a threesome. I wondered how long she would go on about it.

Eventually, I pushed Finch out of my mind and Dakota continued sending options for places to stay, from quaint farm inns to chateaus.

Later that week, she went off on her lingerie-shopping excursion, keeping me apprised by texts and voice messages along the way. In one voice message, as she walked down the street, I could hear the sounds of European honking horns and background conversations of people talking in French.

She noted in several texts what she was looking for and trying on. She asked if I had any preferences or whether she should just surprise me. She was trying on one especially nice set of panties and bra and wondered if I might like them.

> **ME:** I might, but seeing is knowing.

In short order, she texted a photo of herself in the dressing room from the waist up only in a bra.

> **DAKOTA:** Okay, Turner Grant, what do you think? No photos of the bottom half. You'll have to see that in person.

> **ME:** Will you be wearing those under your clothes when you pick me up at the airport?

> **DAKOTA:** Yes.

The most unusual thing about the photo of her in a state of undress in a Paris lingerie shop was that it seemed not unusual at all. I tried to take a step back in my mind to look at all this with a bit of perspective. I found it impossibly hard to believe.

Here I have a woman I've never met, we've virtually ravished each other from an ocean apart, and she's sending me—sexting me—scantily clad photos of herself as if it's the most natural thing in the world.

You've come a long way, said Little Turner. *A very long way.*

I must be on another planet, I thought.

Then the reality of it all began to take hold.

EMAIL RECEIVED: Normandy Beaches + Mont Saint-Michel ...

Turner,

It was wonderful to speak with you twice(!) in one day. Things did get very personal last night. Our discussions keep going in new directions, which at times leads to re-thinking boundaries. To be honest, it's feeling a little bit scary, but also exciting because I trust you so much. I woke up (again!) at 4:30 am and my mind was going in circles. "He had almost 40 different coffee dates, goodness, eventually lowering the radius to 40 miles ... and then this started between us across the ocean." Must, must sleep tonight ...

Dakota xxxxx

EMAIL SENT: Normandy Beaches + Mont Saint-Michel ...

Help me understand what is scary. Scary because of how real it is, or scary, "Who is this strange man coming on so strong?"

EMAIL RECEIVED: Normandy Beaches + Mont Saint-Michel ...

1) Scary because I haven't known you very long and I am telling you so many ultra-private things about my desires

2) Scary to imagine that three weeks from today we will actually be in bed together!

3) Scary because you seem so passionate, and I hope you will desire me (oops, there comes Mrs. Vulnerability)

EMAIL SENT: Normandy Beaches + Mont Saint-Michel ...

#3 is scary for me too. There is a Mr. Vulnerability who is very worried he may be a "dud" to you when we meet.

EMAIL RECEIVED: Normandy Beaches + Mont Saint-Michel ...

Okay, it is SO unreal between us. So so so so so unreal between us ... TELEPATHY TIME!!

I was just in a meeting and tried to focus, but I was worrying you would think no. 3 showed insecurity on my part.

Shall we make another deal? I think we both enjoy negotiating, yes?

Why don't we just eliminate no. 3 and go ahead and forget about no. 1 and 2 while we are at it? :-)

Let us look briefly at the facts:

1) We were interested in each other from the get-go with our profiles and texts

2) There was total chemistry from the moment we started speaking on the phone

3) We have near telepathy when we discuss various and sundry themes

4) Our Skype could not have been better ... and I thought you were even more handsome than your photos

5) We have both been willing to discuss utterly profound and personal themes because we somehow already feel trust

6) We have been floored, moved, and blown away by things

the other has understood instinctively—which no one else ever really "got"

7) There is something magical happening and we both know it—we can't sleep, our hearts race, and we can't seem to talk on the phone for less than two hours!

8) We both described the way we wrote from some otherworldly place about deep thoughts—the unconscious mind was literally spilling onto the page

9) We have had an entire discussion on kindness (I don't want to reorder all of these, but ideally I should have written this higher on the list)

10) We have had wildly erotic discussions going all over the place. Why would we not feel desire the moment we first kiss? Duh of the century.

And what does Mr. Grant say now?

EMAIL SENT: Normandy Beaches + Mont Saint-Michel …

Mr. Grant says he thinks he is falling in love with you.

EMAIL RECEIVED: Normandy Beaches + Mont Saint-Michel …

Ms. Wallace wishes to say she thinks she is falling in love with Mr. Grant.

Would you be so kind as to relay her message to him when you see him next? She would be ever so grateful.

EMAIL SENT: Adventure in Life

My Dearest Dakota,

I have referred back to my profile several times to help you connect the dots to who I really am as a person. Some things are basic information (to the point of being boring), some things perked up your antennas (the white dinner jacket), and other things were probably more cryptic and not well understood because certain blanks needed to be filled in (we've certainly been doing a darn good job of that now, haven't we?).

Do you recall what I said about adventure? I said that "I don't define adventure as skydiving (although that keeps life fun and interesting), rather I define adventure as that which changes the course of your life and those of others." Do you remember, Dakota?

My hope is that I am about to do just that. My reservations to Paris are confirmed; I am coming to see you, to meet you, to make passionate love to you, and to see how my life and your life might be changed forever.

Your lover (I do so like that!),

Turner

EMAIL RECEIVED: Adventure in Life

Darling,

This is the most beautiful email I have ever received ...

When I reflect on it, I don't think anyone has ever really loved me the way I hope we will love one another. Well, I'm sure we have both had moments of passion (thank goodness!), but I've not experienced a deep, mature love, which is also full of kindness, understanding, acceptance, hope, complicity, and a sense of permanence. Maybe I hadn't met the right person or maybe I wasn't ready, but now everything feels so completely right.

Your Dakota love xxooxxooxxoo

****

As the planning progressed and the number of days until my departure dwindled, nervous jitters and doubts continued, intermingled with intoxicating excitement. We exchanged messages and talked openly about our fears on the phone several times.

These scary feelings would come, melt away, then come back again. However, we both wanted this, knew the risks, and shared the same hoped-for outcome. And besides, at this point, there was absolutely no turning back. I wasn't just pushing the limits of my boundaries or comfort zone anymore—I had positively obliterated them.

The Boys were in the same boat I was, but by now, they were totally in *gaga* land. Their eyes were perpetually rolled back into their heads, and they weren't of much help right now.

Ten days before I was to depart for Paris, we finally had our long-talked-about Skype dinner date. We scheduled it for a Sunday at one in the afternoon my time, seven in the evening her time. Since formal wear was the subject of our first correspondence, I would wear my white dinner jacket, and she would be dressed accordingly in evening wear.

The menu for each of us would be simple but special—champagne to begin, salad, then dinner of filet mignon, baked potato, and a nice red wine.

I got the same stack of books I used before under my laptop but now put them on the dining room table. I placed candles behind me so she would see them. I started the baked potato, made the salad, grilled the fillet outside, and then quickly changed into my white dinner jacket.

Doo-dee-do… doo-dee-do, rang the Skype call again on my laptop.

She looked wonderful.

She was dressed in a cream-colored gown with lace and wore pearls around her neck, looking classic and marvelous. She made note that she was wearing the lingerie she had sent me a photo of the week before, but I would have to wait until I arrived and was in her bedroom to see it.

"At least I think you'll have to wait," she said. Then, as before, she flirtatiously flipped back her hair.

While talking and sipping our champagne, she swiveled her laptop camera and pointed it out the window. I could see the sun was going down, but right there, in the City of Light, was an unobstructed view of the Eiffel Tower slowly being illuminated.

I would be there seeing this—with her—in ten days.

In the meantime, our dinner and evening together were nothing short of magical.

Imagine a dinner date in someplace spectacular, say … Paris, with an unobstructed view of the Eiffel Tower from your table as you dine, all during those heady early days of a new relationship when you're filled with an over-the-top dose of excited, anticipatory electricity.

Everything felt perfect, even with 3,800 miles of separation, but our evening together went by way too fast. I was ready to undress her right there—or rather have her undress herself for me.

"Let's wait until you can undress me in person," she said, and I agreed.

Reluctantly, we wished each other goodnight, blowing kisses before signing off.

But I couldn't let the evening end there, so I texted her thirty minutes later.

> **ME:** You remember a few weeks ago I mentioned something that "might amuse you" with your phone?

> **DAKOTA:** Yes, I do, Mr. Mysterious.

ME: Good. Have you undressed yet?

DAKOTA: Partially. Is this a clothes-on or -off activity you have in mind?

ME: Either could work to varying degrees.

DAKOTA: Okay

ME: Go to the bedroom, lie on your bed, and have your phone with you. Turn the ringer off and set it to vibrate. I'm going to call you but don't answer.

DAKOTA: Okay. I think I know where this is going.

ME: I thought you might, you clever girl.

DAKOTA: Are you trying to reach out and touch me from across the Atlantic?

ME: Pretty much. Tell me when you're ready.

DAKOTA: The debutante in me is blushing and scolding me, but I'm ready.

I dialed her international number and waited. … And waited … and then …

DAKOTA: You better get here fast mister! You've got some unfinished business to attend to!

CHAPTER 16

We Will Always Have Paris

THE PLANE FLEW QUICKLY INTO the darkness of the night, and thoughts of what lay ahead went rapidly through my mind.

What will meeting her at the airport be like?

What will it be like in her apartment?

We had boastfully talked about immediately going to her bedroom to make love. *Would that really happen?*

We had never laid eyes on each other before except as pixels on a screen propped up on books. *How is this going to feel when it is real?*

For hours, thoughts rushed in and out of my mind until sheer mental exhaustion set in and I fell asleep for an hour. When I awoke, time began to pass quickly. The skies lightened as we flew into the sunrise.

The coastline of France was now below, and quickly enough, we were over Paris. Looking out the window, I easily picked out the architectural landmarks I knew so well.

As we landed, nervous jitters rushed in full force. Everything we had done before had led up to this moment, and everything that would happen *after* would *begin* from this moment.

Walking off the plane at the gate, I grabbed my phone and tried to find a Wi-Fi signal so we could connect. It was lousy, plus all the instructions were in French, but we connected briefly.

> **ME:** I'm just getting off the plane.

> **DAKOTA:** I'm here, just outside international arrivals. You'll see me with a sign for you. I can hardly stand it. I'm ready to jump out of my skin!

> **ME:** Don't jump!

Then the Wi-Fi signal dropped.

I found my luggage and quickly went through customs. I emerged onto a ramp in the arrivals hall and began walking down, my eyes eagerly and nervously darting around the crowd trying to find her. She was hiding a bit, so I didn't see her until I was a few feet away. I saw her face, then looked down to see the handwritten sign she held.

I felt a bullet rip through my heart.

"MR. FINCH GRANT," read the hand-drawn sign in blue marker, with Xs decorating the border.

FINCH!?!?!?! The Boys screamed.

It was an emotional body blow like I had never felt before. I was hurt and confused.

Finch?! I repeated to myself. *Finch?!!!*

She wants Finch, not you, said The Boys.

Then I looked up to see her face. There was such affection and longing in her eyes, but there was apprehension too. She looked so vulnerable, so beautiful, so …

Shake it off, Turner! Shake it off! Come on!

There was a momentary pause, an awkward pause. Seeing the sign made me feel as though I wasn't the person she was here to meet. I wasn't sure what to do or say. It obviously meant a lot to her, so I pushed hard against the hurt I felt inside.

I reached out to hug her, and she me. We embraced each other as tightly as we could for several minutes as people hustled around us. The emotion of finally having her in my arms slowly began to melt away some of the distress I was feeling.

We released and looked into each other's eyes. She wore her emotions on her sleeve. I thought she was going to cry, and then she did.

We should kiss! I thought. Then she smiled with an eager look on her face, possibly thinking the same thing.

Our first kiss was marvelous … unbelievable … surreal.

I was coming back, albeit with doubt now sowed where I never imagined it would be.

"I'm so glad you're finally here," she said, reluctantly pulling away.

"Me too. Sorry it took so long."

"You should be sorry," she said before coming in for another lovely, longing, wanting kiss.

Our lips hesitantly parted, and we held each other for what seemed like a long time in the now-empty arrivals hall.

Then slowly, we began to walk, hand in hand.

We talked in short sentences, keeping our gazes fixed on each other. The conversation began cautiously—in some ways, like a first date, which this was. We talked of mundane travel things, then Dakota interjected. "You're here …"

She entwined her arms in my mine, her fingers in mine, and pulled herself as close as two people can possibly be while walking together in an airport.

Then pausing, we turned to each other and kissed again.

From there, we hustled out to the parking garage—me, her, and the Finch sign she had given me to remember the moment. We got into her small blue French car and joined the crowded highway to Paris.

It was the beginning of the morning rush, and Dakota remarked she had never seen the traffic this bad. I put my hand on her lap as she drove, and every few minutes, she'd take one hand off the wheel and give it a squeeze. At each stoplight, I leaned over and kissed her, lingering until the light turned green or the traffic moved. Each time, she smiled, both out of pleasure and, I think, anticipation of what was to come.

It took us two hours to make a drive that was normally forty-five minutes. Looking at Dakota along the way, she mostly fit the photo of her that I first saw, except perhaps for not being as tall as I had imagined. Her intelligence, sensuality, mischievousness, and her above-and-beyond womanliness that I had gotten to know the previous weeks were there in full force. But sitting in the car with her, I felt nervous and hesitant.

Did the build-up in the weeks before create expectations that couldn't possibly be met in reality? Was it because of the Finch sign? I wasn't sure. There was too much going through my head and my heart at once to figure it all out.

Give it time, I thought. *Give it time.*

I kept kissing her at every stop, both because I wanted to and, I suppose, hoping things would start to feel better and come into focus.

As we drove, I began to chastise myself for reacting to the sign the way I did. *All she wants is you. Get over it!*

As Finch began to fade from the picture, the electricity of being in the car with Dakota began to take hold. My kisses became more wanting.

The city seemed to go on forever, dense and busy everywhere. We finally arrived in the arrondissement where she lived, well away from the café-packed tourist areas. It was a quieter neighborhood of residential buildings, stores, schools, and small businesses. The architecture ranged from classic Parisian mansard buildings to contemporary. We parked, toted my luggage into the elevator, arrived on her floor, and went into the apartment.

"This is it," she said. "Look familiar?"

She led me into the living room, then to the window with the stunning unobstructed view of the Eiffel Tower a few miles away.

After a tour of every room but her bedroom, she said, "Would you like to see my French lace sheets now? They're freshly washed, ready, and waiting for you."

She then took my hand and led the way.

The bed was neatly made. The corner of the cover was pulled back and laid over as though turn-down service had just been done.

"Are you wearing the lingerie?" I asked.

"Yes," she responded in a whisper, then flipped her hair back in her characteristic way. "I know you're probably tired from your trip, but it's waiting for you underneath if you're so inclined."

I kissed her … then we went for each other, my hands on her breasts, her hands making their way to my chest as she began to unbutton my shirt. Then my hands went down between her thighs, and she did the same to me.

Then she stopped and pulled back.

"Oh, this is *so* strange," she said. "I just met you; this seems crazy."

I instantly flashed back to Joyce and her immediate regret after our first kiss.

I paused, ready to stop if she wanted to, then she resumed taking off my shirt. I grabbed the bottom of her top and pulled it over her head to reveal the bra I had seen in the photo a few weeks before.

"I've been looking forward to seeing that in person," I said. "It was worth the wait."

"It's just half of the matched set, you know."

I unbuttoned and unzipped her pants, gently pushed her onto the bed, then slid them off to reveal her panties.

"Yes, they're nicely matched," I said. "You look luscious in them, but I bet you'll look even more luscious with them off."

Then again, she stopped and pulled back.

"Oh god, this is *so* strange, having sex with someone I *don't even know*."

At that, I stopped.

"We don't have to do this," I said. "I know we talked about it, but I didn't come over here just to have sex with you. I came over here to meet you, spend time with you, and for us to be together. Let's not do this. Let's just get in bed, cuddle, and fall asleep. It's fine, really, it's fine. I don't want this to feel strange and weird."

"No ..." she said. "I want to."

I pulled her from the bed, and we kissed again. I reached behind to unsnap her bra with one hand. It unhooked and loosened in front, then she slipped it off.

I caressed and kissed her breasts. She threw her head back and arched her back.

I followed her body down to her panties, kissed them, pulled them down, then kissed her there again. She stepped out of them, then she finished undressing me.

She then laid back on her bed and gestured for me to join her. We made passionate, hungry, and wanting love. We were insatiable.

Our naked bodies bent and folded into each other afterward—me behind her—cupping her breasts as they fell into my hand. We then drifted off to sleep between the tossed and wrinkled French lace sheets.

****

We awoke an hour later, around noon.

Weeks of build-up from our cross-Atlantic liaison had finally climaxed, both literally and figuratively. It was transcendent by any measure—one of the most amazing experiences of my life.

"Hi," I softly whispered into her ear.

"Hi," she whispered back.

We adjusted our bodies tight and snug to each other. I fondled her breasts and readjusted my hand over them. We lay silent for a few minutes, totally content, entwined, naked, and twisted in the sheets.

Little Turner then asked the question of the moment.

What now?

We had talked about, fantasized about, and pretty much scripted every moment up until this point. But with the script played out, the question loomed large.

What now?

By Dakota's stillness and silence, I could tell she was thinking the same thing.

Finally, she spoke. "I bet you're hungry, Finch. Want to go for a walk and get some lunch?"

I froze. I couldn't speak. But The Boys could and did.

We. Are. Not. Finch.

After I had been quiet for too long, she asked, "Are you awake?"

"Yeah, I'm awake," I said and gave her breasts a gentle squeeze.

"Oh, okay. You went quiet. Is everything okay?"

My heart suddenly felt heavy and guilty; I was about to lie to her.

"Yeah, I'm fine. Just tired from the flight and, oh yeah, pounding you into the mattress for an hour."

She laughed. "Well, yeah-h-h, no jet lag there, mister."

But I wasn't fine. What could I say in the afterglow of making love for the first time? My apprehension hung in the air like cigarette smoke. I felt our connection slip ever so slightly.

Okay, it's time to close out this fantasy script—yours and hers, Little Turner said in no uncertain terms. *It's time to get real.*

But the *real* felt *surreal,* and I had no idea where this might go.

I kept hearing Abby's voice in my head. "You're going to be there for five days. What happens if …?"

We left her apartment, hopped on the metro, and went to the area around the Louvre. We talked along the way about how perfect it felt to finally be together but also how we were both feeling the jitters about meeting for the first time.

We walked over to the Palais Royal, into the garden, and to a little restaurant in the far corner. Dakota greeted the waiter in perfect French, but he quickly switched to English. We ordered lunch, then sat basking in the warm autumn sun with sapphire blue skies above.

"So," she said. "How's your son doing in his first few weeks of college?"

And so began the process of being real.

****

After lunch, we joined hundreds of Parisians walking through the Tuileries Gardens; the tourists were mostly gone in late September. We found a bench to sit on to soak in the sun and each other. I sat with my back against the armrest with my legs stretched out. She lay down on my legs and put her head on my chest. I stroked her hair, and she alternated between shallow, restful breathing and heavier, fast-heart-beating breathing.

I loved that I was here with Dakota, loved that I was in France, and looked forward to the plans she had made for us, including making love in romantic little French inns and a dozen other places she had talked about during the preceding weeks.

Lying now with her head on my chest, she said, "We're like two cliff divers, you know. We made this leap together."

"We sure did," I replied.

With that, she burrowed into my lap and dozed off for a few minutes.

When she awoke, she laid out our choices for the remainder of the afternoon. In planning the trip, I became aware that a major new building was about to open in Paris and asked Dakota if we might see it. The California architect Frank Gehry had just finished construction of his latest tour de force, the Foundation Louis Vuitton, with its billowing glass sails and timber structure. It was several metro rides and a bit of a walk to the Bois de Boulogne Park where it was located. If we went there, we'd be going off the beaten track a bit, but she was keen to see it too, so off we went.

For the next hour, Dakota led us through the ins and outs of the metro and the Paris streets during the early evening rush. Finally, getting to the park, the building began to emerge above the treetops.

Even the design snob in me was impressed, and Dakota was positively floored. She couldn't imagine anything like this ever being conceived, let alone built. But here we were, getting an early preview of a building that was about to hit the architectural press with a splash, and it was incredible to see it in person.

She said she never would've known this was here if I hadn't come to Paris and brought her.

That was good for a long kiss of gratitude.

As we left, it felt like the surrealness of being together had finally worn off.

During the afternoon and evening, meandering through the streets, sidewalks, and parks of Paris, we filled in many of the gaps we had wondered about each other. We talked about our families, marriages, children, and life in general. We could now see each other's reactions to what was said, giving us a better sense of the other's judgments, values, opinions, and sensitivities. Even with the best technology in the world, we couldn't do this across an ocean.

At this point, we realized that walking around Paris and the emotions of the day—not to mention my long travel—had drained us. We were looking forward to getting back to the apartment, so she hailed a taxi.

On our first evening together, Dakota made dinner while I sat at the bar counter, watching and talking with her. The domestic scene felt familiar and comfortable.

After a nice homemade dinner, we had an early rendezvous with the French lace sheets—clothes off and spooned together in what was becoming our way.

We talked for a bit, then lay quietly awake for a while. So many feelings, thoughts, and emotions needed to be sorted out for both of us.

For me, it was a mix.

Wow!

How lucky am I!

How lucky are we!

Ecstatic to finally be here with her!

Apprehensive to be here with her.

Will the fantasy live up to itself?

Will normal seem mundane?

Where can this go?

Ditch Finch!

… and a million other things.

But Dakota changed me, now and forever. I had a new outlook on life—a newfound desire to embrace opportunities and seize the moment. And I did that now, entwined with her here. With very little movement and no spoken words, we slowly and quietly made love in our spooned and entwined position.

Everything else in the world went away.

****

Waking up the next morning, I moved toward her. She turned away, then shimmied back into our spoon position. But our busy travel schedule meant our time in bed was short. In no time at all, we were in her little blue car and heading out of the city.

The drive to Giverny was ninety minutes. Once there, we did our own tour of Monet's home and famous gardens amongst the heavy crowd of tourists. It was an amazing place and easy to see the magic that captivated and inspired Monet. It was also a romantic place, with the dreamy landscape and pond, but for whatever reason, it felt less romantic for us.

There is a famous little green bridge where everyone has their picture taken. Dakota told me to go to the middle, and she would take mine. After she took several of me, I said, "You go so I can take yours." But she declined. When I tried coaxing her, she quickly turned to me—or was it *on* me?

"No!"

What was that about? The Boys said, startled.

Some people are less than thrilled at having their picture taken; I get it. Maybe this was the case or maybe not, but her emphatic no was hard and awkwardly blunt.

We spent two hours touring Monet's home. I eventually got a photo of her and one of us on a garden path, but it was more of a concession from her instead of "Let's take a picture of us together to remember this wonderful place!"

The day before, something had happened to me because of Finch. Now, it felt like something had happened to her. The day felt more like an outing with a good friend, not a lover. I had expected more, especially since I was working hard to expel Finch from the picture.

From Giverny, it took several hours of driving to get to the Normandy countryside, but it had the effect of brightening her mood considerably. Getting off the main highway, we stopped at a travel restaurant for dinner. Being France, it was a cut above what you'd find in the States. It was fast food but served at a table, ordered from a menu, and came with a choice of wine.

As we sat looking at the menus, she said with a happy smile on her face, "So what'll it be, Finch?"

Stop it! The Boys yelled immediately, *just stop it!*

I hesitated, and she noticed.

"Is something wrong?" she asked.

Okay, so I know what you're thinking—why didn't I just tell her that all this Finch stuff bothered me and to please stop calling me Finch?

Because something inside me said not to, and it wasn't The Boys.

One of my goals from the beginning of my time on Venus was to find out as much as possible about the women I met as soon as possible. I'm sure most of them did the same to me.

I tried to encourage, even coax, them into being comfortable enough to reveal themselves—personal things, secrets, and any noteworthy quirks—in an unfiltered way. This meant not always responding to things they said or did. If something about them was odd or off in any way, I wanted to know what it was. I didn't want to say anything and then have them hide whatever it was.

Coming here to meet Dakota was not some sort of game—me taking advantage of an opportunity to go to France and get laid over and over. I cared about her, wanted to be with her, and wanted to get to know her. But this whole Finch thing—while not a red flag for some—was odd to me and hurt every time she brought it up. It was the first thing she wanted me to see at the airport at the *big moment*, and one of the first words out of her mouth after we made love in her apartment, so clearly, it was important to her. She was looking at me and us through Finch-colored glasses, and I needed to understand why, all the while hoping it would just go away. Right or wrong, I decided to let it play out, not to tell her how much it bothered me, and to see if it was a cautionary tip of some larger problematic iceberg.

So I told Dakota I could feel myself holding back a bit but not intentionally. We revisited how this was all uncharted territory for both of us, and there was bound to be some hesitation at times.

This seemed to get us past the moment.

Driving a short time later, it was now pitch-black in the French countryside. We had trouble finding the farmhouse inn where we would be staying the next two nights. No neon signs out here—just stars, lots of wheat fields, and narrow roads. We finally found the farm and the wonderfully warm woman who owned it. We settled into our room and began asking questions about preferences for this and that.

It was a little funny as the getting-to-know-you process continued. Here were two people, on the most intimate of terms, trying to figure out if the other preferred a shower or a bath, where to put one's clothes (hanging or in drawers), which shelf will be for your toiletries, which will be for mine, and so on.

It was cozy in our little farmhouse bed, something I will never forget. We made love by candlelight for I don't know how long. Whatever went on earlier in the day was now gone. Between the sheets, we were in sync and one.

It was all surreal once again.

****

The lazy, unhurried morning was more of the same as the night before, but we finally agreed we needed to get this show on the road.

Normandy was incredibly moving and sobering. Dakota had never come to see the American Cemetery and walk the beaches, and we couldn't help but focus a bit less on each other and more on the events that had occurred here. If you've ever been, you know what I mean. But generally, it was a continuation of the day before—a touring-with-a-friend sort of day.

As evening approached, we drove into Bayeux, a wonderful town nearby with a stunning medieval cathedral. We walked the old part of town and had dinner.

By now, we had gotten to know each other well enough to be able to anticipate the other, like couples normally do. So it was even more apparent that something was off. Moments of awkward silence occurred too often as we walked. For me, the silence was filled with a singular thought swirling in my head—this wasn't working out as planned. I didn't feel toward her the way I thought I would.

My mind raced, looking for reasons why. I was beginning to think it was as simple as the chemistry and connection weren't there, except between the sheets, of course. The fleeting jitters I felt earlier now returned, but this time they stayed.

Back in the room, Dakota put on a full-court press, coming out of the bathroom in her long-talked-about bustier and panties.

"Okay, buster, get to work!" she said, ambling across the bed on her knees.

In short order, I unhooked the zillions of little hooks on the back of her bustier and unwrapped her, just as I had imagined.

While our time between the sheets was as steamy as ever, I made love to her with an awareness that my passion was ebbing and my feelings were changing.

As we turned out the lights to spoon and go to sleep, I thought, *I don't think I can do this anymore.*

Making love makes a statement, as it should. But it was a statement I could no longer back up nor commit to. I'm not good at leading someone on, especially someone I respect and care for. Some guys can put on an act day after day, having sex every night until the rooster crows in the morning, then walk away without a second thought. But I couldn't do that with Dakota.

I began to feel the same guilt I had with Emily when I realized we had no future together. After everything Dakota and I had been through, all we had hoped for, it felt like our greatest fear was coming true, and our exotic-erotic romance had run its course.

The voices of The Boys *and* Abby now spoke in unison.

Okay. We have Sunday, Monday, and Tuesday to go. What are you going to do?

The day before, I experienced a few allergy symptoms—sneezing, sniffles, and itchy eyes. I presumed it was the fall French ragweed. I mentioned this to Dakota the next morning, exaggerating and feigning the possibility of coming down with a cold. It was the only way I could think of, under the circumstances, to start pulling back and take the pressure off having sex every morning and evening.

In Bayeux on Sunday, we went to the museum to see the incredible 230-foot-long Bayeux Tapestry depicting the victorious conquest of the Normans in England.

Losing a war in 1066 AD was pretty lousy, in more ways than one.

We had lunch and visited the British Cemetery in town. But early on, she knew something was up, and I think she correctly suspected the worst.

WE WILL ALWAYS HAVE PARIS

Moments of awkward silence from the day before found their way back. We went into a polite and be-kind-to-each-other mode for the rest of the day.

The drive to the hotel near Mont Saint-Michel was a quiet one. Lovemaking was absent that night as the cold had taken my energy level down a few more notches, or so I said. We went to sleep naked and spooned together, but we were not in sync; we were not one, not tonight. We were two people together but apart.

****

The next day was Monday, our last full day together. The drive to Mont Saint-Michel noticeably lifted our spirits. There was a newness to the day, and a sense of excitement found its way back to us. We shared the thrill of catching our first glimpse of the medieval fortress in the early-morning mist, the assemblage of buildings rising to a point on the island. It was an incredibly special place to visit and to share with Dakota, certainly a better *couple* activity than the solemnity of Normandy.

We excitedly walked through the medieval gate and up the steep and winding main street. We went in and out of the many stores, buying little things here and there—gifts for my sons and Mary. We took side excursions into what seemed like blind passageways, only to learn they led us to new places of discovery.

Over several hours, we made our way to the top of the island. A service was underway in the abbey church, so we went next door to the sun-drenched cloister. There, Dakota took one of the best photographs of the trip: me standing amid a forest of Gothic columns around the edge of the loggia. Then, with no hesitation on her part, we had someone take a wonderful photo of the two of us sitting together in the cloister.

On the way down, we found a place for lunch, a tourist-type place where she tangled with a rude waitress. Dakota was furious and told her off in French.

She was great! We alternated between fuming and scheming how to "stick it to her," laughing the entire time.

I still remember thinking how wonderful and surreal it all felt in that moment. Our spirits had lifted. We were riding high in the warm, autumn sun, on an outdoor terrace, above the sea, together at Mont Saint-Michel.

Then, the feeling of this soon coming to an end washed over us, and we sat in silence. The 3,800 miles that would be separating us this time tomorrow was too sad to think about, let alone talk about. This had been one of the most memorable experiences of my life, experiencing France with this incredible woman. It had been, and still was, as long as I was with her, a time apart from the rest of the world, and I didn't want it to end. The blissful feeling of being with her in the moment was impossible to reconcile with the feeling of not seeing us as a couple going forward.

The conversation turned tender, wistful, and intimate. We began to reminisce about our time together and all that we had done, seen, and felt. Then she brought up the questions that had been hanging in the air seemingly since our first embrace and kiss at the airport. "What now? What next?"

She was waiting for me to say, "When can you visit me?" but it's not what I was thinking or wanting. I knew it would not be the happily-ever-after ending we dreamed and talked about.

For the several-hour drive back to Paris, Dakota was quiet and terribly sad. I reached over many times to squeeze her hand, as I had done on the drive from the airport that first morning. I tried to be reassuring, indicating everything would be okay, but I knew it was of little comfort. Besides, what was I saying would be okay anyway?

We both knew it was *not* going to be okay.

Dinner that night was planned to be the same meal we had during our Skype dinner date a few weeks before. Once we arrived back at her apartment, she silently went to work on dinner. I worked on packing and confirming flight reservations. Dakota set an exquisite and romantic table in front of the large window with a striking view of the Eiffel Tower. It was a gorgeous setting with a bittersweet air.

She spoke first, saying she had no regrets about us before or now and this was the most incredible experience of her life, but she felt so very sad it was coming to an end with an uncertain future. I shared similar sentiments, and we ate more in shared silence than in conversation.

Then a big smile came to her face.

"Okay, Mr. Ballroom Dancer. I haven't seen your moves on the dance floor. Let's go, buster!"

She walked over to her iPhone and put on some music. The sun had gone down, and the Eiffel Tower shone bright and golden in the distance, along with the twinkle of a million city lights. With candlelight illuminating the room, we slowly took each other hand in hand, body to body, and we danced ... and we danced ...

At first, we swing danced to upbeat music. Dakota beamed an incredible smile of delight and laughed as I led her through various moves. It was happy and cheery for a while. But then, in the most ironic and prophetic of twists, the last night in her apartment became the last-night scene from *Out of Africa*.

It was her candlelit room, several stories above the City of Light, instead of an almost-empty plantation house on the remote plains of Africa. While fireflies had blinked in the African night, we had the rapid-fire blinking of the glittering golden lights of the Eiffel Tower at the top of each hour.

The coming morning felt foreboding. We clung to the night and each other.

We were sad, and our hearts were heavy. It was as much about her sadness that I was leaving as it was our collective sadness that this was not ending as we had hoped. It was going to be the same sad ending as had happened in the movie. We slow danced late into the night, our bodies in a perpetual embrace; our arms, hands, and fingers entwined together; and our emotions melting into one another's. Tears were shed, moistening each other's cheeks. We slow danced to the point of not moving anymore but not wanting to let go because if we did, it would be the goodbye we dreaded.

Dakota blew out the candles just after midnight, now Tuesday morning. She left everything as it was, and we went to bed. We spooned naked and tight, holding fast to each other as if our lives depended on it. Both our pillows were moistened with tears, and I felt her body tremble several times as she cried. I felt terrible for feeling like I had failed not only her but me too; I was heartbroken. I had written an ending to this story, but this wasn't it.

The next morning, we put on brave faces to get through what was already a difficult time. Being strong for each other was the mission of the day.

She did the driving through the crazy, early-morning Paris traffic out to Charles de Gaulle Airport. In the post-9/11 era, airport security in Europe— and in Paris, specifically—was insane. I knew the drop-off would be quick, and we had said our long goodbyes the night before.

I hopped out of the car, pulled my luggage out of the back, and we embraced, but found ourselves at a loss for what to say.

She said, "Safe travels back, my darling," and gave me one final hug and kiss.

She quickly hopped back in her car and moved away as the police were blowing their shrill whistles at the crunch of cars. I quickly walked inside and looked back, but she was gone.

The departure area was disorienting and packed with people. I paused for a minute to gather myself in front of a monitor with my flight information. Then, walking around the first roped-off area to head toward security, I thought I heard a woman's voice shouting my name over the din.

"Turner! Turner!"

I wasn't sure if I was hearing my name or if a little voice in my head was playing tricks. Turning around several times, I couldn't pick out anyone in the crowd. But then Dakota was right there beside me on the other side of the rope. She grabbed me, hugged me tightly, then gave me a long kiss.

"I'm going to miss you *so* much," she said with eyes red and tears streaming down her face.

"I'm going to miss you too. But we'll always have this, Dakota … always," I said with a breaking, tearful heart.

She let go and quickly ran back out to her car, where police were already circling warily.

I stood there, wracked with guilt.

Why don't I feel about her the same way she feels about me? I thought. *This just isn't right. I can't do this to someone like her … or anyone else. What an awful person you are, Turner Grant.*

"You're a walking *disaster*, you know that, Grant?" I said out loud.

****

"What happened?!" Abby asked.

I told her about the Finch sign at the airport and pulled it out to show her.

"Oh no!" she said. "That was the first thing you saw?"

"Yeah. It was a real blow. I don't think I ever recovered from it," I said.

"From then on, the chemistry came and went at different times," I went on to explain, "but it went downhill for me. I wondered if it would come back as we got to know each other better or if I could *make* it come back. I felt awful, and I didn't know what to do. I didn't know if I was being dishonest in being there, or what, but I knew I went there with the best of intentions, with hopes for the possibility of an incredible future with an incredible woman, but instead, I broke another person's heart. I feel so awful for doing that. I don't think I can do this dating thing anymore, Abby. If this is what's going to happen, I mean, I can't handle it. I just can't. It's terrible."

Abby listened patiently and quietly as I poured it all out to her.

She knew exactly what to say. "You did nothing wrong. Your intentions were good. You both knew something like this could happen, even if you tried to push it out of your minds. I gotta tell you, if you don't risk heartbreak, you'll never find someone. I'm sorry. I'm really sorry."

A few days later, a letter arrived in the mail from Dakota.

Dearest Turner,

As I write, you have just landed at Dulles Airport, and yet, it feels like only moments ago we embraced with emotion as you departed Charles de Gaulle Airport in deep fog. So many memories rush to me now … It was all perfect, somehow existing out of time, as if we had known each other forever, though we had only just met.

Now you are back in your home, maybe looking at us in the distance through the prism of the immediacy of your life. You are trying to grasp the profound changes taking place as your son has taken flight and some past pain slowly begins to recede. Seismic shifts can only be undertaken with infinitely small steps, listening for inaudible whispers guiding you to the next destination.

Somewhere deep inside me, I understand all of this. I know you are unsure, hesitant, unwilling to go any faster than what feels possible. I respect your deep sense of honor and wanting to proceed with caution. I admire your steadfast commitment to your children and your ability to stay grounded in the face of soul-revealing challenges. I am simply here on the horizon, bringing you heartfelt birthday wishes. May it be a day filled with joy, insouciance, laughter and delight.

Sending you my love,

Dakota XXXXXXOX

Reading these words, my heart broke more and more. But what was about to happen next would positively crush it.

****

I quietly slipped out of Mary's bedroom. It had been a long two weeks, and I was emotionally and physically spent. Her son and granddaughter were now there, and I felt like I could finally step away.

We had said our goodbyes many times in the last two weeks. Over the twenty-five years I had known Mary—but especially during the last four and a half years—I experienced and learned the depths and true meaning of trust, respect, honor, friendship, kindness, and love. Mary was the most amazing and wonderful person I had ever known in my life. She was my rock when my wife took her life, she pushed me to go find life and new love again, supported my walking away from my terrible job, and so much more. She had been the foundation of my life, and I would do anything for her. With all the loving devotion and supportive resolve I could muster, I was there for her every minute during these last weeks. Now, as I left her room, she was only moments away from her last breath on this earth after ninety-two years.

On my return from Paris, I showed Mary every photo and told her everything I had seen and done. As we sat together in her home, she excitedly reminisced upon seeing the places where she and her late husband had also gone during their decades of marriage. Her scrapbooks came out, as did stories of her travels in the France she knew and loved.

Unbeknownst to me, a tin box of cookies I bought for her in Mont Saint-Michel—at Dakota's suggestion—came from the gift shop of the hotel she and her husband had stayed at during their honeymoon. It was a marvelously happy coincidence, and she was excited and touched beyond words. A wistful twinkle came to her eyes, with knowing smiles for memories still close and dear from long, long ago.

Eventually, Mary asked about the divorcee I had gone to meet in Paris. I told her she was a nice woman, a kind and warm host, but that was about all. I found it hard telling her something so very untrue.

"Well, never give up on France. It's my favorite place in the world," she said. "And never give up on travel—it's stupendous, superb, and necessary."

A week after my return from Paris, Mary and I drove in my Mercedes roadster to the foothills of the Blue Ridge Mountains and the remarkable French restaurant, The Inn at Little Washington.

We got to the area a little early, so with time to spare, I headed for the entrance to Skyline Drive. We drove top-down through the Blue Ridge Mountains on what was becoming a chilly night. Imagine a ninety-two-year-old woman, full of life, riding in a sports car with the top down on a late fall afternoon, with a long scarf tied over her head, whooping and hollering as we zipped through the tight and twisting turns up the mountainside.

"Mary, you're having way too much fun! People are looking at us!" I shouted.

In fact, a few cars honked at us. I figured it was either because I was driving too fast or because they loved the wonderful sight of a great-grandmother zooming along in a sports car with her scarf blowing in the wind, grinning ear to ear.

Our drive that day summed up the joy she brought to me and always sought out in life. It is an indelible memory of her I will never forget.

Five days later, Mary's health went into a precipitous decline. A week after that, she was mostly unconscious and lay in her bed for six days.

I sat in the room with her from early in the morning to mid-afternoon that last day. I was told that even though she couldn't respond, she could hear me. I told her that all was as she had wished, that she had done it her way, in her own home, that I loved her dearly, and I would miss her so very much. I said she was a treasure in my life and my heart.

With the arrival of her son and granddaughter, I handed the last hour of the vigil over to them. My job as her rock was done.

****

Dakota had kept in constant contact during those weeks, supporting me with Mary, even as we dealt with the difficult subject of *us*. We exchanged numerous painful voicemail messages on WhatsApp.

"I don't understand ..."

"Please tell me ... why?"

"If that's the way you feel ..."

"Let's try again, Turner ..."

"Let's see someone to work out whatever it is. Anything worth having is worth fighting for ..."

"I've never had the love that we had ..."

"My heart is broken into a zillion little pieces ..." she said with such heartbreaking emotion.

I still have the voice messages we exchanged, and I listened to them again during the writing of this book. They are raw, anguished, and painful.

I finally told her I couldn't handle this right now and to please give me time and space to deal with Mary's care and say my goodbyes.

In her last voice message on WhatsApp—two weeks after my return and a week before Mary's passing—she tried to soothe my grief in her incredible caring way and begin to turn the page on us.

"Good morning, Turner, in several more hours. It's about eight o'clock here. Just wrapping things up and getting ready to go to the office. I have been ... thinking about you ... so often ... and ... just kind of living this thing with Mary in real-time, if that is possible from this far away. A myriad of emotions come to me, and I'm guessing you and I might have some of the same emotions ... so ...

"I— I do— I do— I don't know what to say. ... I do feel for you and support you deeply. I admire the fact that you called in someone to speak to about all this. It makes perfect sense to me—it makes me very sad—but it makes perfect sense to me that this event with Mary is making you, at a deep level, making you unconsciously, subconsciously relive things you experienced with the loss of your wife not five years ago. I'm so, so sorry, but I think it's wonderful that you called someone in. It's yet another testament to how grounded you are and your ability to ... to ... face what I've written in my letter, soul—what did I write?—soul-stirring challenges ... or something like that ...

"I have a nice little metaphor. I'm looking out my living room window at Paris, the Eiffel Tower, and as I finished my coffee, there were these unbelievably dark and menacing gray clouds, and it sort of made me laugh, and I said, 'Oh my gosh, can there be a more menacing sky this morning? This is unbelievable.'

"And then I turned and did something else, and a few minutes later I came back, and there were these tiny slivers of pink coming through. I'm looking at them now, they're coming through everywhere.

"You're in a very very difficult place, and it's not over yet, but there are slivers of pink on the horizon … and that's you … and in my life, that's me, and that's—that's life, and that's what's next … and you'll get through this, I have no doubt about that.

"And I'm here, and you can call me … whenever you like. There's no rush. Okay. I'm thinking of you. Bye."

****

Dakota decided not to take the job offer from her company in Washington.

"I love Paris too much to leave," she said.

We were able to reconcile as friends over the ensuing months. She said she would always remember and treasure what we had and our time together in Paris, and I told her I would as well.

We were able to genuinely support each other in life and love over the next couple of years. After all, we knew each other more deeply and intimately than two friends ever could. To be there for each other, after all we had been through, was a testament to Dakota and the incredible person she is.

About a year after our time together, I happened to pass through Paris on my way home from a vacation in Greece and Turkey. While waiting at Charles de Gaulle Airport for my connecting flight, we exchanged several emails.

EMAIL RECEIVED: Catching You on the Backside

Hi Turner,

What great pictures and so glad you had a wonderful time!

I believe the third picture was taken at Ephesus, yes? It's so special that you felt it was the trip of a lifetime, and you made some new lasting friendships.

I thought at one point I would write to share some news with you, so it's uncanny that you wrote me passing through the City of Light.

I went back online last summer, on a lark, to show my cousin in Illinois how it works, and then a man wrote to me, and we started an extraordinarily deep correspondence … then he flew to Paris to meet me (sound familiar?!), and now it's all systems go. Charles is Scottish, so our commute is not so long distance and much more doable than ahem … across the Atlantic. We've connected on myriad levels, and I really think this is it. As of June next year, I will be free to move to Brussels where he will be.

Charles contacted me first. The funny thing is my line about "fabulous prose, flawless grammar and fitting metaphors, as well as having in your closet and feeling at ease in a tux will give you bonus points" was what actually compelled him to write to me, whereas I thought it might be eliminating too many men—you liked it too, I believe, so my point is: never be less than you are. :-)

Warm regards,

Dakota

CHAPTER 17

Enigma – Part II

THREE MONTHS HAD PASSED SINCE I'd said goodbye to Ava. Seven weeks after our awkward parting, I had flown to Paris to meet Dakota. During the entire time, for whatever reason, Ava and I remained Facebook friends.

In mid-August and early September, I posted trip photos as I took my son to start his college career, then others from my time in New England with son number two. She had several unremarkable posts, except for one in September—it looked like she was at an extravagant party.

Among the photos was one with a vintage Rolls-Royce parked in front of a spectacular house. Another was of an elegant, sequined-dressed woman hanging from a chandelier in the middle of a large white tent. It looked like she was swinging back and forth and pouring—splashing—champagne down into the glasses of the fashionably dressed party crowd below. It was outrageously decadent, so I sent a brief Facebook comment of Wow!

I was surprised when Ava responded in a separate long text.

She described a friend—a rich friend who made his money doing such and such—who decided to throw a Great Gatsby party just for fun. It was one hell of a party and clearly a world apart from what I knew. But she made it sound like it was just another weekend party with clients and friends ... before she was off to London and Italy.

She ended her text with a perfunctory "Hope you are well."

I didn't respond.

Later in September and early October, I posted a few photos of my Paris trip and my birthday dinner with Mary at The Inn at Little Washington. From then on, I was silent until, with the heaviest of hearts, I posted a remembrance and tribute to Mary at the end of October.

I was adrift once again.

My children were both gone, and the house was far too empty. With the heartache from Dakota and the devastating loss of Mary, I was back to the familiar, one-foot-in-front-of-the-other method of getting through each day, the same as I had done after my wife's passing.

Ava knew from our many conversations about family how important Mary was in my life, and she sent a thoughtful email in late October.

EMAIL RECEIVED: (no subject)

> Dear Turner,
>
> I saw your post on FB and just wanted to express my condolences. I am so very sorry.
>
> From all of our conversations, I could tell Mary was not just a mother-in-law, but your best friend, confidante, and guru wrapped into one. I know she is continuing to watch over you and the children from above.
>
> This certainly has been a challenging year for you on many levels. Change is hard but also brings new growth. Hopefully one full of great joy and creativity in whatever and wherever your heart leads you.
>
> Keeping you in my thoughts and prayers.
>
> Warm hugs, Ava

EMAIL SENT: (no subject)

> Ava,
>
> Thank you so much for writing. We knew this was coming, but still … I'm so numb at this point I hardly know how to react.

Sometime and somewhere, maybe we can have a glass of wine. But right now, I think I still need time.

A hug back to you. Take care.

Turner

EMAIL RECEIVED: (no subject)

No worries, Turner. Just try to stay positive. Trust me when I tell you there is a silver lining to everything, and I mean everything. Shall share when and if.

Peace and blessings –A

She followed up a few days later with several more chatty emails, seemingly trying to strike up a correspondence. I took them as nothing more than thoughtful kindness for the tough times I was going through. It was nice, and I appreciated her reaching out, but I kept my responses polite and brief, trying not to engage too much. I just wasn't up for it, especially after having come home from a weeklong trip to Massachusetts, where I had fought a few more battles on behalf of my son.

EMAIL RECEIVED: Special Needs Law

FYI—Garrison Florence was just on the news. He practices throughout Virginia on special needs law and has written a book on the topic. Maybe you should connect with him.

Ava

EMAIL SENT: Special Needs Law

Thanks for the thought, but I finally won for my son by NOT using a lawyer. As I mentioned before, they have difficulty thinking outside the box and their egos know no bounds.

Just glad to be home, so much to deal with at the moment. Can't imagine trying to do all of this and work at the same time. When and where is your next trip to?

Turner

EMAIL RECEIVED: Special Needs Law

Just got back from Los Angeles and San Francisco for a week. A friend just built a gorgeous state-of-the-art house near L.A. I also lived there for a while, so I go out a couple of times a year to see friends.

Am in NYC 'til Wednesday. It's the height of the season, so busy with business and charity benefits I have to attend. Then shall be home 'til I head down to Palm Beach in December.

EMAIL SENT: Special Needs Law

In days gone by, you would be called a "jet-setter." Happy trails and stick to the warmer climates for sure.

All the best, Turner

I thought my "happy trails" and "all the best" comments would be taken as intended, an end to our correspondence.

The Boys were suspicious. *Why is she writing to you all of a sudden? What's she up to?*

EMAIL RECEIVED: Special Needs Law

> Haha, most of my trips are work-oriented, and I'm blessed I can squeeze in seeing family and those I consider family on my travels.
>
> Hope things have somewhat calmed down for you.
>
> Without this being awkward, a close friend of mine was going to go with me to a gala at the Museum of Fine Arts. It is a very big deal and I'm hosting a table for friends and clients. Anyway, he now has to go to London for business and will not make it back for the gala on the 22nd. Perhaps you might enjoy going as my escort? Just let me know. Promise lots of incredible food, great dancing, and wonderful company.
>
> Either way, happy to catch up sometime in DC and be a neutral sounding board if you need an ear and/or shoulder.
>
> Smiles,
>
> Ava

Say what?! said The Boys.

No kidding! I thought.

I had suspended my OkCupid account a few days into my correspondence with Dakota in late August, but I reactivated it so I could look at Ava's profile again.

I bounced between curiosity—*why in the world would she possibly want to see me again*—to not wanting to do anything social right now. Mary's memorial dinner was scheduled for Thanksgiving weekend, and I was in charge of the planning. Fun with Miss Grind-a-crotch-then-show-you-the-door was not on my agenda.

As I went back and forth, I remembered my conversation with Mary more than two years before.

"I think I need to get the burden of the past off my shoulders and move on. I just can't carry it with me anymore ..."

I didn't have a clue where I should be moving on to and had zero interest in doing anything dating-wise, but I thought my own advice to get out and do *something* might not be a bad thing. The Boys shared their thoughts on the matter too.

Okay, life really sucks right now. Can't we go and do something fun for a change? asked Darrell.

I don't like it, said Charles. *Be careful. She's a schemer.*

Little Turner spoke up and sided with Darrell. *I agree; it might be fun, and we could use a little bit of that right now.*

EMAIL SENT: Special Needs Law

> Ava,
>
> That's a thoughtful and wonderful invitation, and it might be a very nice diversion that weekend.
>
> Would be very nice to see you and would enjoy the chance to dance. For me, dancing can help cure what ails you, and to be in your environment with you would be quite special.
>
> A smile back to you and thank you,
>
> Turner

****

Saturday-night traffic to Richmond was positively awful. I left thirty minutes early for the drive down but arrived at Ava's home almost thirty minutes late. Instead of being annoyed as I had supposed she might be, she was pleasant and cordial when she came to the door, and we exchanged a polite hug.

She looked *stunning*.

Totally.

She wore a strapless, full-length vintage gown—held up in eye-catching suspension by her generously sized breasts—with matching gloves up past her elbows. A fashionably draped wrap covered her bare shoulders. The ensemble was highlighted and finished off with superbly elegant dangling diamond earrings.

This woman could work a wardrobe like no other, and I admired every bit of her style.

As I was late, she was ready to go, and we immediately went to the car. She was happy to see I had driven the Mercedes for the occasion.

The conversation was simple and friendly as we drove to the museum, but it felt so weird given how we'd parted three months before.

Why were we invited to this? The Boys asked over and over. They were now of one mind with Charles: skeptical and wary.

The best read I could get was that this was a gesture of simple kindness, a well-considered diversion she wanted to give me from the grief of Mary's loss. An escort-only role at an elegant, black-tie gala seemed to be the gist of the evening, which was fine by me. No pressure, no worries, but the nagging question of *why* never left my mind.

Driving into the packed parking lot, she directed me to an area reserved for special museum patrons, and I pulled in beside a Bentley. The couple inside got out just as I was opening the door for Ava to rise out.

And rise out she did.

This woman, with the subtlest of gestures and movements, knew how to make an entrance just getting out of a car.

The Boys admired her in silence, as did I.

The couple next to us instantly called out, "Ava!"

Ava smiled, took my arm, and led me over for introductions.

They were an older couple, but clearly well known to Ava. After a few pleasantries, there was some chitchat about needing to return an email to set up a meeting.

We walked into the entrance of what looked like a new, contemporary museum addition to find the cocktail reception well underway. Ava narrated the history of the museum and prepped me about the friends and clients I would be meeting. As usual, I had no idea who they were, but she quickly summarized what they did and how they made their money.

The museum was impressively staged for the gala evening. An eight-piece ensemble from the Richmond Symphony Orchestra serenaded guests with classical music in the grand entrance hall. Dining tables were set up throughout the galleries, highly unusual since the chance of damage to the art from food, drinks, people, and utensils was high. Meandering through, we made our way to the atrium, where music and dancing would be held later on.

Given our late arrival, we only had time for a quick walk-through before being seated for dinner. I was introduced to the couples around the table who all knew Ava and each other. Given I was the new kid on the block, curiosity was high as to who I was, and the questions started immediately.

"So, Turner, what do you do?" a woman asked.

I finished the unspoken part of her question in my mind. *And how much money do you have?*

And off into the evening we went.

Conversation flowed easily. Ava's friends were gregarious and interesting, and they shared great stories. I picked up the evening's program and scanned the list of donors. Donations ranged from $1,000 to $250,000, and I saw a few of their names listed under the five-figure amounts. I knew Ava had donated, but her name wasn't there. She was nothing if not consistent in the protection of her privacy, and I was left trying to guess which high-dollar anonymous donor she was.

About halfway through dinner, a couple to my left mentioned a family member who was disabled. That led to a discussion about my son, typically not a topic of party conversation. I shared some rather difficult details and a few stories about the battles my wife and I had fought. I explained one particular battle ten years earlier with my local school district and then my congressman, which had led to my run for Congress.

The couple and Ava were seemingly riveted by my stories, but I found myself getting a bit emotional. I realized I had probably gotten a little too deep for such a festive occasion—and with strangers to boot. I reached over to Ava under the table to find her hand. I wanted to give it a quick squeeze as a way of apologizing, to make sure I was okay having gone down this path of profoundly personal conversation, and to signal I was done talking about it.

To my surprise, she eagerly took my hand in both of hers, caressed it with tenderness, pulled it tight to her lap, and didn't let go. Her reaction was more than a gesture; it seemed to be a sign of genuine affection.

I looked over at her. She looked back at me.

I was *not* her escort anymore.

Okay ... NOW what just happened? asked Darrell.

After a delightful dinner, we walked to the atrium where music was playing and people were dancing. It was more rock and current hits, not much for dancing, really, plus it was too loud for conversation. We walked back through the galleries to an out-of-the-way spot where we could talk in private.

"I'm very sorry about Mary," she said. "I know how much she meant to you. Can I ask what happened?"

Thinking we might have this conversation, I brought a copy of a goodbye letter Mary had written to family and friends, and I let Ava read it. It wistfully reminisced about life and family. She expressed pride in her many accomplishments, offered wisdom from a life well-lived, was at peace with what was to come, and left us all with her eternal love.

As I continued to share the details, tears came to my eyes. Looking at me with sorrow and understanding, Ava kissed my cheek, then offered a hug of support, holding me tight for almost a minute as my tears continued, then finally began to dry.

Then, somewhere in the moment, her hug became something else. She parted her legs so that mine slid between hers.

I immediately pulled back, let her go, and let it rip.

"Okay! Wait a minute! *Why* did you invite me here tonight after what happened this summer?! And, oh yeah … what the *hell* happened this summer when you *dumped* me?!" I asked angrily.

With a look of guilt and remorse, she looked down at the floor, reached for my hand, pulled it to her, then looked back up.

"I thought—I thought when you said you were going away to do all those things with your boys that it was … that it was really just an excuse to see other women."

"What?!!!" I shouted in astonishment.

She looked over to where people were standing to see if they had heard me. She then reached out for both my hands and gripped them in hers.

She said, with apology rippling through her body, "I thought you wanted to go out with other women and that was a convenient excuse."

Standing there with my hands in hers, I turned my head and looked away in total disbelief.

"An excuse to see other women?" I whispered, shaking my head. "Wow, you really thought a lot of me, didn't you?"

"I'm sorry, Turner. I've been hurt so many times. It's what I thought. But I saw your Facebook posts. You did everything you said you were going to be doing, and I knew I was wrong. When I saw Mary had died, I felt even worse. Then I thought maybe I could reach out to you."

I now looked at her with a sense of sorrow.

"Boy, you *have* been hurt. *I'm* the one who's sorry," I said gently, "for *you*."

I didn't know what to do, so I gave her the heartfelt hug she deserved.

"I thought you were dumping me because of my parenting responsibilities and it *really* pissed me off," I said, recalling the anger I felt in August. "Family always comes first, Ava. I won't apologize for that … ever."

"And you shouldn't ever apologize for that. It's what makes you so different from every other man I've ever met."

While still in our embrace, she tilted her head back from mine, looked into my eyes, then kissed me with her lunging tongue I remembered from before. We went at it for a few seconds before pulling back to see who might be watching.

I put my hands on her hips and pulled her tight.

"I could straddle you right here," she said, lunging in for another kiss. She pushed her breast into my chest and shimmied her body.

Needing a breath, I asked, "Are we done here?"

Catching her breath, she said, "Yes, but we need to say goodbye to a few people and pick up our swag bags. They have some good stuff."

We left our out-of-the-way corner and went back to the milling partygoers. Ava found a few people needing personal goodbyes and air kisses, then we walked back to the grand entrance hall. Walking out the doors we had come in four hours earlier was a decidedly different experience. We couldn't get out fast enough.

In the car, we kissed, and my hands made a beeline for the top of her strapless dress.

"We'll be home in ten minutes," she said. "Let's just go!"

We walked into her house, and she led me toward the sofa. I sat down; she kicked off her shoes, hiked up her long dress, and mounted herself on my lap as she had done three months before, both here and on the park bench a few blocks away. Down came the zipper on her dress, and out came her breasts.

"Okay, this isn't fair. This tux needs to come off," she said after a few minutes.

She then led me to the stairs and up to the bedroom.

The lights were out—as I knew she preferred—and we fell on the bed, still partially clothed but barely. After a few minutes of wrangling each other in the sheets, she paused.

"So, what do you want to do tonight?" she asked. "Do you want to stay here or go home?"

"I think I know what I want to do, but what do you want me to do?"

"It's up to you," she said.

Okay, stop it you two! The Boys shouted. *Stay already, you dumbnut!*

"To be honest," I said. "I'd like to stay here tonight with you if that's okay. I want to be with you."

"I was hoping you'd say that."

The rest of our clothes were off in short order, the sheets were pulled back, and nothing could have been better. I was fine with whatever she wanted to do—or didn't.

"What are you waiting for?" she said after a few moments of silence.

After two hours of making love, we finally fell asleep. But sometime in the middle of the night, I had a dream someone was kissing me. It was four in the morning, and I awoke to find Ava naked and on top of me, in full tongue-lunging mode.

"Oh, hi, ehh … you okay?" I said, barely awake.

"I couldn't sleep. I thought you might be awake too.

"Well, I am now," I said.

She then tightened her grip, wrapping her arms and legs around me. "If you want it, just go for it," she said.

****

When morning came, last night felt like, well, so last night.

That was then, and this was now.

We lingered in bed but just a little. Ava said she was glad we reconnected and that last night was fun. She was affectionate, but only subtly so, with minor gestures and few words.

She said she had some work to do that Sunday, implying I needed to get a move on so she could get on with her day. She offered to get my gym bag with clothes from the car trunk. At least I could leave in something other than wrinkled and disheveled black tie. She offered tea after my shower but no breakfast.

Okay. What now?

The hour and a half drive between us negated any thoughts of getting together soon. Thanksgiving was only a few days away, and we would both be busy.

"Let's get together after Thanksgiving," she said as I prepared to leave. "But let's talk before then."

She gave me a simple kiss, then lifted the veil from her gotta-get-to-work demeanor for an instant. She laid a full-body, leg-up, crotch-grinding kiss on me, then, seemingly without a thought, turned away and closed the front door.

Odd, I thought. *So odd.*

But a hell of a fun night! The Boys piped in. *Don't even think twice about it. You needed that, pal.*

****

Ava drove up to see me in northern Virginia the first Saturday in December. We had talked about her coming up so she could get to know me better and see my world. Entering my house, she seemed genuinely impressed by the mix of midcentury modern furniture and art.

"Wow! You've put together some great things. I just love it!" Coming from her, that was high praise.

In my bedroom, she admired the material on the bed and the drapes, running her hand gently over them. "This is *gorgeous!*" she said.

Walking back to the living room, she looked at each piece, much like what I had done in her home four months before.

"I received more classic modern furniture from my mother-in-law and put it in a new storage unit in town. It's not your warehouse full of stuff, but it's some nice things she wanted me to have."

"Can you take me there?" she asked.

"My storage unit?"

"Yeah. I'd like to see it, if that's all right?"

"Okay, but that's not where I planned on this date going," I said.

We drove to the storage building; she was the first person other than my brother-in-law to come here since everything had been put in a month before. Ava was crossing into a more emotional and raw part of my life.

After a run-through of everything, we left and had lunch. Afterward, I drove her around town and then into the surrounding neighborhoods. I showed her the old Kennedy house, along with a few other notable, high-profile homes of famous figures past and present.

"Let's go back to your house," she said around four.

I knew she had to leave around four thirty, so I wasn't sure what she had in mind, but I found out quickly enough after closing the front door.

"Let's go to the bedroom and have sex."

"But we only have twenty minutes before you have to hit the road," I said. This was new to me. Every other woman I had experience with wanted or needed a ton of foreplay before sex. They made it clear I wasn't making it good for them if we didn't.

We quickly walked back to the still-fully-lit bedroom. Ava carefully pulled off the bedspread with the "gorgeous" fabric, jumped on, and gave me the get-on-here look.

We undressed each other and were done in all of ten minutes.

"See. I won't be late getting back," she said, looking over at the clock with a grin on her face.

****

The next day, we talked on the phone and went over December calendars to see when we might be able to get together.

"I want to cook for you," she said.

Now any guy knows those are serious coupling words, and I was fairly pleased to hear them from Ava. She asked about what foods I liked but also let me know the things she liked to cook. Her taste in food was no less than her taste in everything else—refined, detailed, and discriminating.

After our dinner plans were set for Sunday evening, she went on. "I know you have the boys home for Christmas, and I don't know what sort of flexibility you have, but I wanted to ask if you might be able to accompany me to a friend's wedding on the twentieth."

"A wedding?"

"Yeah, in Zurich."

"In Zurich? Switzerland?"

"Yeah," she said. "I don't know if I'm going to go, but I would if you could. I want to dance with you."

"Okay-y-y-y. Dancing would be nice, and a wedding in Zurich at Christmas sounds pretty magical. But daddy-duty begins then as the boys start coming home. I'm sorry."

"No worries," she said. "Just thought I'd ask."

That's quite an ask, I thought.

The week went by with several nice phone calls. When Sunday afternoon arrived, she texted to ask if it would be okay if she took me out for dinner instead of us eating in. Work had been busy, and she hadn't been able to grocery shop.

I told her that was perfectly fine.

She wanted to take me to a great Indian place nearby where, of course, she knew the chef and the owner. She told me to bring a jacket since it was a fairly nice place.

I arrived at her home to find Ava nicely dressed in an expensive-looking blouse under a black leather vest, wool slacks, and elegant flats, all set off with sparkles of diamonds here and there. We had a little "sofa time" before walking over to a high-end condo building nearby. It was one of several elegant, high-rise, prewar residential buildings in the area. The restaurant was on the ground floor and identified by a small, discreet sign; it was a place you had to know was there. It was superbly elegant in its old-world charm, clearly a few levels above "I want to cook dinner for you."

Ava made menu suggestions in consultation with the waiter, and a dinner of curated appetizers was marvelous from beginning to end.

She's putting on her A-game for you, The Boys remarked.

After a wonderful dinner, the check arrived. The waiter discreetly placed the leather check holder on the table. Given this was at Ava's invitation, I assumed she'd be picking up the tab. But she went silent, froze, and gave me a what-are-you-waiting-for look. After an uncomfortable few seconds, I reached for the check, and she unfroze.

The bill for our little Sunday-night dinner of appetizers was $180.

Did I have a right to be annoyed? I thought so. It also made me wonder about my ability to keep up with her financially. I wondered if I had said yes to the wedding in Zurich, how much of the expense would've been put onto me.

After a little more sofa time, the generally nice evening ended, and I drove the ninety minutes back home. But I couldn't get the check thing off my mind.

The next week, she let me know she was coming to Washington to go to a concert with friends. I had a meeting and couldn't join her, but she texted from the concert.

> **AVA:** The music is wonderful. Makes me think of you. If you were here, I'd take you to the bathroom and lock the door. Just thought you'd like to know how much I'm thinking of you right now and what I'm thinking about ;-)

A couple of days after Christmas, she offered to come up my way again, this time for dinner on a Saturday evening. We went to the club for a casual dinner since my kids were out with family. Somehow, we got on the subject of life in general, and I talked about all the changes in my life since my wife's passing.

After listening for some time, she casually said, "I know what you mean."

"You mean from losing your father?"

"No … my husband."

Now it was my turn to stop cold and go Mount Rushmore.

The subject of prior marriages, divorce, or anything in her background had never been discussed. It seemed to be off-limits, and I had let it go. She hadn't mentioned having any children, so I assumed a short marriage was somewhere in her past that ended in divorce, and that was the extent of it.

"You were married, and you had a husband who died?" I asked incredulously.

"Yes."

"Oh my gosh, I'm so sorry. I didn't know … you never said … you never told me."

"No, it's like I've said. It takes me a long time to trust and share about myself."

"But don't you think … don't you think I would've wanted to know given my situation? I mean, really, how could you have not told me?" I was surprised, hurt, and now aware of how far at arm's length I was being kept.

"But I *am* trusting you now and telling you things. It takes me time," she repeated.

"Can I ask how he died?"

"In a chain-reaction car crash."

"Were you in the crash too?"

"No."

"How long ago was this?"

"About twenty-five years ago."

"Oh my gosh, Ava! I'm so sorry. I wish I'd known."

"It's okay," she said.

"So … wow! You were married. Did you ever marry again?"

"No. I lived with a guy for a few years but never married again."

It was like she had turned on a fire hose of information for a few seconds and aimed it right at my face. It was a lot to take in, but oddly, she said it without any emotion. The fact she hadn't told me, either back in the summer or during the past month, made me wonder.

Charles didn't hesitate to offer his opinion: *She seems like one cold-hearted woman to me.*

We went back to my house to get her car. I wasn't able to have her stay over since my sons would be back shortly, but she asked if she could come inside briefly to say goodbye.

After kissing in the foyer, she said, "I want a quickie before I go."

"A quickie?"

"Yes. A quickie," she repeated.

"O-o-o-kay, a quickie. Any preference where?"

"Well, here would be good," she said, grabbing my hand and pulling it to her crotch.

We went downstairs to the guest bedroom and repeated the previous quickie process from several weeks ago.

"Thank you," she said. "You're good for any time. My on-call man. My one-man swat team!"

Darrell was relentless after that. *Hey, on-call man, somebody be needin' some swat?!* He roared with laughter.

****

Ava and I made plans to be together on New Year's Eve. Since I had daddy-duty, she was coming to my house to meet and have dinner with my sons—a big deal. She would stay the night in the guest bedroom since the boys would be upstairs with me.

But two days before New Year's, she called on a Monday morning, an unusual time to hear from her.

"I really need to talk to you about something."

"Okay. Is everything all right?" I asked.

"Well, I don't know. I don't know what to think."

"About what?" I said, concerned.

"One of my girlfriends said she saw your profile on OkCupid. Are you dating other women?"

That came out of nowhere, and momentarily, I felt like a deer in the headlights.

"Ah, well, I'm on OkCupid. We both are, you know that," I said.

"No, I'm not on OkCupid. I turned off my account."

"Oh. Okay. I didn't know that."

"Are you seeing other women?" she demanded to know.

"No!"

"Then why are you on OkCupid if you're not seeing other women or wanting to see other women?"

I paused to take all this in and catch up with what she was asking, saying, and accusing me of. Then I loaded up.

"I turned off OkCupid after we met back in June, then turned it back on in August after you *dumped* me for no reason. As I got busy with my sons and before I went to Paris, I turned it off again. Then Mary fell ill, and I had nothing to do with it, dating or anything. Then, out of the blue, *you* contacted me— three months after *dumping* me—and asked *me* out, so I turned OkCupid *back* on to see your profile and look at you again. I never bothered to turn it back off, I guess. I just didn't think about it."

"Okay," she said grudgingly. "I guess that makes sense."

"But damn it, I'm pissed! I mean, you never even told me you were married, let alone that your husband died, because you can't trust me? How am I supposed to trust you? You can drop me like a sack of potatoes because of some *nonsense* you cook up in your crazy head, that I'm making excuses to get away from you to see other women and using my *kids* as the *excuse!* And now I get *this?!* This crap?! Just because I turned that damn thing back on to see who you were again!"

The next words to come out of my mouth were loaded and ready to go. I was ready to tell her to forget about New Year's Eve or *anything else* for that matter!

But she spoke first. "You're right. I'm sorry. I'm sorry, really."

I sat in silence, stewing away with the phone to my ear, but I didn't know what to say or which way to go on this.

Maybe we should just call it, whatever this is, I thought.

But before I could decide what to say, she spoke. "I look forward to seeing you on New Year's Eve and meeting your boys. I know it's a big deal, and it tells me how important I am to you. I know you've done that with only one other woman, the one you were with for a year. This is *really* special, and I can't wait to see you, Turner."

"Okay, thanks for that," I said. "And yes, I look forward to seeing you too."

****

I prepped my sons about Ava and her coming over for dinner. My college son had little interest. He was more focused on the New Year's Eve party he would be going to with friends after dinner. My other son was curious, but in a who's-coming-to-dinner sort of way, not with any curiosity about who this new woman was in Dad's life.

I made their favorite dinner—chicken pesto pasta with veggies on the side. It was certainly a bit strange, the four of us sitting around the table. I didn't know how well she'd do with children since she had none of her own. She was pretty cool with them, but experienced parents have a certain way with kids. It's a thing you can see, and she didn't have it.

After cleaning up in the kitchen, my college son left for his party. My other son went to his room upstairs and closed his door, generally preferring to have privacy in the evenings. Ava and I went downstairs and settled into the sofa to watch a movie until the ball dropped in Times Square. Squirming a bit, she nestled cozily and nicely into my arms.

Around nine thirty, she looked up. "I want a quickie!"

"Another quickie?"

"I think I'm going to be too tired by midnight to want to do anything, so I want a quickie right now. Then we can come back and finish watching the movie."

"Ahhhh, well, we'll have to do it in the guest bedroom again, and we'll have to be quiet about it."

"No problem. Let's go!" she said and bolted off the sofa.

Fifteen minutes later, we were back on the sofa, watching the movie.

Eventually, midnight came, the ball dropped in Times Square, we kissed, and we waited for my college son to arrive back home safely. Once he did, I joined Ava in the guest bedroom. She was the opposite of "too tired to do anything," and we tore up the sheets until two in the morning.

****

On January second, I was doing my up-and-back routine to Boston, returning my son to his school. His ride came to the airport on time, I had dinner at my usual Logan Airport restaurant, and everything seemed to be routine.

Then snow and sleet began to fall.

Takeoff was delayed twice, and we began a second hour of sitting on the plane at the gate. It was full of people going home from the holidays on this Saturday night, so crying babies, fidgety kids, and already exasperated parents filled every seat. My usual savvy travel planning had failed me, and my long legs were folded into the cramped confines of the window seat instead of sticking out from an aisle seat.

I had been thinking about Ava a lot since our last night together, not in a fond way but in a what-is-her-deal kind of way. I mostly enjoyed my time with her, but there were big holes and unknowns that weren't being filled in or making any sense.

Looking out the window for an hour, I remembered that it had been the first Saturday night in January some twenty-six years before when I met my wife-to-be on the ballroom dance floor here in Boston. It was a cold, snowy, sleety night just like tonight. And it was the first Saturday in January two years later when we were married at the Washington National Cathedral on a cold night, like tonight, with light snow falling.

With all the memories flowing as I looked out the window, I was overcome with emotion. My heart ached for her, for what we had, and for what I had lost. I became almost panicky with emotion, something I hadn't felt in a long time.

I pulled out my iPhone and went to the photos of our wedding night. My heart became heavier still, and my eyes moistened with tears.

I logged on to my Facebook page to write a tribute and remembrance to her. I desperately needed to share the memories of her and feel the support of family and friends.

With two photos from our wedding—one of us walking down the aisle of the Cathedral and another of me spinning her on the dance floor—I wrote:

> Twenty-six years ago today, we met on the ballroom dance floor in Boston. Twenty-four years ago tonight, we wed at the National Cathedral and danced the night away at the Anderson House. Five years ago this year, we lost her. If you only have 'one' in your life, you're lucky. So count me as one very lucky guy.

When I hit the button to post, the flashbacks and raw emotions evaporated, and I became calm. It was an amazing thing to experience because it happened so fast.

I had passing thoughts about Ava seeing it and knew she wouldn't like it. I even thought she might dump me again because of it, but I didn't care. I was no longer interested in being the scratch pole for her pussy cat, if that was all I was to her. I realized in this hour of memories, emotions, and tears that what my wife and I had—the love, the devotion, the *for better, for worse, for richer, for poorer, in sickness and in health, until death do us part*—wasn't possible with Ava.

The next morning, I sent Ava a message, telling her I had hit a rough patch of emotions the night before on the plane and posted a remembrance to my late wife on Facebook. There was no message from her that day, nor the next day, the day after that, or ever again. A few weeks later, I unfriended her on Facebook and sent her a final email explaining what happened on the plane, as well as a few parting words.

EMAIL SENT: Lastly

My parting thought to you is to show yourself to whoever you may meet in life and think you may care for. A mystery woman is like the dark room you prefer. It's rather difficult to see and understand who you are. It may work for some, but for someone like me, for whom the connection and sharing of hearts are paramount, it does not work well (admittedly, guys like me may be few and far between).

You are a wonderful woman, and I'm very glad to have met you. Good luck to you in life and love.

Turner

CHAPTER 18

I Can Be a Very Generous Woman

A FEW DAYS INTO THE New Year, I felt emotionally spent and physically exhausted. Thinking about the year that had just ended, I realized it was one for the books.

I had left behind my job and career, one of my children had left behind his adolescence and home to start college, I became an empty nester, and I said goodbye to my best friend and mother-in-law. It had been four years and seven months since the passing of my wife and two years and seven months since I arrived on Venus. In the past twelve months, I had met twelve women, broken up with three—including one twice—and had flown across an ocean, hoping to find love with a truly amazing woman—only to find it wasn't there. I was no closer to finding my future than I had been at the beginning of all this.

I decided I needed some big-time rest and a major reboot. I booked a week of the Life Enhancement Program at Canyon Ranch in Tucson, Arizona, in February. I needed to improve my physical and mental health; I wanted to improve my diet and begin turning whatever pages needed to be turned to move forward. Knowing I had all this planned allowed me to more calmly and deliberately look at things in the here and now—most notably, dating.

The urgency I felt when I first blasted off for Venus was gone, but my interest in possibly meeting someone was not. So, having declared my need for major rest and a reboot, I did the most counterintuitive thing possible—I tripled down on online dating.

After meeting Emily eighteen months before, I had abandoned eHarmony. Now I decided to try it one last time. I also kept up with OkCupid and explored the newer dating app Tinder. It would be one, final, colossal effort.

One, final, colossal, bonehead disaster in the making, was the opinion of The Boys.

Please leave us out of it, they begged.

With all I had been through on Venus, I decided to set my sights on finding someone who was also widowed. I reasoned that finding someone with the same filters in life as mine, that is, the ones I acquired when I lost my wife, might make for better compatibility. It also meant one less thing to deal with, as in the "ghost of wife past" that Emily complained about in our breakup emails.

Navigating and sorting through women on three dating apps was not particularly difficult, but as I've said before, it was incredibly time-consuming. I can't overstate this enough—time gets sucked out of your life when you're on these dating sites.

****

Christine popped up on my screen in mid-January. Many of the must-have boxes were quickly checked off as I read through her profile. Photos showed her in exotic locations around the world, and her appearance was stylish and sophisticated. She had an intangible quality that was hard to pin down, but it was extremely attractive and one I was drawn to. Looking at her face in several of her photos, I thought I saw a knowing, a been-there-done-that sensibility, and perhaps a kindred spirit.

She was a widow who said she was fifty-four—although I thought she looked older—and lived in Washington. I sent her a direct message, skipping the nonsense of preliminary communication steps.

She responded a day later with cautious interest, but I wasn't surprised. In the way she presented herself in her photos and words, I got the impression she was involved in a major business, was very successful, and *should* be cautious. We exchanged a few messages, always after work between eight and eleven. Eventually, she said a phone call would be welcome.

We arranged the call for one evening at eight thirty, and I made note that the caller ID said "Unknown." Even as she sounded warm and inviting on the phone, I got a clear sense during our conversation that certain questions weren't welcome.

When I asked what she did, she hesitated, then answered like she was walking through a minefield. She said she had several areas of business involvement, but between the lines of her answer, I also heard, "Please don't ask me anymore about it."

It was like that for almost everything.

She was born in the U.S. but raised overseas, and her work had taken her to live in many different places in the world. She had married someone "not from the U.S." and was widowed years before. That's about all the info I got on the personal front.

At some point, I heard background noise and asked what it was. She said she was out on her balcony.

"Can I ask where you live?" I said.

"City Center," she responded.

City Center was a new, high-end, mixed-use development in downtown Washington, and I knew it well. Several high-profile architects had designed the buildings.

"So what's your view like from the balcony?" I asked.

"Ah … well … how about you see it for yourself sometime?" she responded.

Another answer that didn't answer the question.

At some point during the call, I half-jokingly called her my "mystery girl." Her pause at that and her follow-up email let me know she didn't appreciate the comment. But it did prompt her to begin explaining her cautiousness.

EMAIL RECEIVED: Meeting You

Dear Turner,

I wanted to say how easy it seemed to talk to you and to listen to you. That's a bit special. The only time I felt awkward was when you called me "mystery girl." Just a little …

I don't mean to be mysterious. Perhaps you could assume that if I seem "mysterious," maybe it's just a topic I'm not comfortable with. In fact, I'm not always comfortable talking about myself until I know someone better. That probably goes for all types of situations. Not just "dating." So, it's not you; it's me. And when we decide to meet (should I say "if"?), we can probably clear all that up.

You have a nice voice; clear, uncomplicated, pleasant, and a nice laugh. :).

Have a wonderful day.

Christine

EMAIL SENT: Meeting You

Christine,

Regarding your comfort level in sharing with me who you are, I know enough about you to understand you have much to protect, your need to be very cautious, and that, in turn, means it takes time for one to get to know you. I understood that when I first read your profile, and it was confirmed by your first messages. It requires me to be a little more thoughtful and cautious in steering the conversation as we continue our interest in wanting to get to know one another—me the boy and you the girl (I like taking it to its simplest form :-)). I want to be both respectful and a gentleman as I get to know you—not just the facts but what is in your heart, your soul, what makes you smile and laugh, what gives you joy (really interested in the "what gives you joy" part), and what puts that twinkle in your eyes (I know it happens, but I don't yet know how :-)). Of course, I hope you want to know the same about me.

I look forward to reading more about your thoughts, and I very much would like to continue getting to know Christine.

All the very best and warmly,

Turner

Ava was infuriating when she said over and over, "It takes me a long time to trust and share about myself," but at least she was concise. Christine, on the other hand, was positively scholarly on the subject in her next email—or rather, her dissertation.

EMAIL RECEIVED: Let's Change the Subject

Dear Turner,

So, here I am trying to organize my thoughts to respond to your email. :)

On a macro level, "who we are" is so many things. On a more direct and personal level, dimensions and texture are SO important. So, I'll ramble a little on what that means to me.

I know who I am. I really like myself. I have foibles and weaknesses, but I know how to forgive myself. But in human relationships, there is the ever-present question of what we reveal, how we reveal it, how much of it we reveal, and when we reveal it. I approach things as an "unfolding" because that's become my nature. We all are a product of where we've been and who we've met and how we've experienced people and situations. The uncomfortable situations are when you reveal yourself and discover one or more of many reactions; the most obvious is that you find out you have little in common—not so easy to solve. Or, you revealed yourself in stages, but perhaps in the wrong order, or you didn't reveal things because you overthought it, or you didn't "catch" the timing correctly. SO many other possibilities; but you get the point.

My history is, let us say, textured. Because I crossed cultural, geographic, economic, class, and yes, even political boundaries, who I am is largely from how I navigated, absorbed, rejected, experienced, fled, embraced (and so on) life as it came at me …

Her email went on again four times as long, explaining why she was cautious in sharing details about herself. Talk about not breaking the ice in the getting-to-know-you phase! I mean, seriously! We needed a nuclear-powered icebreaker to cut through this ice. I can't imagine how long it took her to write it, but it made the "mystery girl" even more mysterious.

Clearly, she was keeping something secret; I just didn't know what.

The next night after the gym, I drove into Washington and City Center. It was a cold, crystal-clear night, and I drove around the buildings several times, looking for a condo with a balcony. There were numerous balconies, but none with special views of anything except the street below.

A few more emails later, we ventured into a little flirting, but only a little. She sent photos of her children and grandchildren, which were nice, and our emails finally got more relaxed in an everyday, conversational way. But seeing the photos made me circle back to her age. Fifty-four didn't quite make sense given the apparent ages of her children and grandchildren.

A couple of days after our first call, I suggested we speak again. I asked for her number, making note that the Caller ID on my phone from our first call said "Unknown."

"That mystery thing …" I said at the end of my email.

"Ha ha ha ha ha! Yes, and remember what that is about?" she said in her reply.

She gave me a number with a New York area code. She said it was an old number that had an international roaming plan, as a way of explaining why she didn't have a Washington, D.C., area code.

Nothing, it seemed, was simple with her.

Our phone call that Sunday evening was much like our first. I tiptoed around with questions—trying to be careful but probing—while she was evasive, measured, and short in her answers. But this time was even stranger than before—she talked to me like I was her plumber, not a potential romantic interest. It was odd. After the call, she explained in an email that she had a house guest staying with her. Afraid her guest could overhear us, she "thought it best to keep the conversation neutral."

Then why have the phone call at all? was the obvious question.

After that rather convoluted explanation, she went on to ask about my daily routine, my home, if I'd remodeled it after my wife died (she had after her husband passed away), and more normal questions. But they were the types of questions you usually asked a few days in as you got to know one another, not after ten days, which was where we were. I mean, ten days in with Dakota, I was looking to book a flight to Paris!

It's not like Christine and I weren't communicating often with each other, but information was sorely lacking. I intentionally avoided answering *her* questions in one of my emails that night, wondering how she'd feel at not having them answered.

Not well, it seemed.

EMAIL RECEIVED :-)

> Dear Turner,
>
> So, if you've noticed, we both ask questions and many of them get missed in further discussions. DID you notice?
>
> There is much to discuss in person.

I had hinted several times over the past few days that I thought we should meet, but she always avoided or deflected the suggestion. But now with her comment of "much to discuss in person," I had the opening I'd been waiting for.

EMAIL SENT: A Thought for You

Dear Christine,

Yes, I noticed how many questions get dropped in the conversations of the moment in our emails. Soooo much we have to share, I think …

You know my preference to meet, and I think I know your preference not to meet but please do consider it. We could do a leisurely museum crawl at the Portrait Gallery perhaps and talk endlessly. Then maybe have lunch at one of my favorite restaurants nearby or a favorite of yours.

Sending you good wishes tonight, or rather, I'm going to be bold here and send you a cyber kiss on your cheek and a hug goodnight.

Turner xo

EMAIL RECEIVED: A Thought for You

Dear Turner,

I want to gather my thoughts and write. Perhaps I'll get to it before you fall asleep, but more likely it will be waiting for you in the morning.

I have to decide how to proceed, dare I say, progress this. There are, as you say, several (perhaps many) things to share, and as you said so nicely, it would be better to say them in person. Some things can feel hollow if not accompanied by reassuring eyes and words.

So, that's where I am. Best to go to sleep and leave me to it.

Sleep well.

Christine xx

EMAIL RECEIVED (the next morning): Not Done Yet

Dear Turner,

I'll need more time, if that's okay.

Christine

It was now Monday morning; there didn't seem much else I could say or do to move us forward, and it was all wearing pretty thin by now. We exchanged a few more emails and texts that day and the next, and she even confessed to getting "a little flutter" whenever there was an email from me, but meeting me seemed to be out of the question.

I couldn't figure her out.

Finally, exasperated, I decided to give her time and space, especially since she was about to travel to Europe on business. I would simply wait until she was ready to engage, if ever that time came.

EMAIL SENT: Hmmmm

Christine,

It was not at all my intention to cause flutters, confusion, or distractions from everyday life and so forth. I am concerned I have made this too difficult and/or uncomfortable for you, and that was not at all my intent. I spoke from my heart at a given moment.

I'll just stand down in my communications for the time being, okay?

You are leaving Saturday for Europe, and I would like to do more than just meet you before you leave because then I will quickly be leaving for Arizona about the time you return. I would like to spend a bit of time with you so these many conversations we seem to want to have with each other can just flow in an easy and natural way. I thought the distraction of browsing through a gallery or museum might be nice in that regard.

I'm here and all is fine ... breathe ... smile ... and let me know whatever you want me to know when you want me to know it.

With flutters as well,

Turner xo

EMAIL RECEIVED: Hmmmm

Dear Turner,

You're terribly sweet, but don't do that. Don't stand down from communicating, writing. That's not what I meant.

By confusion, I meant I'm having trouble sorting through the order and the pace of things as they are, or rather of how I think I'd like them to be. You've been terribly kind and quite adorable—really.

Of course, I understand your intention was positive and constructive. I do want to meet. There's more to say and more to learn between us before we do and hopefully after. Maybe that seems difficult, but I have a feeling about this. Too much too soon; I don't want to miss important signals. I think it takes time. Remember the days of dating when we never knew what the other person was thinking or feeling? We have the opportunity to sort those things out early and focus on the positives. What is special here is you also seem comfortable to "speak" openly. It may be easier to write though. Let's practice for when we meet.

What I've liked so far is the gentle unfolding of things about you. You've revealed some lovely things, volunteering feelings about things that are quite special. Of course, I'm very curious about many more things, as you are, but I think the trust we build sorting through things is important.

I think I agree that speaking on the phone will help a lot. But I wouldn't want to stop writing also. We can talk before I leave and after and from Tucson if you want. Will you be able to?

Bye for now

Christine xx

EMAIL SENT: Hmmmm

Christine,

You have a nice way of saying "no" to my suggestion that we meet.

I will admit that I'm struggling a bit to understand what it is you are looking for, but the keywords and phrases you use are "more to say and learn ... trust ... too much too soon ... important signals ... takes time ... sort things out and focus on the positives ..."

I take this to mean you are looking to distill some very specific and important things by means of wide and varied conversations, but at the same time, the thought enters my mind that there may be a wrong thing and right thing I might say, and it puts me in a "cautious" frame of mind.

Christine my dear, all I can possibly do is be me, and you have a little sense of who that is, and if your xx's are any indication, our hearts are operating on the same wavelength. I AM open; I share feelings that many struggle to even understand, let alone articulate and be willing to share. I know that makes me unique. But it also makes my heart more vulnerable (and I have become a bit more protective of that as of late), but it also makes me value the feelings and the heart of the other person.

I've learned that one can write, talk on the phone, and do all kinds of things to try and to be the best one can be, and it can seem quite wonderful. Then you meet, and the chemistry, the personal interaction, the little things that never come through in phone calls and emails may not be there for one or the other. For me, that is the measure—that personal chemistry—and to take that measure, two must meet.

For my sake, for protecting my heart and for protecting yours, I don't want to build up to something that "seems" certain either this way or that, then we meet and, well, it's just not there. There is the opposite too ... something is said or written that is taken the wrong way and prevents us ever from meeting, when perhaps we really should have.

Christine, I will be cautious of my heart until I look into your eyes, feel your touch, see if I can make you laugh and you me, see if things I say make you happy or frown, see if that spark is there, and more importantly, wait to see what my heart says to me.

So ... there you have it.

What do we do, Christine?

I'm going off to the gym, but you are going to be on my mind and, yes, in my heart.

Turner

EMAIL RECEIVED: Hmmmm

I understand.

And I agree!

More later.

Christine (rose emoji)

That evening, Christine began a barrage of text messages, but they all went in the same direction as before—nowhere. I finally told her I was confused, didn't understand her reluctance to meet, didn't know why we were even still talking, and I thought it best to just wish each other well and move on.

> **CHRISTINE:** Please, no. Can we talk? Can I have one more chance?

> **ME:** No, I really don't think so, Christine. I don't want to talk anymore. I don't see the point.

> **CHRISTINE:** Can we talk tonight? Please. I'll share with you what I've been holding back. You can ask me any questions you like, and I will answer them all. No more secrets. Please

> don't go away. Please,
> please don't.

At this point, The Boys decided to pipe in after their short abandonment of me. *Just say yes already! You know you want to know the big secret.*

So I said yes.

She called that night around eight thirty.

"Hi, Turner."

"Hi, Christine, are you okay?"

"Well, no. I'm really nervous and a little scared too," she said.

"I can't imagine what this is all about, Christine, but it's not worth making you feel this way. Really, it's not. There's nothing I need or have to know. I'm certainly not worth making you feel like this."

"But I don't want you to go away, and I want to share some things with you. You've been very patient and kind. But ... I'm afraid of what you might think about me," she said.

"Well then, why don't you just tell me?"

"Okay ..." and after a long hesitation, she said, "I'm not calling you from Washington."

"Oh, okay. Where are you?"

"I'm in Singapore," she said with trepidation.

"You're in Singapore? Are you visiting?"

"No ... I live here."

"You mean you have a second home there?"

"No, I mean this is where I live."

"You live there now?"

"Yes. I've lived here for twenty-four years," she said.

"Ah okayyy ... I don't—Ah ... so ... you don't live here in Washington? At all?"

"No. Singapore is my home, and it's home for most of my children, although I was in Washington over Christmas visiting family. I was born there."

"Okay ... I'm-mm lost. Tell me how this makes any sense? Is there some sort of plan at work here? What's the deal, Christine?"

"Well, yes, I did have a plan. It's sort of like this. The world's very small for me, Turner. I've lived and worked all over. I have properties in London, France, and a few others. I can live and do my work anywhere, but not necessarily find love anywhere. So, I came up with a plan. I made a list of major cities where I thought I could live, then I decided I would try to find a man—to find love—in one of them. If I found someone and love followed, then I planned to move there to live and run my businesses. Washington was one of the cities on my list, and it's where I'm originally from, so I decided to try it first … then I found you."

Whoooaaaaaa!!! said The Boys. *Holy-y-y cow-w-w!*

After a long pause, she said, "So, what are you thinking, Turner? Please tell me … I'm scared."

I sat in silence, processing it all.

Should I be hurt? Should I be angry? Is she a total wacko, and should I run for the exit? I wasn't quite sure what I was supposed to feel or do, so I let it churn around, even as I began to speak.

"Well … I think … I think I'm flattered," I said. "I mean, you decided to search the entire world for a man—for love—and you found me? I mean … that's kind of—like 'wow!' it seems to me. So, I guess my first thought is how flattered I am, Christine."

"Oh my! That's such a relief, Turner."

After getting past her big secret, we talked for almost three hours, to near midnight. Well, midnight for me, lunchtime for her. So many questions got answered, including some of the quirky ones.

Like, why did her emails and texts usually only come in the evening?

Because it was morning for her, the only time when she had any time to spare.

She typically woke up early, played tennis every morning for an hour, took a bath around eight thirty, worked in her home office until noon, then was driven to her corporate office. The afternoon and evenings were always full of business appointments and meetings, so from bath time until lunch was her time to be Miss Chatty with me. Being almost twelve hours apart, it was the evening for me. I thought she was emailing, texting, and talking at the end of her day, but it was really the beginning.

She filled me in on everything about her marriages and divorces—including her last husband, how they met, were married, and how he died—and all her children and grandchildren. I told her the true story of how my wife took her own life, everything leading up to it, and the aftermath. As with Ava, I decided to tell Christine everything in hopes of gaining some amount of trust.

She then shifted to matters of the heart by asking what love meant to me. After pausing for a moment, I spoke.

"Christine, we all give love and receive love differently. While the act of love is beautiful in its simplicity, love is difficult, complicated, and never perfect. I think I've learned—as you may have—that it's during the most difficult times when true love shows itself and matters the most. In those times, simply being there is often the most profound expression of love. We've both learned, too, that love remains after great loss, and we don't have quotas on how much love we have to give. I still love my wife and you said your husband was the love of your life, yet here we both are, looking to find love again.

"We can choose who we give love to and who we receive love from. That's one of the things that makes love complicated and often elusive. Getting how you give and receive love to work with someone else and how *they* give and receive love is pretty tricky business. So what you and I are doing is scary stuff.

"During the happiest of times, you can't assume love is there. And by saying 'I love you,' that doesn't mean it's there. Living the love you profess is harder than saying the words—you have to show it in a thousand different ways. I think people say it too much and then don't back it up with the hard work it requires.

"To give love and be open to love, I think you have to be pretty brave, because it means leaving yourself open to be hurt, as well as hurting others. Honestly, I've been having a hard time with the hurt part lately. So … I'm a bit more cautious right now, Christine.

"In the end, love is a choice, which, of course, makes it all the more precious. I know there's more, but I'm just rambling now. Sorry about going on so long."

"That's beautiful, Turner," Christine said. "I don't think I've ever heard a man say what you just said. You and I are similar I think."

Through the sharing of these and other more intimate thoughts, we built some measure of trust in each other. Later in the phone call, Christine told me about the several businesses she either owned outright or was a major investor in; she was basically a business mogul. True to her word, she answered every question, including telling me her last name.

We were both mentally, emotionally, and physically exhausted as our call came to an end. We agreed to see where this crazy long-distance relationship might go. It wasn't an all-in sort of thing like it was with Dakota; it was an undefined *let's-get-to-know-each-other-better* and *see-what-happens* kind of thing.

She was off to Europe in a few days on business but would be able to stay in touch with one of the many phones she used for international travel—like the one with the New York area code. At the moment, she had no plans to come to the U.S. but said she could possibly arrange a business trip so we could meet.

When I got off the phone, I was stunned by it all.

I did an internet search on her name, and the results were all obscure regulatory filings for Asian businesses. Digging into each one, I was amazed at the breadth of her business holdings and investments. I mean, this woman ran a small slice of the world.

One of the filings was five years old and noted her age then as fifty-five. So she wasn't fifty-four as she said in her profile; she was sixty—deception number two.

Later that evening, she sent several emails about a personal arts project she was passionate about for which she footed the bill. It wasn't quite like Larry Ellison, the CEO of Oracle, spending billions on his America's Cup racing passion, or Elon Musk and SpaceX, but it was in the same vein.

So after all the mystery, drama, confessions, and revelations, what did we have?

"Let's just stay in touch," Christine said. "Me the girl and you the boy, and we'll see what happens."

****

We used WhatsApp to communicate on her way to Europe, but it took some doing to keep up with Christine as she switched from one phone to another for different continents and countries. Our Singapore conversation began under one phone number, then hopped over to another number on another phone, then another.

"Hi, it's me," she texted each time, so I would know who it was.

Once she was in Europe, we found it difficult to find time to talk. It turned out that the six-hour time difference made it harder to schedule phone calls than the difference between Washington and Singapore.

"See?" she left in a voice message, laughing, "My being in Singapore isn't all that big of a deal after all, is it?"

The result was that we used the WhatsApp voicemail-message feature quite a bit as a phone call substitute, the same way Dakota and I had. We shared the goings-on of our days and evenings in texts, voice messages, and emails and soon had the pace and pulse of each other. We flirted a bit in our messages too. In one email, she sent a link to a *New York Times* travel article, wondering if we might take a trip together in the upcoming summer to one of the exotic destinations it featured.

When I shared that I was finally going through another closet of my wife's things that had sat untouched for five years, she sympathized in a way only another widowed person could, and it was very much appreciated.

Less appreciated was her food-shaming about meals I made at home. She jumped all over me about the quickie rice I made, among other things.

A couple of weeks into February, while she was still in Europe, she asked if I might fly out to meet her in San Francisco later in the month. She had business there and would be flying in from Singapore.

"Could you join me for the evening?" she asked.

I said my schedule was busy and couldn't make that date, but what I *didn't* say was that I also couldn't afford to fly across the country for a one-evening date on the West Coast.

She then mused in another message that perhaps I could join her in Europe before she left for her next stop in a few days. It felt a little like Ava again with her wedding invitation to Zurich.

The world may be small for her, but it's damn big and expensive for you! The Boys said, pointing out the obvious.

Finally—with obvious exasperation—she said she could probably add a stop in Washington after San Francisco as she made her way back to Europe again at the end of February.

Her frustration at my inability to fly long distances to join her would become an issue. Each time, it made me question what business I had pursuing this; I couldn't keep up. But for the time being, curiosity about *her* and the possibility of *us* got the better of me, and *we* continued along.

****

With a small bouquet of flowers in hand, I waited for Christine to arrive at Dulles Airport. It was seven in the morning in late February, and she had taken the red-eye from San Francisco to Washington for a three-day visit for us to finally meet.

In the previous three weeks, we had spoken on the phone at least every other day. In our texts, she had embraced the use of my heart-flutter symbol (~) for ending messages, along with lots of XOs. We were certainly curious about each other and this halfway-around-the-world liaison. We were having fun too, but it was far from simple; it was downright complicated. Having been on Venus as long as I had, my eyes were open and my was mind wary, but I decided to go with the flow.

More often than not, Christine called me in the morning from her bathtub. It was her favorite place to call from because she could avoid being overheard by frequent house guests, employees, or staff. Anywhere else, she often apologized for having to "disguise" her voice when someone was nearby. When that happened, I became the "conversation with a friend," as she would say. She implied I was a secret to be kept under wraps lest there be complications on her end. Sometimes I felt more like a bath toy being played with while she lounged in her bubbles.

Now standing next to the luggage carousel at Dulles, I saw her in the distance walking my way. She was smartly dressed for the cold weather in Washington with a colorful scarf fashionably draped around her neck—she looked every bit the world-traveling pro she was. Having flown on a red-eye all night, she still looked fresh and ready to take on the world.

She looked a bit older than in her photos and carried a few extra pounds, so that was a bit of a surprise. But that knowing look in her eyes, the way she carried herself, and the obvious been-there-done-that look of confidence was there too. This was not a Jane Fonda-Ted Turner sex-attraction connection; this was a connection of shared life experiences—love, pain, loss, and those filters in life.

A big smile came to my face and hers as well.

"Hi, Turner."

"Hi, Christine. You look terrific!"

She was friendly but coy, not unexpected in a situation like this. I was only five months removed from my meeting with Dakota in Paris, so the scene felt familiar. I did my best to help us get past the first-meeting jitters.

We exchanged a hug; I kissed her cheek and offered her the flowers. During the one-hour drive to her hotel in Washington, we decided on our plan for the day. She would rest first, then meet me for drinks around four o'clock at her hotel. After drinks, I'd take her to dinner at one of my favorite restaurants in nearby Georgetown. Given my experience with Dakota, where we spent every minute together for five days, Christine's hotel arrangement and our scheduled times for seeing each other were more than welcome.

When she met me that afternoon in the hotel lobby, she had a warm smile on her face. We hugged, then found a cozy spot to sit. Having talked during the drive that morning, we were already into multiple topics of conversation, and we picked up where we'd left off. We stayed there for two hours before venturing into the cold night for dinner.

Our two-hour dinner was nice ... and interesting.

She was a fascinating and accomplished woman who had traveled to just about everywhere in the world—and I mean *everywhere*. It was mesmerizing, at times, listening to her.

My life seemed rather mundane compared to hers, but when she asked about the details of how I got from a small town in the South to Harvard, to architect, to stay-at-home dad, to investor, to special needs parent and advocate, to congressional candidate, she seemed equally fascinated. As she gently inquired about the details of my wife's depression and suicide, she showed a rare kindness and consideration that was generally hidden behind her more typical businesslike façade.

And businesslike was the general tone of the evening, clearly the type of interaction she preferred. Date-night subjects were kept at arm's length, and there was no flirting.

We circled back around to one of her favorite subjects—food—and the food-shaming began again. She said rice was one of the foods that most defined a country's culture, and my quickie rice was an apt—although sad— commentary on food in America. I suggested it was more a statement about a single man who eats to live, instead of the other way around. A rice-cooking lesson—challenge—was offered and accepted for the next day at my house.

I picked her up at ten in the morning and took her on a tour of my neighborhood. We then went to the grocery store, where she gave me a lesson on the different kinds of rice. She insisted on paying for our groceries and pulled out a crisp one-hundred-dollar bill from her purse. From there, with ingredients in hand, we went back to my kitchen to prepare a Middle Eastern rice dish.

At my home, she spent a lot of time looking at the family picture wall. She took note of many things, but as with the evening before, everything— including me—was kept at arm's length.

I shot video on my iPhone as Christine carefully prepared the ingredients and used various techniques in preparing the rice dish. As she did, it dawned on me that perhaps she was trying to think of ways to keep us busy so there would be no uncomfortable pause that might then put the focus on *us*. So, moments after she sat down at the dining room table to enjoy our meal, I walked over to her, slowly leaned down, and kissed her.

She seemed terrified.

"I'm sorry if that wasn't welcome," I said.

"It's okay, you did nothing wrong … but that's the first time I've been kissed since my husband died almost nine years ago."

She sounded like me when I first kissed Joyce over two years earlier, so I knew how she must have felt. But I was surprised she had gone this long without a kiss.

"You seem … scared," I said.

"It's just that it's been so long."

"That long and never a kiss?"

"Yes, that long. I've kept myself busy all these years, avoiding it," she said.

"You mean like you've been doing the entire time you've been here?"

"Have I? Sort of, I suppose," she said, "but what *are* we doing here, Turner?"

"Well, I think we found each other, liked each other, and decided to see what might happen. I've had no expectations other than to meet you and go from there, but I confess, I wanted to kiss you to break through the ice a bit. But I won't do it again. I don't want you to feel uncomfortable."

"It wasn't uncomfortable; it was nice. Your lips are very soft, and you're very tender."

"Well, I'm honored that I'm your *first*," I said with a smile.

She smiled back and laughed. "Why don't we have some rice?"

And with that, we were past the moment.

I took her back to the hotel that afternoon but returned later in the evening to take her for drinks at the Four Seasons, where I was determined to make the conversation more about us.

Christine seemed to be of the same mind, and we quickly became more intimate and flirtatious. We got on the subject of dating in general, and I remembered she hadn't been truthful about her age on her dating profile. As I was about to say something, she confessed.

"I was reluctant to do eHarmony, but my friend made me do it. She did a lot of the writing of the profile and even selected the photos. She also said I couldn't give my real age because men wanted younger women. I'm not fifty-four, Turner ... I'm sixty."

"Yes. I know."

"You know?! How?"

"I did an internet search after our phone call when you told me your last name and came across a corporate filing. It gave your age as fifty-five, and the filing was five years old."

She looked surprised and then gave me a wary look. "Does it matter?"

"Age isn't an issue; my wife was ten years older, you know, but the deception is a problem," I said.

Embarrassed, she apologized, then sat quietly, trying to figure out what to say next. To get past *all* the deception issues, I then shared the story of my evening drive around City Center two months before trying to guess which "condo with a balcony" might be hers.

"You did *that*?" she said in astonishment and further embarrassment.

"Yes. I was really curious about my *mystery girl*. I wanted to unravel some of the secrets. But obviously, I needed to be circling the globe, not a few blocks in downtown Washington."

"I'm sorry I put you through that. I didn't realize what—it never dawned on me—I'm sorry, Turner. You're really a very sweet man."

We finished our drinks, and she thanked me for a wonderful day. I took her back to her hotel; we exchanged a quick kiss and said goodnight.

The next day, she was flying to New York on her way to Europe, but before her evening flight, she wanted to do some shopping at the local department stores. She wanted to get some gifts for her grandchildren, but she wanted to look in the kitchen department first.

"They don't sell pots and pans in Singapore?" I asked.

"I want to buy you something for your kitchen—a rice cooker."

I laughed. "You're trying to change me, aren't you?"

"Now, now. I'm not trying to change you, just help you," she said.

We found a little rice cooker for twenty dollars. At the register, she pulled out another fresh one-hundred-dollar bill to pay for it.

"Do you always travel with that kind of cash?" I asked.

"I prefer not to use credit cards."

From there, we went to another mall, where she bought a few things for her grandchildren ... paying with one-hundred-dollar bills. After, she asked if she could buy us some ice cream.

As the server was handing us our cones at the counter of Ben and Jerry's, I said, "If you pull out another hundred-dollar bill to pay for these, I'll drop my two scoops on the floor."

She smiled, searched through her wallet, and pulled out a twenty-dollar bill like she'd found a needle in a haystack.

Driving to the airport, we talked about meeting again soon, although it was all left open. We decided we would stay in touch and keep on with whatever it was we were trying to do—me here and her everywhere else in the world.

"Let's see what might happen," as she now liked to say, "between this girl and this boy."

****

"You know," Christine said during her morning bath-time phone call with me three weeks later, "if it weren't for *your* schedule, we could be at my beach house in Bali."

She was referring to my two-week schedule of upcoming spring break activities with my sons.

Since we had met in Washington, we'd spoken on the phone almost daily, but they were generally ten-minute calls, just enough to catch up on each other's day. We were fairly good friends by now but always aware we were trying to be something more. She made a point of asking what I was doing and what was coming up on my calendar. It made me feel like she really wanted to be involved with my life as best she could, but I felt she was usually less than forthcoming about what she was doing.

Her comment that we could be together if it were not for *my* schedule took me by surprise and sent The Boys into orbit.

IF NOT FOR OUR SCHEDULE?! What the hell?! The Boys shouted. *What about if you didn't live on the other side of the world!*

As Emily had done, the finger was again being pointed at *me* as the reason *we* weren't together. It pissed me off to no end, especially since—again—my parenting responsibilities were cited as the problem. Also being ignored was that my financial ability to hop on a plane for Bali was pretty much nil—a fact she wasn't getting *at all.*

I let her comment go and nonchalantly asked about the beach house.

"It's quite nice, but you'll need to see it and decide for yourself."

Another non-answer to a question.

In going over my spring break plans, I let her know I would be in New York City the three days leading up to Easter Sunday. I would stay with friends of my late wife, and I was looking forward to being there. It had been quite a while since I'd been in New York, especially with time to myself.

Two weeks later, we were talking on the phone when Christine begged to cut the call short.

"You have a meeting to get to?" I asked.

"No, I have a plane to catch."

She hadn't mentioned any travel coming up, so I asked where she was going.

"New York."

"New York City?" I asked.

"Yes."

"For how long?"

"For the week and weekend," she said.

I paused. This made no sense.

She knew I would be in New York later this week, and now she would be there, too, but didn't say anything?

"How long has this been in the works?" I asked.

"The plans have been iffy for a while as we worked to line up meetings with potential clients," she said.

"But you remembered I was going to be there, too, right?"

"Actually no, I didn't," she said.

I paused. What to say?

"I don't understand," I said. "Remember when you said we could be at your beach house in Bali if not for my spring break schedule, which included New York?"

"No, I really don't remember. Anyway, my business partner is coming with me, and I'm not sure of our schedule. We'll be making pitches to a lot of potential clients, and I may be looking for property to buy as well. I don't know what my time will be like," she said.

"I still don't understand, Christine. This makes no sense to me. We're going to be in the same city for three days, and we can't find time to see each other, even for a drink? Really?"

"Well, I think it's all a bit complicated," she said.

"Clearly."

"Well, let's do this. Let me get there—I arrive late Tuesday—and figure out my schedule. It certainly would be nice to see you, darling," she said in her parting words.

Okay-yy, Dar-r-r-rling. What are we going to do now? asked The Boys.

****

She arrived in New York on Tuesday, and I arrived early Thursday afternoon. We had been texting all week but didn't yet have a day or time to meet. It looked like Friday night was going to be best, but she wasn't sure.

Friday morning arrived, and Friday afternoon was getting close to evening, when she finally texted.

> **CHRISTINE:** We can meet for drinks after my dinner party. Should be back at my hotel by 9 latest. Meet somewhere nearby?

She was staying in Times Square and suggested we meet at a speakeasy place called the Flute Bar. It was one of those downstairs, dark and mysterious-type places.

I arrived at nine o'clock and texted. She texted back to say she had returned from her dinner party and was finishing changing in her room.

> **CHRISTINE:** Is there a big black Suburban parked outside the hotel?

> **ME:** Not that I can see from the bar. Secret Service or something?

> **CHRISTINE:** Almost. The driver I hired is Protective Services. He often waits outside for a while after dropping me off to be sure I'm okay.

> **ME:** I'll go out and have a look.

> **CHRISTINE:** Tall Caucasian guy in a light gray suit.

> **ME:** All clear.

> **CHRISTINE:** K. Coming :-)

Walking back down the stairs into the bar and looking around—dark and hidden from the street—a picture began to emerge in my mind. My "mystery girl" had made it clear that my existence was—and had to remain—a secret from anyone and everyone in Singapore. And now, enlisting me to help her elude her security detail and wanting to meet in a dark basement hideaway, it felt like I was being kept under wraps here too.

She came in with her familiar warm smile. We exchanged a nice hug, then a peck of a kiss. We ordered two glasses of champagne, got a corner table, then proceeded with the familiar businesslike small talk she preferred for about an hour.

I sat there thinking how incredibly strange this was. Here were two people trying to navigate a long-distance … romance? friendship? … or whatever it was, in one of the most exciting cities in the world, and she wanted to meet in a basement bar and do small talk.

As usual, she wanted to know everything I was doing but not share what she was up to. Our small talk soon got old, was no fun, and was becoming uncomfortably forced. I was about ready to say goodnight—and perhaps goodbye and good luck—when she asked a funny question.

"Do you know who makes the best hot dogs on the streets of New York?"

"No idea," I said.

"The Egyptians," she said. "The. Very. Best. Hands down."

"Whaaaat?" I said with surprise.

She explained and then offered to treat me to the best hot dog in New York.

Times Square was a refreshing change from the dark basement bar. Our conversation was more animated, and she seemed much more at ease. She led the way to a particular hot dog vendor on a street corner. She greeted him in Egyptian Arabic, and it seemed like they were old friends.

She translated a bit and then asked me, "What'll you have?"

After my first bite, I confessed my hot dog with a bit of mustard was pretty darn good, and she smiled with satisfaction as she ate hers. She decreed the evening was now "a marvelous success." But then, as we walked, she became more demure, shy, cautious, and well, mysterious. It became uncomfortable as we mentally searched for how to say goodbye. But finally, we did, on a street corner a block away from her hotel, lest her returning security man catch me—some unknown guy with his arms around her.

"He might come after you," she said, "and I'm not kidding."

She texted me after I arrived at my friend's place.

> **CHRISTINE:** It was fun, time flew by … wasn't that a great hot dog?!?! And a lovely glass of champagne?!?!

I spent the next day traversing the city with my friends. Before hitting the road early Easter morning, Christine and I exchanged several texts. Her last text described a marvelous, sumptuous Saturday-evening dinner party.

> **CHRISTINE:** You really
> need to spend more time
> with me. Life's never dull!!
> (followed by a rose emoji,
> clapping hand emojis,
> musical note emojis, and
> celebration confetti emojis)

Well, The Boys said, *you gotta give it to her. She teases you with suggestions of more time together and talk of lavish dinner parties, but she forgot you were even going to be here, then given the chance to invite you to join her, it's a dive-bar drink and a street hot dog instead, all the while evading Bruno the hitman security-guy in the black Suburban. Why wouldn't you want to spend more time with her?*

I replayed in my mind everything about her since we'd first met.

It seemed she was working desperately hard for me to simply be her friend, not a boyfriend—certainly not a lover—but just a friend in the rarified air of her closed-in bubble world. I felt a little sad for her but also knew that whatever we were trying to do, it wasn't for me.

During the drive home, I thought about how to bring all of this to an end. It was too strange, and that was saying something in this place called Venus.

****

My text to begin our breakup was not terribly clever.

> **ME:** We need to chat about
> something.

I texted about the disconnect between her comments of wanting to be together, actually getting together, the secrecy of our bath-time phone calls, her not remembering we would both be in New York, our short time together once we were there, and then circled back to her last text, "You really need to spend more time with me ..."

ME: Do you have any thoughts as to how the 'spend more time with me' part would actually work?

I went on at some length, and in her reply, she did the same. She recollected dating when she was young and how she and one of her husbands communicated and found a way to bridge what sounded like another long-distance romance.

CHRISTINE: It worked well then, why can't this work with us? What's the problem? I don't know if there can be any expectations, but it would take more effort and compromises to spend more time together.

The compromises she referred to were clearly on my side of the equation. Two days later, we talked on the phone.

"Hi, darling, how are you?" she began.

Did she really not know what was coming next? Our long text messages were all questioning what we were doing, what we had, and what we didn't have.

After exchanging a few pleasantries, I said, "Christine, this isn't working for me. You're a wonderful woman, but it's just not going to work."

We went back and forth for twenty minutes—me saying this wasn't working and her coming up with all sorts of reasons why we should keep going.

Exasperated that I kept saying no, she finally said, "You know, my friends will tell you I can be a very generous woman."

Is she putting money on the table if I agree to be her boyfriend? I thought.

Sounds like it to me, said Charles.

"Christine, you *are* a very generous woman, and I'm so glad I met you. Is it possible … we could be friends?"

"Why?"

"Because you're a wonderful woman, and you don't come across wonderful people in this world every day."

After a long pause, she said, "No, I don't think I can do that, Turner. I just don't think I can."

Sounding like she wanted to get to the end as fast as possible, she said, "I guess this is goodbye, Turner. I will miss you," then she hung up.

****

Four years later, I received a surprise message from Christine. She was to be in Washington on business and asked if we might be able to have breakfast. Intrigued to no end, I agreed, and we arranged to meet at one of my old favorite meeting places, the Ritz.

I arrived a few minutes before she did and took a seat on the same sofa where I had met Marilyn six and a half years before—the evening before the *Date Lab* story was published.

Talk about déjà vu! Here I was meeting a person from what felt like another place and time, in a setting from another place and time. That other place and time, of course, was Venus.

Then there she was.

She walked in the door, saw me, and headed my way with open arms and the same warm smile I remembered.

She looked terrific.

She had lost weight, and her face had a fresh, rejuvenated look. She was relaxed and looked very happy. We walked to the dining area for a light breakfast.

I asked what brought her to town, and she explained she was here to deal with some banking issues related to the passing of her mother a few weeks before. It was the ridiculous, drive-you-nuts stuff only banks can dish out. She was forced to come in person to finish sorting it all out, no little thing since that meant coming from the other side of the world.

For the next hour, we shared the details of our lives from the past four years.

She had stopped or sold several businesses and was involved with a few new ones. She was still a business mogul, and I could tell it still excited her. She told me a friend had talked her into going to a special spa in Europe, where she transformed everything about the way she ate and cared for herself.

Among the foods she said she never ate anymore was rice.

Given she had forgotten that I was an architect until I reminded her, I was pretty sure she had also forgotten the rice-cooking lesson and rice cooker she had given me way back when.

After she finished sharing everything, but before I began to catch her up on my life, I asked if she was still looking for that special guy in faraway places. She smiled knowingly and looked a little embarrassed. She said no.

"I realized, not long after we last spoke, I shouldn't keep trying to make something happen that wasn't there. It was futile and a waste of time. I should just move forward with the life I have. In the process, I found more time to be with my grown children, I have gotten closer to them, and I'm so very happy about that. I do more of what I enjoy, and that's simply my mission in life.

"And you seem very happy too. Really happy, and you haven't changed a bit. You look great!" she said.

I caught her up on my children, my new investing business, my travels around the world, and my personal life. It was nice to see her again, to see her happy, and to reconnect for a brief moment of enjoyable and easy conversation.

As we parted, she kissed each of my cheeks. "As we do in Europe," she said, and we exchanged a warm hug goodbye.

CHAPTER 19

Tinder

IT WAS AN ARTICLE IN the *Wall Street Journal* that introduced me to Tinder.

Anything you can buy, sell, invest in, or make money on is reported in the *Wall Street Journal*, and Tinder had become a gold mine. With so much money involved, it wasn't surprising to learn a dispute had broken out between Tinder's creator and a business partner.

The story described how the app was originally designed as a hookup/dating app for twenty-somethings. It was so simple to use and so obvious in its purpose that it caught on fast and was now being used by a lot more than just twenty-somethings. When I downloaded the app and looked at it for the first time, it looked pretty mainstream.

My college son's reaction, however, was anything but.

"Ewwww!" he cringed out loud after seeing the app on my phone one day. "Dad! What are you doing with Tinder? That's a hookup app! That's gross!"

"It's not just for hookups; it's used for dating by grown-ups too," I said with full parental authority.

He would have none of it. "That's *so gross*, Dad! Just get away from me! Get a-way!"

Regardless of my son's "gross" declaration, the current state of my dating life left me open to pretty much anything. I tried Tinder with the same attitude I had in applying for *Date Lab* over two years before. Why not?

Here's how Tinder works.

After downloading the app on your smartphone, it asks you a few basic demographic questions and prompts you to upload at least one photo. In two minutes, you can be up and running.

Immediately after completing the basic registration steps, the app opens and presents you with your first card-like picture of a possible match. You can see the person's name, additional photos, and a short bio. You now face a decision—a decision that made Tinder a cultural phenomenon and introduced the digital-dating lexicon of *swipe left* or *swipe right*.

If you don't like the person in the photo, flick it to the left, and they are gone, never to be seen again. If you like them, you swipe right. It's like going through a deck of cards, one card at a time. You'll start slowly at first, but pretty soon, you'll be flicking through them rapid-fire, with each one getting about two or three seconds of your time. On a plane waiting for takeoff, I once saw a young woman flicking through photos left and right so fast that she could have been a Blackjack dealer in Vegas.

And that's pretty much it—no matching, no questions; you just get right to it. It's simple, uncomplicated, and highly addictive.

Matches are made when you and someone else have both swiped right on each other. You get an instant celebratory graphic on your phone with your two pictures put together and a "You've Matched" banner. After that, the app allows you to text back and forth.

When I began using Tinder, ninety-nine percent of the women began their profiles with "Not looking for a hookup." The other one percent clearly *were* looking for a hookup. Often, they were scantily clad or provocatively posed—always with a boob shot—to reinforce what they were looking for.

I had numerous matches on Tinder over several months and engaged in quite a few text conversations. But for all the effort, only two meetings occurred before I left Venus. For whatever reason, both women were from Persia (Iran) and were daughters of privileged families who had come over before the fall of the Shah in 1979. As I learned in my brief time with each, they were raised to be *Princesses* with a capital P.

Adrianna was fifty-three years old, stylish, refined-looking, and attractive with high cheekbones and a regal-looking face. Her notably expressive lips, large penetrating brown eyes, and prominent eyebrows gave her an air of dominance, adding to her classic beauty.

I texted her to say hello, and our back-and-forth correspondence became a painfully one-sided affair. She gave only one-word responses to my various questions, mostly "yes" or "no."

Chatty girl, The Boys remarked. *She's really knocking it out of the park! Maybe she should've been a swipe left and not a righty.*

Deciding to end our conversation, I mentioned I was at an architectural luncheon with several fellow Harvard grads, should probably go, and perhaps we could chat later.

> **ADRIANNA:** You went to Harvard? Wow! I've never met a man who went to Harvard. You must be really smart. You went to Harvard? When were you there? I just love that you went to Harvard!

Good grief! Said Charles, *a Harvard groupie? That's a first.*

Over the course of two dates, I was "Mr. Harvard this" and "Mr. Harvard that," as in, "You're *so* much more handsome in person than in your photos, Mr. Harvard."

But I was running a few minutes late for our third date—and to borrow a line from Finch in *Out of Africa*—I "was demoted" from Mr. Harvard to Turner and given the boot.

> **ADRIANNA:** Where are you? I'm here waiting for you. Why aren't you here? I'm leaving. Goodbye!

Adrianna, however, was just a warm-up for the main Tinder event.

****

When I first saw Sabrina's picture on Tinder, she looked stunning in her one photo—beautiful, poised, and sophisticated but also serious and a bit stiff in her demeanor. She didn't smile; instead, she had a what-are-you-looking-at, indignant, pouty-face look. Nothing was silly or superfluous about her.

In her profile, she mentioned a love of travel, elegant evenings, and a desire for a sophisticated, worldly, and well-traveled man. She didn't list her age, but I guessed she was probably in her early fifties.

Swipe right! Swipe right! shouted Darrell.

I thought she was out of my league—always the wingman, never the leading man—but I swiped right anyway and didn't give it another thought. That's the way Tinder works. So imagine my surprise when, twenty minutes later, a celebratory banner popped up on my screen saying we had matched.

Seriously?! said Charles.

Sabrina sent the first message and was quite chatty. She complimented my photos and my looks—*a red flag right there,* The Boys pointed out (thanks, guys). Over several long exchanges, I learned she was a freelance executive recruiter, and what she did sounded pretty impressive. She was on a deadline for a presentation in New York the next week at that very moment.

She lived in Washington near Dupont Circle. I had a dinner meeting that night near the Portrait Gallery not far away, so I took a chance and asked in a text if she'd like to meet for a drink at the Monaco Hotel around nine. The Monaco is a self-styled chic hotel, with a destination bar off the lobby.

> **SABRINA:** The day will be over by then. I will be tired and getting ready for bed.

> **ME:** Sorry. I'm sure you have some very long days in your business. But if the hotel is convenient, I could meet you there early tomorrow evening. How about drinks at six thirty?

> **SABRINA:** Yes, that would be fine for meeting you. Could you get there before me and have a table for us, so we don't have to stand around waiting?

> **ME:** Of course.

I drove into the city the next evening and grabbed a rare parking spot on the street a few blocks away. I walked into the very chic, very noisy bar and found a nice spot with a high-top table and chairs where we could sit close to each other and talk. I texted her where I was and waited. Since the bar was crowded, I didn't see her until she was right upon me.

Wow! said The Boys, as she stood there, elegantly dressed to kill.

She was about five-foot-eight in heels, slim, with shoulder-length, perfectly coiffed hair that framed a stunningly beautiful face. She had the most perfect skin I had ever seen, elegantly delicate facial features, and expressive brown eyes. She wore a short, snug red dress with a similarly snug waist-length red leather jacket. Her dress was modest in that it wasn't revealing in any way, but it was a killer in that it cut a line of eye-catching femininity. She had on white stockings and red high heels that were just right.

"Turner?" she asked in an accented voice.

"Yes! Sabrina? So nice to meet you!" I said, standing up, smiling, and gesturing to her chair.

Moving to the other side of the table, I tried to help her with the bar-height chair, but she struggled in her tight dress. She gave several exaggerated eye-rolls as she climbed up. Once seated, her serious and dour expression was in striking contrast to how she otherwise looked. I tried to counter the less-than-good start to the evening and hopefully bring a smile to her face.

"I have to say, you look absolutely fabulous."

"That's what I would expect a true gentleman to say," she said matter-of-factly, with her pouty-face look unchanged. "Obviously you are."

Okay-y-y, I thought. *I was thinking more of a "thank you" and a friendly smile, but whatever.*

329

"How are you tonight?" she asked.

"I'm good! How was your day? Not another long one I hope, working on that proposal," I said, grasping for any sort of conversational footing.

"No, it was fine," she replied.

"Would you like a drink?"

"Yes. I'll have champagne."

An interesting choice, I thought. *A hint of expectations for the evening, perhaps?*

While waiting for our drinks to arrive, we slowly got into the rhythm of a conversation of sorts, but the seriousness of her face, and the fact that she never smiled, made it seem like everything I said, every gesture I made, was open to judgment.

When our drinks arrived, we clinked glasses. I thought I might try an obvious, half-sarcastic, first-date question to lighten the mood.

"So, what kind of things do you like?" I asked.

"What kind of *things* do I like?" she said, repeating my question with a tinge of judgment.

"Yeah," I said with a simple tilt of my head and an easy smile.

"I like champagne and caviar. What do you like?" she replied seriously.

Oh no! She's one of those, I thought.

High maintenance alert! yelled The Boys. *You're gonna need a solid gold toolbox with diamonds inside to maintain this woman!*

I on-ly like cham-pagne and ca-vi-ar! Charles added mockingly.

I've never met a woman with such overt expectations of being put on a pedestal and finding a sugar daddy, but instead of dread, I suddenly took it as a challenge to see what this woman with the goddess-good looks was all about.

Talking with her for the next forty-five minutes, there was no doubt she was well-educated, well-traveled, and generally well-informed, but as I asked more about what she did in her work, it sounded less impressive than the night before, almost like she was between jobs, if I was reading her correctly. She asked a lot of questions about architecture, then seemed alarmed when I told her I was on a sabbatical of sorts.

"What do you mean 'of sorts?'" she asked, concerned. "Don't you make any money?"

Most people would have framed the question a little more like, "Sooo, it's okay that you're not working right now?" or something like that. But her anxiety and focus on money relaxed after I told her about my investing activities.

I tried not to stare, but as we talked, I kept wondering how her face could be so perfect and expressionless for so long—never smiling—and what her perpetual pouty-face look was all about.

Charles was the one who figured it out. *She's Botoxed to the max!*

Just as I was wrapping my head around that little piece of reality, she lobbed an unexpected grenade my way.

"So, are we okay here?" she asked.

"What? Are we *okay* here?" I said. "You mean like, do I *like* you, and do I want to keep going on with the evening?"

"Yes, of course. What else would I be asking?" she said with some indignation.

At that moment—over the shouting voices of The Boys saying, *What just happened? What is she asking us to say yes to*—another voice entered my head: the legendary TV voice of Rod Serling.

"Consider the question carefully, for it is not a simple one. Especially when you are on the precipice of entering … *The Twilight Zone*. Do-do do-do, do-do do-do!"

The Boys were frantically shouting by now.

Is she a hooker? She's a hooker! Why don't we get the hell out of here, now!

But it had just gotten really weird and so much more interesting. This was something I had never experienced—an executive recruiter of a different sort—and I was keen to know more about what I didn't know.

"Yes," I said, "we're good."

There was one more thing I wanted to know before we moved on, however.

"You didn't mention your age in your profile, but you know mine. May I ask yours?"

"You know you should never ask a woman her age," she said.

"Yes, I know, but it seems only fair. Besides, you know a lot more about me than I know about you."

While giving me the answer-this-truthfully-at-your-peril look, she said, "How old do you think I am?"

Even with her immaculate complexion, figure, and everything else, there were telltale signs that made me think she was older than I was. To gauge the age of a woman, I often look at her hands and eyes. You can tell by the skin on her hands. There is a thinness and transparency to it as one ages. For the eyes, it's something indescribable, something you can't Botox away, lest you go total zombie.

But like any guy with half a brain, I low-balled it. Thinking she was probably mid-fifties, I said late forties. With the compliment in hand, she didn't hesitate.

"I'm sixty."

Surprised and not surprised, I could only admire—she looked fabulous for any woman at any age.

With that behind us, I made the pivot to the evening ahead.

"Are you hungry? Would you like to go somewhere for dinner?"

"Dinner? Yes. I would like that. What do you have in mind?"

I mentioned one restaurant, but she said, "And what's nice about that?"

The Boys rolled their eyes at her in disbelief, and at me for playing along.

I then asked where she might like to go. She mentioned a well-known Italian restaurant as being a favorite.

"Okay. Why don't we go there?" I said.

"Do you have a car?"

"Yes, I'm parked about two blocks away."

"You want me to *walk* two blocks to your car? In this dress I wore for you and in these shoes? You *can't* be serious," she said. "What kind of car do you have?" she asked, seemingly more out of curiosity.

I had driven the minivan.

Upon hearing that, she looked at me like, you *really* have to be kidding.

I mentioned the Mercedes and my preference not to drive it into this crowded part of town, but that did little to appease her.

"Let's do an Uber," she said, before correcting herself, "an Uber Black."

I had the Uber app on my phone but had only used it once. I was less familiar with the differences between one Uber and the next.

"Sure, that's fine," I said.

I paid our check and helped her down from her perch on the chair. We walked out hand in hand, then I stopped in the vestibule to flip through the Uber app. As I did, she moved in close, touched her body to mine, pushed my back to the wall, then nuzzled her head into my neck. Thinking she wanted a kiss, I pulled back to see her face and leaned in.

"No!" she said. "No wet kisses. I don't like them."

"You don't like kissing?" I asked.

"Kissing is fine but not wet kisses."

"Kissing is fine but not wet kisses?" I repeated.

"Yes," she said.

"I'm not sure how that works," I responded.

"It works fine," she said nonchalantly, coming back in close and nuzzling me once again.

She then put her mouth to mine, held it there, and made the smallest pucker with her lips. I immediately flashed back to my first high school kiss where we touched lips, then had no idea what to do from there. It was totally weird then but even more weird now.

Back to the Uber app, there were no Uber Blacks to be found. Unbeknownst to me at the time, a big political event was going on in Washington, and all the Uber Blacks were tied up. I showed her the screen of my phone to prove there were none.

"Why don't we just take a cab?" I said.

"I don't like taxi cabs," she responded quickly. "They're so dirty."

"Just get an Uber," she commanded impatiently, then leaned back in and pressed me against the wall.

When our Uber arrived, she looked at the Prius and frowned.

"This is an Uber? How am I supposed to get into this?" she said, raising her voice.

I opened the door, and she somehow contorted her tightly dressed self into the back seat. I went around and got in on the street side. Once in, she complained it was like riding in a shopping cart. You'd think she was being tortured during the half-mile ride. The Uber driver heard everything and looked back with wary glances. But he knew better and kept his mouth shut.

Arriving in front of the restaurant, I thanked the driver while she said it was the worst Uber she'd ever taken. Offering my hand to help her, she stuck one leg out the door, putting one high-heeled shoe on the pavement, then bent and dragged the trailing leg out. In the process, her legs splayed, and she gave an up-skirt view of her white tights to everyone in front of the restaurant, but she seemed to care little.

The restaurant was clearly on the more exclusive side and much more to her liking. With the big event going on somewhere else in town, they were able to seat us without a reservation, and her mood lifted. She almost even smiled but not quite.

At our table, the conversation was thankfully more of the regular first-date variety. Sipping on another glass of champagne and reading through the menu, she decided on a rotini pasta dish.

When the waiter came to take our order, she offered specific instructions.

"Please tell the kitchen to make sure the pasta is cooked. I don't like it hard or chewy; it's impossible to eat. You know what I mean, right?"

After a bit of back and forth, and confident her order was clear, she let him go.

For the next fifteen minutes, she was quite the enjoyable dinner companion, but that ended when dinner arrived.

The waiter put down our plates, and she looked skeptically at the vegetables and pasta. Hesitantly, she picked up her fork, poked at one of the spirals, and took half a bite.

"They did *exactly* what I told them *not* to do!" she said, dropping her fork to the plate with a clank. "They *didn't cook the pasta!*"

The waiter was not far away, so I motioned him over.

"Yes. Is there something else I can get for you?" he asked.

"You can take *this back* to the kitchen and tell them *to cook* the pasta like I *told you to!*" Sabrina said, picking up her plate and dropping it into his just-in-time outstretched hands.

"I'm sorry, ma'am. The pasta is not cooked properly? It's not to your liking?"

"*Not* to my *liking?! No one* could eat this pasta! It's *not cooked!* All I wanted was for it to be *cooked!* Can't they do that?!" she demanded to know.

"Yes, ma'am. I'll have the kitchen re-cook the pasta if that's acceptable, or you can order something else if you prefer. I'm so sorry," the waiter said, apologizing profusely.

"Have them *just cook the pasta!*" she said again. "How *hard* can it *be?!*"

The waiter left, carrying her plate like a radioactive bomb.

"I'm sorry," I said.

"No! *They* should be sorry! How is yours? Is it cooked? I bet it's not cooked!"

My veal stuffed ravioli was fine.

Ten minutes later, the waiter brought out a new dinner for her. He put it down, stepped back, folded his hands in front—striking a subservient pose—

then waited for her to try it. He should have put his hands up to shield himself from what was about to happen.

"Oh my god! It's raw! How can this be! It's worse than before!"

"It's not cooked again?" the waiter asked warily.

"This is an Italian restaurant! How can you not know how to cook pasta?!" she said.

Picking up her fork, she speared a little spiral pasta and pushed it toward the waiter.

"Here! *You* try it!" she said.

He put one hand up in a gesture. "No, I can't do that, ma'am."

"*Eat it!*" she ordered again.

Now he put both palms out to decline.

"How can you do this?! How can an Italian restaurant not know how to cook pasta?! *How?!* I recommended this place to my friend here because I wanted to enjoy a nice dinner with him, our first dinner together! You know he went to Harvard and ran for Congress! He's an important person, and I wanted to impress him. What do you think he thinks of me now?!"

"I'm sorry, ma'am," the waiter said, almost whimpering.

She shoved the plate away, almost knocking over her glass of champagne.

"This is inexcusable! I'm *sorry* he's *ruined* our evening together, Turner. I *hope* you're happy!" she said, glaring back at the waiter who had the look of a man in front of a firing squad.

"I can take it ... take it away, ma'am," he said, fumbling for words.

"No! What good would that do! You don't know how to cook pasta here! I'll eat the vegetables and leave the pasta for you to throw away or feed to the rats! This is *inexcusable!*"

The waiter began taking small steps backward in an effort to shrink away, but then he ventured to ask, "Could I bring you more champagne, ma'am? On the house?"

"*Yes!*" she said imperiously. The waiter quickly skedaddled.

She stabbed another piece of pasta with her fork.

"Here. *You* eat it and tell me if I'm wrong," she said.

Putting it in my mouth and beginning to chew, I could see that she was right: the pasta was oddly undercooked. Not even close to being al dente.

"Okay, that's pretty bad. I don't understand; it's an Italian restaurant," I said, "but *he* wasn't the one who cooked it."

Sabrina tried to simmer down, but as she pushed around the pasta to pick out the vegetables, she still fumed. Hanging on to indignation was clearly a part of who she was or maybe part of acting like who she wanted to be, I wasn't sure.

As dinner was nearing an end, she looked at me with her big brown eyes.

"I want to say something to you, but I don't want you to judge me or think I say this to just anyone," she said.

No judgment here! said Charles. Darrell and Little Turner just laughed.

"Okay," I said.

"I don't do this normally, I want you to know that," she repeated herself, "but if you would like to, you can come to my apartment for a drink. But I *don't do this* normally, I just want you to know that. Don't think I do this with everyone I meet. I'm not that way," she said emphatically.

"That's very nice of you," I said. "Thank you."

She gave me a look that said, *I really don't think you believe that I don't always invite men to my apartment on a first date.*

She was right, of course.

We repeated the earlier Uber experience—her being unhappy, complaining, and telling the driver she didn't like his car. Four years later, as I began writing this chapter, an article in the *Wall Street Journal* discussed how low passenger ratings from Uber drivers stay with you forever. By now, I had taken about eight or so Uber rides, so I looked at my passenger rating. It was 4.4 out of 5. Dumbfounded at how it could be less than 5, I reviewed my ride history. They were all 5-out-of-5 except for the two rides with Sabrina. Both drivers had given me a rating of 4.

Just another way your history in the digital world never goes away.

The Uber dropped us off in front of her apartment building. It was an older, half-block-long, 1960s building, nine stories tall. Taking her hand, I started toward the front entrance when she tugged me back.

"I prefer to go in the side entrance—this way," she said, walking toward the street corner to the end of the building.

Using her keycard to open the small side door, we went into a sparse vestibule. She opened another door that led into a stairwell.

"I hope for your sake, in that dress and those shoes, you're just one floor up."

"No, I live on the seventh floor," she said. "I prefer coming in this way and taking the stairs."

You mean with men you've just met, added The Boys.

This must be her strategy for preventing the building's reception desk people from keeping score of all the different men she brings home, I thought.

It made total sense for someone who only likes champagne, caviar, and Uber Blacks to walk up seven flights of stairs in high heels, when only two hours ago, she couldn't walk two short blocks to my car.

This is not good, The Boys said, still trying to get me to listen. *No one sneaks up the backstair of an apartment building without a damn good reason. She's got her swaying hips inches from your face as we walk up the steps behind her, and there's not much left to the imagination up her short skirt. This is trouble! You—we—need to get out of here!*

I was worried too; it felt unseemly.

On the seventh floor, we arrived in a narrow hallway. It had been cheaply renovated, the kind of thing you see all the time in older apartment buildings, even in good locations.

Arriving at her door, she said again, "Okay, don't think I do this with just anyone. I think you and I will be friends, so it's okay."

Her one-bedroom apartment was much like the hallway—old, tired, and with only the smallest attempt at renovations to make it look nice. In the development business, it's derisively called "putting lipstick on a pig." There was a little vestibule, off which was a small galley kitchen. It had a granite bar counter that separated it from the main room for dining and living. Another little hallway off to the side went to a bathroom and her bedroom. It was pretty standard fare.

"Nice place," I said.

"Thank you," she said back. "That's a Roche Bobois sofa. It's the *best*, you know. Do you know Roche Bobois?" She nodded over to the large, L-shaped sofa that dominated the room.

It was as tired-looking as the rest of the place.

"Yes, I know Roche Bobois. They make some nice things."

"Come in and make yourself at home," she said, taking off her red leather jacket and kicking off her high heels.

"I have some wine. Come choose what you'd like. I buy it from the wine store on Connecticut Avenue. It's the best wine store in Washington you know."

She opened the refrigerator and pulled out two already-opened bottles of white wine. From the cabinet, she pulled out an unopened red.

Standing close to her, I chose one of the whites. She poured and handed me my glass. "Cheers!"

After a sip of wine and a moment of silence, she asked, "Why are you so quiet? Are you getting *shy* on me?"

Deciding I would keep this little sojourn to her apartment short and simple, I walked around to the other side of the bar counter so it was now between us.

"If I can't kiss you the way I want to right now, what else am I supposed to do? I'll just enjoy the wine and your company for a few minutes before I take off. You mentioned the other night you don't usually stay up late. It's almost eleven o'clock now, and it's a school night."

She missed the "school night" reference, one of several lost-in-translation comments that evening.

"Then I don't know why you bothered to come up," she said.

"An invitation by a beautiful woman to come to her apartment? How can I say no to that?" I raised my glass to toast her.

Oh geez! Said The Boys. *Just stop it! This is stupid! Can we just go home, please?!*

She gave me a frustrated look. I wasn't playing the game the way it was supposed to be played.

Across the counter, we chatted for ten minutes to kill time as we drank our wine. She picked up the bottle and came around the counter to offer me more, reiterating that it came from the best wine store in Washington.

Without a word, I put my glass down, took the bottle from her hand, her glass from the other, then picked her up and sat her up on the countertop, facing me.

"Oh! You *do* have passion in you. I was beginning to wonder," she said in an unemotional and mocking tone.

I pushed her dress up above her hips to expose her white tights and leaned in to kiss up and down her neck.

"Oh! So passionate!" she said again and again in the same emotionless, mocking voice. "You have my *dress up*. I *wonder* what you have in *mind*?"

Then I moved to pull away. Not liking that, she wrapped her legs around me and pulled me tight. I took my hands and grabbed her nicely sized breasts through her dress, but she jerked back and slapped my hands away. There was something about her breasts she didn't want me to know, but I had a pretty good idea.

Foam rubber is what came to mind.

After a few more minutes of, "Oh! You're so passionate! I think you're about to be on fire!" I reached around and forcefully unlocked her legs from behind me.

"I should go. It's late. But I really enjoyed our evening," I said.

"You have to go?" she asked, with more real emotion than I'd heard from her all night.

Then, thinking for a moment, she said, "Sure you don't want another glass of wine? You *do* like the wine, don't you?"

"Yes, the wine is nice, but no thank you. It's getting late."

"Well okay," she said. "I'm sorry the wine wasn't better. You can go back down the same stair you came up if you like."

"How about the lobby and the front door?" I asked. "Am I not allowed to go out the front door?"

I wanted the security cameras to see me leaving through the *front door*, not the backstair, for my own protection.

"Yes, you can go out the front door. It's up to you. Of course, you can," she said.

Saying my goodbyes and giving her a *dry* kiss, I left with palatable relief.

****

Sabrina texted the next morning about how much she enjoyed our evening and thought we could be "good friends." Clearly, the word "friends" was a euphemism for her kind of relationship with men. For my part, I was curious to see her one more time, preferably during the day. Without a doubt, she cloaked herself in the night, but in the light of day, I thought she might be a different person. Perhaps the games would diminish and maybe the nice, smart person I thought she was deep inside would come through.

> **ME:** Are you free Saturday afternoon? Maybe we could take a walk on the National Mall. Weather will be nice.

> **SABRINA:** Yes, maybe. The afternoon or the evening are fine.

> **ME:** Great. How about 2:00? I can pick you up or meet you.

> **SABRINA:** I think the night would be better. Why don't you come to my place at 8:00? You can pick up some wine at the store I told you about on Connecticut Ave. They're the best.

I had to think twice, three times, even four times about it. Over the objections of The Boys—that is, them screaming *noooo!!!* at the top of their lungs—I replied:

> **ME:** 8:00 works. Happy to bring the wine. See you then.

****

When Saturday evening came, I grabbed a chilled bottle of white and a bottle of red and headed to the city. Traffic was a nightmare, with early spring activities going on everywhere. Trying to find a place to park meant block upon block of crawling around, looking for a spot. After finally parking and walking several blocks, it felt almost as creepy walking in the front door of her building as it had been going in the side door two nights before.

Opening her apartment door to greet me, she was dressed the opposite of what I had expected—a loose, semi-sheer ruffled top that barely covered her midriff, white jean shorts hemmed above the knee, and bare feet. She looked more ready for a walk on the beach than a Saturday evening date.

"Hi," she said, opening the door. "How are you tonight?"

"I'm good. How are you? Traffic is crazy out there. Really nuts," I said, walking in.

Closing the door, I somehow knew what was coming next.

"So it was a *problem* coming to see me? Is *that* what you're wanting to tell me?"

"No, I was commenting on traffic tonight. That's all."

"It sounded like you weren't happy to come here," she said sourly.

"Sabrina," I said, turning to look her square in the eyes, "if I didn't want to be here, I wouldn't. I have plenty of things I could be doing with my time, I assure you."

"Okay. It just sounded like you weren't happy to be here," she muttered under her breath.

"So … how are you, Sabrina?" I said in a let's-do-a-reset tone of voice.

"I'm okay. I'm fine," she said. "You brought the wine, I see. Didn't I tell you the wine store has great wines? What did you bring?"

"Actually, I brought two bottles from home I thought you might enjoy."

A silence came over her.

One Mississippi …

Two Mississippi …

Three Mississippi …

"Why didn't you go where I told you to? They have the best wine in the city. What are *these*?" she said, taking the bottles and looking at the labels. "I have some good wine here, but I *thought* you'd bring something special from the store on Connecticut."

"They *are* special," I said. "The white is very nice, very dry, very crisp, and one of my favorites. The red is a great cabernet."

That was two strikes against me, and I hadn't even been in the door five minutes.

"I don't understand. Why didn't you go there? Can you please tell me?"

"Because parking there is impossible. I have some nice wines at home. I wanted to get here and not be late," I replied.

She mumbled on as I opened the wine. I knew she'd hate it—if nothing more than on principle—but then she let it go … for now.

"Cheers." Trying to turn things around, I raised my glass to her. "To a beautiful woman."

That seemed to work for the moment.

"Please, make yourself at home," she said, gesturing toward the living room with a "whatever" wave of her hand.

A continuous window ran the entire width of the room. It gave an expansive view of the busy street below and the city beyond. It was easy to admire the nighttime city lights from our seventh-floor perch. She kept the lights off in the apartment except for a small one in the kitchen, so the room was illuminated only by the lights from outside.

"What a great view," I said.

"Thank you," she responded. "I never tire of it."

We walked to the sofa with our wine and sat down. She folded her legs and sat sideways to me as I looked at her and the view out the window. As I was thinking she wouldn't be able to pass up a chance to comment on the sofa again, she read my mind.

"Isn't this Roche Bobois sofa so comfortable? I mean, there's nothing like it," she said, passing her hand across the fabric before placing it on my shoulder and touching my neck.

Pausing momentarily, she then said, "You know, you can spend the night here if you want. You don't have to drive back late tonight. You can sleep here on the sofa. After all, it's Roche Bobois. It's very comfortable."

It was now my turn to pause; I decided to simply play along.

"Where would you be? In your bedroom?"

"Yes, *of course*. But you can be out here. There's nothing wrong with that. It's perfectly fine."

"But that's not fair. How am I supposed to sleep, knowing there's a beautiful woman right next door in her bed? That's a lot to ask of a guy. I'd be up all night, thinking about you in there."

"It's up to you," she said nonchalantly.

Pretending to consider it for a moment, I said, "I think I'll go home for the night, but thanks for the invitation."

"That doesn't make sense to me, but do as you please," she said, sipping her wine and looking away.

Trying to move on, I saw photos and personal items on a shelf across the room I hadn't noticed two nights before. I asked about a particular photo, and that began a conversation on her life that went on for ten or fifteen minutes. Then, slipping out from under her hand, I got up to look at the items on the shelf. She followed and started an isn't-this-great tour of every item.

She then asked personal questions about me, offering condolences on the loss of my wife. As she talked and I got a little emotional, she reached behind me, grabbed the bottle of wine off the counter, and filled my glass to the top.

"So why do you like to dance?" she asked, shifting the conversation. "Most men hate it."

"What's not to like? It can be so romantic, personal, and intimate. Especially when you slow dance together and you become in sync with one another. Slow or fast, though, it doesn't matter, as long as you're touching."

"I think that's very nice too," she said, then, after pausing for a moment to think, "I want to dance."

As I turned to put my glass down, she added quickly, "No, I want to dance, but *not* with you."

"Oh? How does *that* work?" I asked.

"Your way to dance is not the *only* way."

She grabbed her iPhone, plugged it into a speaker on the shelf, then began to search for music. Soon, what sounded like festive Middle Eastern dance music filled the room. She then gave a two-handed shove to my chest to push me away. Not having moved me far enough, she pushed again, putting all her weight behind it, a push that said, *Get back! Get out of my way! I'm serious!*

She pushed so hard, wine sloshed out of my glass onto the floor, but luckily, not on the *Roche Bobois*.

What followed can only be described as The Dance of the Seven Victoria's-Secret Veils.

As the fast-moving music flowed, she moved to the beat, spinning back and forth in an open area in front of the window. As she spun, she lifted her top above her head, revealing a lingerie-type bra that was very sheer and very small.

Holy cow! exclaimed Darrell.

Is she belly dancing? Or stripping?!

I stood there gawking, not quite sure what this was supposed to be. Was it some sort of dance of seduction? All I could do was watch and wait as she pranced around the room, spinning and lifting her top. But my previous guess about her breasts was confirmed: it *was* a foam-filled bra—she hardly had any breasts at all.

After ten minutes or so, she spun and hopped around with her top lifted high in a flourishing finale. Then she calmly walked over, turned off the music, and did a bottoms-up of her wine glass.

"That's how *I* dance. What do you think?"

Yeah, Turner, what do you-u think? Said Darrell, mocking her and taunting me.

"I confess that's a first," I said. "Was that belly dancing?"

"No," she said. "It's simply how *I* like to dance."

"With your top up?" I asked.

"I do what feels good. I feel free with the music. I don't care what you think."

"Well, thank you," I said, "for showing me your dancing … and your bra."

"You're welcome. I like nice lingerie."

I grabbed the bottle of wine and refilled her glass.

"Thank you," she said. She raised her glass to toast. "To dance!"

"To dance!" I said, then we clinked glasses.

"Now … show me how *you* like to dance," she said.

"Okay, we'll need a little different kind of music," I said, pulling out my iPhone. "Do you know Diana Krall?"

"Yes. I know who she is. You like her?" she asked.

"I like her music a lot. She's phenomenal." I plugged my phone into her speaker.

A few seconds later, Diana Krall came on, singing about love, and I reached for Sabrina. She came in close, placed one hand in mine, and we began to slow dance to the sultry jazz. Almost immediately, she put her head on my shoulder and cuddled into my arms. We moved together, enveloped by the music, the darkness of the room, and each other. Once the song ended, we kept our embrace and kept dancing until the next song came on. We continued slow dancing until the second song faded away.

"Okay. Enough of that," she said, abruptly breaking off. "I don't like dancing to the music of a dead woman."

"What?" I said. "Who's dead?"

"Diana Krall," she said. "She's old and now she's dead."

I looked at her, dumbfounded. She knew how to take a tender moment and make it a Tinder moment.

"What are you talking about? She's not old or dead! She's younger than either of us and very much alive! I saw her in concert a few weeks ago."

"She's *dead*!" she repeated, unmoved.

"Good grief. Here, I'll show you." I did a quick internet search and held my phone out to her. "See! Here she is, an attractive *younger* woman. And here's her bio too."

"She's *dead*!" Sabrina repeated insistently after glancing at the photo on my screen.

I threw my hands up in the air. "Poor Diana," I said, shaking my head in disbelief. "And she looked so good just a few weeks ago."

I picked up my glass of wine and plunked down onto the Roche Bobois.

Where can this possibly go from here? I thought.

She stood across the room from me with her arms crossed. She alternated staring at me and staring out the window.

A few silent and awkward minutes passed, then she said in a quiet voice, "Can we cuddle?"

Oh geez, said The Boys. *This is nuts!*

"Sure, we can cuddle," I said softly.

This is so-oo weird. When's this going to end? asked The Boys.

I took off my shoes and laid down, stretching out against the back of the sofa. She laid down facing me and buried her head into the crook of my neck as we entwined our legs and arms. After that, she said nothing, nor did she move. As with everything about her, I wasn't sure what this was supposed to be. After a bit, my gaze drifted to the window and the nighttime city outside. A while longer still, and I thought perhaps she'd fallen asleep. Somewhere along the way, I began to gently stroke her back.

The room was silent for the longest time.

Just when I thought all the tension might have melted away, she spoke.

"Can you stop doing that? It's *really* annoying."

I stopped stroking her, and we just lay there in silence for a while.

She then moved, pulling her head up to look at me, then sitting up all the way.

"I don't know why you don't stay. You look comfortable here on my sofa. Isn't it comfortable?" she asked.

"It's *very* comfortable, but as I said before, I don't think I could be out here knowing you're in there."

In silence again, and a little annoyed, she moved over to the short part of the L-shaped sofa and lay down on her back. I got up and moved to sit at her feet. She bent her knees up, and I moved in closer. From there, she looked up at me from between her legs, and I looked down at her. We began a meandering conversation for a few minutes before she made a pivot.

"You know, you can do with me whatever you want."

"Whatever I want?"

"Yes, of course. What do you want to do? You were so passionate the other night when you had me on the kitchen counter and my dress was up."

With that, she pulled up her loose top and bra to reveal her breasts and erect nipples.

I reached through between her knees and pulled her bra and top back down.

She looked at me, not understanding.

"Are you a biter or a nibbler," she said, pulling her top and bra off over her head. "Do you like my nipples?"

"It depends on the moment, I guess, whether I bite or nibble."

I leaned in toward her but ignored her breasts and kissed her—a wet kiss— and she reciprocated.

Then our lips parted.

"Okay," she said. "You're pretty good at step number two ... but you're lousy at step number one."

"I'm good at step number *two* but lousy at step number *one*?" I repeated, then kissed her again.

"Yes," she said, breaking our kiss.

I didn't ask the next obvious question, "What is step number one?" so she shifted gears again.

"Are you short of cash?" she asked.

"What?"

"Are you short of cash?" she repeated.

Damn! She's a hooker! I told you! yelled Darrell.

"Am I short of cash?"

"Yes."

"No, I'm not short of cash," I said.

"Then why didn't you bring me flowers, and why did you bring this *shit* wine?" she said, annoyed.

And with that, I froze.

Be very careful what you say next, said Little Turner, *be very careful.*

I sat up and stared down at her.

Looking up at me, impatient with my silence, she said mockingly, "So are you going to take your little ball and leave the sandbox now?"

I turned from Sabrina and looked out the window.

Get. The. Hell. Out! The Boys yelled. *Now!*

And this time, I listened.

"Yeah, I think I am."

I put my shoes on, then stood up to straighten my clothes before grabbing my jacket. She watched, still and silent.

"I'll go out the front if that's okay," I said.

She got off the sofa and stood, still naked on top.

"You don't *have* to go," she said.

"Yeah … I do. I can take the rest of this 'shit wine' if you don't want it."

"Do whatever you like," she said. "I won't drink it."

"Sabrina. You're a fascinating woman," I said, walking to the door and stopping for one last look. "Goodnight."

****

The next morning, scrambled eggs with a side of amnesia would have been welcome. Instead, Sabrina sent a text.

> **SABRINA:** Hi, Turner. Even with what happened last night, I think we can still be friends. You want to come over today?

Looking at my phone, I could only shake my head in disbelief. *That's amazing.*

ME: Sabrina, true friends are very precious. They are understanding, loyal, and above all, kind. You are none of these things. We cannot be friends.

CHAPTER 20

Last Orbits Around Venus

IF LIFE IS A CIRCLE—THAT all things end where they begin—so, too, was my journey on Venus. Spring was now in full swing, and I was back to the way it all started—meeting one woman after another, after another, after another.

Slim and petite, with dark hair and a fair complexion, Irene was forty-eight years old. She worked in banking and was still in the throes of major life changes after her divorce a few years earlier. She mentioned in one of her emails that she had just bought a new home, passing a big post-divorce milestone.

We had a typical first-date interview at a local bar and restaurant near her home, about a half hour away. It was generally unremarkable and made me feel like I was back in *Dating 101*. But in the end, she said she enjoyed meeting and would like to see me again.

The Boys' comments about a second date succinctly captured the current state of dating affairs. *Yeah, fine, whatever. Let's just get it over with.*

For our second date, I drove out to her new house in my Mercedes and picked her up for dinner and a movie. Her house was one of the first completed in a new development on a new street, so I drove warily, wanting to avoid any construction debris that could damage the car.

Once we were on our way, Irene spoke pretty freely about everything. You know, when you first meet someone, you typically use fairly polite language, no slang or sexual stuff? She peppered her conversation in the car with "getting off," and "screwing," and "orgasm," among other choice words.

Then, after twenty minutes, she paused. "There's something I want to tell you, but I'm not sure if it's too early since this is only our second date."

My first thoughts went to sex. What else could it be the way she was talking?

"You should probably know," she went on to say, "I see ghosts."

"You see what?"

"I see ghosts."

"You see ghosts?"

"Yeah, all the time, and I talk to them too."

"You see ghosts and talk to them too?"

"Yeah."

"Oh … ahem … okay, where do you see ghosts?"

"Usually at night. At home. They come to see me."

"Ah," I said, trying to maintain some sort of composure. "Well, I have to say, that's not something I have any experience with. Do you know why they come to see you?"

"I think they're just really comfortable with me."

"Ah, okay, what do-o-o they-yy usually like to talk about?"

"They want to use me to communicate with someone who's living. Ghosts are dead, you know."

"Right, yeah … I-ii think I've heard that before."

I went on, "I have to say, I'm not sure I believe in ghosts and all that stuff. I know some things happen that are hard to explain, but I'm not sure about the ghost thing."

"Yeah, I know, most people don't, so I thought you should know."

"Thanks! Feel free to fill me in some more. Maybe I'll become a believer."

Have you lost your mind?! The Boys chimed in. *Don't you dare get wacky in the head for this chick.*

The conversation moved on, even as the ghost thing lingered in my mind. Dinner went well enough, and there were no ghosts in the movie theater. During the drive back to her place, she shared another personal tidbit.

"I have a collection of crucifixes, mostly very old ones. They're really neat. I just love them."

Of course, she has a collection of crucifixes! The Boys said. *Maybe she has some voodoo dolls too!*

Arriving back at her place, she asked if I'd like to come in and see the house. Given that the date had not been particularly flirty, I assumed it was a straight-up invitation on her part that, as an architect, I might like to see and look around her new home.

It was nicely furnished, but for whatever reason, she turned on only a few lights. Looking around, there was a mysterious feeling about the whole place.

"They're down there on the wall." She pointed through the living room to the dining room at the far end.

Crucifixes large and small were hung all over. Others were sitting on tables around the room. It wasn't just creepy; it was shit-fucking creepy.

The comments that came out of my mouth were subtly sarcastic, but she took them as genuine interest. She picked up a crucifix, told me the story about it, then pointed to a large wooden one on the wall, talking about where it came from in Europe.

I wasn't sure where the evening was headed, but I knew where I was headed, and I began saying my goodbyes. We exchanged a hug and a brief kiss, then she walked me out to my car.

I was careful as I drove away not to run over anything on the ground from the construction, but the next morning, I discovered I hadn't been careful enough.

I went out to my car to do a walk-around, and I saw it—a bright-green plastic tab attached to my rear tire ... with its accompanying one-and-a-half-inch-long roofing staple.

"Shit!"

I looked carefully to see if it might have gone through the bottom of the tire. A tire can be repaired if a puncture happens on the tread, but if it's in the sidewall, you have to replace it.

It was in the sidewall.

How the hell did that get in there?

"Shit!"

Them ghosts didn't think too much of your fancy-schmancy car and shoved that sucker right in there! said Darrell. *Too-o-o bad!*

"Shit!"

****

Lisa was a Washington lobbyist. Her eHarmony profile noted she was a couple of years older than I was and widowed seven years earlier. Her photos showed a slim, smartly dressed woman with a simple hair bob—the kind that's ubiquitous in the nation's capital.

Saying she "wanted to touch base with at least a brief response" to my first message on eHarmony, it was easy to see she was a busy, heavily scheduled person. But she told me to feel free to Google her, gave me her email address, and ended her short message with, "More later—will be in touch. L"

A quick search revealed she was all over the internet. There were countless photos of her with prominent movers and shakers of society, politics, and finance. In our first email exchange, I used the subject line *Girl on the Go!* and happened to mention I was dealing with taxes as April fifteenth approached. She let me know she had "people" who handled these and most other things in her life.

The Boys piped up. *We're your people, Turner. Go ahead, tell her.*

Then, more seriously, *So how far do you think this is going to go with Ms. 'L'? Your dates will be scheduled to the minute by one of her "people," when she's available, that is.*

Once again, The Boys were well ahead of me.

In our first twenty-four hours of correspondence, Lisa's emails were frequent but short. In one, she let me know she was about to attend a business lunch in New York City, with a dinner to follow that evening. She would be seated next to the CEO of General Motors at dinner, Mary Barra, who had been named head of the company only a year earlier. I followed her with interest, given my investment activities, and gave Lisa a quick summary of Barra. She thanked me cheerfully.

She continued sending emails during the dinner, name-dropping as she went along. She had attended a cocktail reception for Lester Crown, the son of the founder of the precursor company to General Dynamics; he was always on the Forbes 400 list of the wealthiest individuals in the U.S. (for my fellow architects, think Crown Hall by Mies van der Rohe). David Rubenstein, Warren Buffett, and other super-wealthy names soon followed.

The next day, she sent a brief rundown of her schedule.

EMAIL RECEIVED: A Girl on the Go!

Picked up at airport, stopped at home, headed to 9:30 am dentist. Meeting friend at Hay Adams at noon, lunch w old boss at the White House at 1, doctor appointment this

> afternoon, then pick my daughter up at DCA at 5:30 pm. That's
> my schedule!
>
> L

Yeah ... almost your schedule too, The Boys wisecracked.

EMAIL SENT: A Girl on the Go!

> Whoa! ... When does it get to be Lisa time? And what does
> Lisa do when she gets Lisa time?
>
> Turner

I got no response to that one.

She sent ten emails in twenty-four hours, and a picture of her began to emerge.

She had a second home on the Chesapeake Bay and horses stabled in Maryland. In her waking hours, she rubbed elbows with the rich and famous and didn't hesitate to name names. It seemed like she could've given Ava a run for her money—literally—and for all I knew, their paths may have crossed.

Things were quiet the next day, but Saturday morning, she called out of the blue. She was in Florida with her college-aged kids on spring break. We talked all of two minutes before she said she had to run.

What the hell was that about? asked Darrell.

She emailed the next day, apologizing for calling only to say she couldn't talk.

A fleeting moment of self-awareness? asked Charles.

A few days later, she sent a detailed email about a spontaneous trip from Florida to the Caribbean. More beach time with the kids, golf, dinners, and a massage on the beach. The relaying of personal travel logs, business travel, conferences, and meetings was the gist of her frequent correspondence.

We did finally speak for about thirty minutes a week later when she was in New York for the weekend. She spoke casually—mostly about the activities of daily life—but absolutely nothing in the way of what two people would normally talk about who had just met on a dating site. However, we did coordinate our calendars and scheduled a dinner for about a month out.

When the time came, I took her to another one of my favorite restaurants, and we had a nice evening, for the most part. She was smart, well-informed, and accomplished, but it felt like a work dinner with a client more than anything else, and I was the client.

At the end, she offered an invitation for me to join her the following week at the Kennedy Center for an all-hands-on-deck evening for their company to entertain clients. They were one of the sponsors of a private event: A Conversation with a Living Legend: President Bill Clinton and General Colin Powell on stage with moderator Bob Schieffer.

Holy cow. This is awesome. What an opportunity! I thought.

As a news junkie, this would be unbelievable. To top it off, the Yale a cappella group, *The Whiffenpoofs,* would perform on the Eisenhower Theater stage at the end. I was excited at the invitation and honored she felt comfortable enough to take me to a work event with her heavy-hitter, power-broker colleagues. Then, as an afterthought, she mentioned one more thing—she would have to leave early to catch a flight to Dallas that evening.

"But you can stay and enjoy the event," she said breezily.

As we said our goodbyes, I got a quick peck of a kiss, and off she went. It was the kind of quick kiss you'd get from a spouse before hustling off to work on a busy morning.

We corresponded that week about logistics for the coming evening. She said she could bring her bag to the Kennedy Center and cab it to the airport, but I offered to leave early and drive her.

She accepted.

When I arrived at her large and very nice home in Washington that Tuesday evening, she gave me another millisecond-kiss hello, then asked me to sit down and make myself comfortable as she finished packing. Three staff were there, who she said were cleaning people, but as she asked questions and gave directions, they were clearly some of her "people" people.

Into the Mercedes with her bag and off to the Kennedy Center we went. She explained that clients would be there, as well as the leadership of her company. I asked how I could be most helpful during the cocktail hour.

"You ran for Congress, so I assume you can work a room as well as anyone. I'll introduce you to a few people, then just talk. You'll be fine."

We arrived in the grand foyer to a throng of dark suits, loud and lively conversations, and bar drinks flowing like water. Other companies were in attendance with their guests, and it looked like it would be a full house in the Eisenhower Theater that night.

She saw familiar faces, and we dove right into the middle of the crowd. It consisted of well-known CEOs I recognized from Wall Street and Silicon Valley. She introduced me to several senior directors in her company, who gave me wary looks at first. But after sizing me up, they treated me like I must have had a few million dollars here or a few million dollars there.

Lisa then introduced me to one of her company's senior people. Coincidentally, he had played football at the small college where I had recently designed a new football facility. He immediately went into stories of his gridiron-glory-days of forty years before. Lisa quickly disappeared, leaving me to smile and silently nod my head as he reminisced for the next fifteen minutes about all the big games. I was finally saved by the bell when the chime rang for us to be seated in the theater.

I was bummed at not being able to stay for the whole event, but given I was trying to impress Lisa, I said, "No worries," whenever she apologized for having to leave early.

The event started at six thirty, and we had to leave at seven fifteen, so I figured we'd grab seats on an end row and not be too close to the stage. But no, that's not what happened. Her company had a block of seats up front, and we made our way to the fifth row.

Surely, we'll sit on the end, I thought, to be the least disruptive as possible when we left.

No, not that either.

Lisa saw people she wanted to sit with in the middle of the long row, so we sidestepped our way in twelve seats deep. We were center stage, right in front of where former President Clinton and General Powell would be sitting.

As the program began—with several long-winded introductory speeches—I could see we were close enough to the stage to be visible because of stage-light spillover. We wouldn't even be able to slip out unnoticed in the dark.

At 6:55, President Clinton, General Powell, and Bob Schieffer were finally introduced to a thunderous standing ovation. I could have reached out and touched them, they were so close.

"Should we slip out now?" I asked Lisa. "We have to leave in twenty minutes anyway."

"No," she said, clapping enthusiastically and smiling toward the stage.

Bob Schieffer moderated a conversational-style format, offering questions for extended discussion. It was truly fascinating to hear their thoughts about events, past and present. But I was nervous and uncomfortable at the prospect of our exiting in the middle of this amazing program with a former president, an important general, and half a trillion dollars of wealth in the theater. We were going to look incredibly rude.

I nervously glanced at my watch over and over as the minutes ticked away.

Finally, Lisa gave the signal.

Of course, there was no easy way to slip past twelve seats without people having to stand up to let us by. As the *wave* of people stood up and down to our "Excuse me, sorry ... excuse me, sorry," I tried to keep my head down and just go, but I chanced a glance at the stage.

Bob Schieffer was in the process of asking his next question when Bill Clinton saw the commotion of our leaving. He glanced from Bob down to us. Colin Powell saw the president look at the wave of people standing up and down, so he looked too. Then Bob Schieffer, seeing the two of them distracted, stopped talking and turned to look at the commotion in the audience as well. With the pause on stage, now the whole frickin' audience of 2,300 turned to look at Lisa and me sidestepping ourselves out.

God damn it! I thought. *This is just so inconsiderate.*

Lisa and I long-stepped our way up the aisle as fast as we could. As we burst through the doors into the lobby, fourteen white-tie-and-black-tail-clad *Whiffenpoofs* were startled, jumping like a waddle of penguins on snow.

"Is it time for us to go on already? It's go time guys! It's go time!" said a few, as they adjusted their white ties and gloves for the performance.

I can't remember ever feeling as embarrassed as I did in those few moments when we left the theater with all of those eyes on us, but Lisa was nonplussed.

I drove her to the airport, got my millisecond-kiss goodbye, and my evening was done by a quarter 'til eight.

Emails from Lisa over the next few weeks were more of the same travel logs. Two dates in, I could see nothing in the way of a connection, let alone anything in the romance zone, but we made a pivotal third date for dinner on a Sunday evening at an elegant waterfront restaurant in Georgetown.

Over drinks and dinner, it was shaping up to be another business-type affair, so I thought I'd spice it up a bit with a little flirting. Awkward doesn't come close to describing how it went; she gave me a confused look and a lot of silence.

With confirmation that things were going nowhere, I decided it was time to lay the groundwork to part ways with Ms. L.

I knew from my time with Christine that topics about money were not particularly welcome. So I tossed out in conversation that I knew she was of "much greater means than me" and wondered how a relationship like that "might work if we were together."

"You have *no idea* what my means are," she said with glaring indignation.

Well ... that was easy, said Charles.

And my time with Ms. L was over.

****

Janet lived forty-five minutes away in a neighboring county. Her profile description was rather brusque. She said she wasn't looking to be anyone's girlfriend but wanted to meet men, go out, and enjoy life. Unlike Margaret two years before, who told me she only wanted to be friends at the end of our first date, Janet was upfront about it.

I sent her a fairly no-nonsense message, and much to my surprise, she responded. She was a fellow empty nester, a divorcee, and head of admissions at a private school. We made a dinner date for the following week at a restaurant about halfway between us.

Janet was in her early fifties, more handsome than pretty, trim, and athletic. She was a smart conversationalist—in an academic sort of way—and a great dinner companion for two hours. Our conversations were wide-ranging, in depth, and thought-provoking. There were no games at all being played, which was refreshing. She was a woman I could simply enjoy being with, period.

As we were saying goodnight, I leaned in to offer a hug and peck of a kiss on her cheek. Surprisingly, she zeroed in with a lip-locking, tongue-wrestling kiss as we stood by her car. As I walked away, I thought she was the first professional kisser I had ever experienced—a real dynamo in that department—especially for someone who just wanted to be friends.

Well, okay, said The Boys, *she really likes to kiss. Just go with it.*

From that enjoyable evening, we made a date a few weeks later for me to come her way to play tennis and have dinner.

The day came, and I was heading to the tennis facility in the late afternoon when it began to rain pretty hard. We talked by phone while I was driving and decided it was a washout, so I went straight to her house. At least we could spend some time together and have a nice dinner.

She was in her tennis-skirt outfit as we sat at the bar counter in her kitchen. We had some wine and munchies and chatted for a bit. That's when I found out what she was really about.

She said she had bought the house not too long ago, and that the property, access, and layout would make it great for the sex parties she was hoping to host.

"Oh good," I said, like I held sex parties all the time too.

Darrell said, *Oh baby! Jackpot!*

However, she said, a complication had arisen.

A new family had moved in a few houses down, and one of her new neighbors was a student at her school. She fretted that her sex-party hosting just got a bit dicey. She went on to say that there were great sex parties in a community right next to mine, and she had been to one last week. After a few sex-party questions, I steered the conversation to something else that I have absolutely no recollection of whatsoever.

After thirty minutes of chitchat, she said, "Let's go to the bedroom."

As she stood by her bed, in one swift motion, she pulled off her clothes, stepped out of her panties, and was totally naked. She had my clothes off in short order, then produced a condom that was nothing short of a NASA spacesuit—nothing would get through that thing. But I was pretty grateful for the best condom NASA had to offer, given the situation.

In short order, we were done. We each showered, then went out for a nice dinner nearby. Sex was no more than a scheduled activity for her, just like playing tennis or walking the dog. All of it was fine, in any order, and at any time.

As I was driving home, I thought the whole episode was the most unsatisfying thing I had ever experienced. Most men would be chomping at the bit to have this—sex at the drop of a hat with no strings attached—but I found the whole thing devoid of emotion, feelings, and desire. There was no sense of connection at all.

I never spoke with her again, and I never mentioned this particular episode to Abby or anyone else, for that matter. As much as Abby and I were willing to share, I decided to keep this one to myself.

****

Saturday mornings are typically the busiest times in the online dating world—looking at dating profiles, making new matches, and exchanging messages while lazily lying in bed. On this particular Saturday morning, I received a message on OkCupid that was one sentence long.

"So, Turner, have you figured out yet that all women are bat-shit crazy?"

I froze.

What the hell?

Has my account been hacked?

Has my life been hacked?!

I couldn't believe it.

The Boys were jolted too. *This is freaky! ... Cue the Jaws music.*

Thinking I *had* been hacked somehow, I shut off my phone in a mild panic and sat frozen while my mind raced.

What does she know, and how does she know it?

Finally, convinced I couldn't have been hacked, I turned the phone back on, stared at the message, and then went to her profile. There wasn't much there except her name, Allison.

Slowly, I typed a reply and sent it with both trepidation and curiosity.

> **ME:** As a matter of fact, I think I have figured that out. But how did *you* know?

> **ALLISON:** Because all women are. I'm bat-shit crazy too.

> **ME:** And you contacted me just to tell me this?

ALLISON: I thought you needed to be warned. I liked your profile. You seem like the only nice guy out there.

Allison lived ninety miles away in Washington, Virginia, where The Inn at Little Washington was located, the incredible French restaurant where Mary had taken me for my birthday three weeks before she passed away. Allison had no picture on her profile, but her age was listed as fifty. No picture usually meant a woman who was not confident in her appearance. I pointed out the missing photo, and she asked for my cell phone number so she could text me one. Given the ability to block anyone if needed, I gave it to her.

She texted a photo of an early-twenty-something woman. It had a yellow cast to it, so clearly, it was an old photo. The woman in the picture was a stunning beauty.

ME: Wow! That's you when you were young? Stunning! Were you a model?

ALLISON: They tried to get me to model for Playboy, but I wouldn't take off my clothes.

ME: Well, that's a good thing. Smart girl. What about a picture of you now?

ALLISON: I'm very self-conscious about how I look now; I'd rather not. I want to get back into shape, I really do.

> **ME:** I understand.

My curiosity satisfied, I was ready to end the correspondence. I told her I needed to get going for the day, but that perhaps we could touch base later.

Never would be better, said Little Turner.

The rest of the weekend and the following week passed without hearing from Allison, and I pretty much forgot about her. That Friday night, I was home watching *Shark Tank* on TV when she texted.

> **ALLISON:** I hope you're home and not out with some crazy woman. You'd be wasting your time.

Good grief. She's back … and what timing. How does she do that? asked Charles.

> **ME:** No. I was waiting for my bat-shit crazy woman two hours away to get in touch with me tonight, and here you are.

> **ALLISON:** Ha! You're funny.

> **ME:** And you're crazy.

> **ALLISON:** I told you I was.

> **ME:** Let's talk.

> **ALLISON:** Why?

ME: Because I've never talked to a self-professed bat-shit crazy woman before. It would be dating research.

ALLISON: I don't think I could talk to you. You went to Harvard, didn't you? I couldn't talk to someone who went to Harvard.

ME: Then why did you text me?

ALLISON: I don't know. I like you, but I don't want to talk to you.

ME: So you're big in the messaging department, but when it's game time, not so much.

Then my phone rang.

"Hi," a meek voice said.

"Allison?"

"Yes."

After a bit of verbal sparring along the lines of our earlier text exchanges, she went into the most bizarre story—yes, this gets more bizarre—of her marrying into elite society, being used for fifteen years, then being dumped.

"He discarded me and left when he was done using me," she said.

In the immediate aftermath, she was childless, broke, and on her own. But now, some ten years later, she had a little confectionery store that she had been able to start with the help of loans from local businesspeople.

From there, Allison pivoted to asking provocative questions about sex. She was trying to embarrass me and gain some sort of upper hand. But to her surprise, I kept up, giving her direct answers and then turning it right back on her.

"How can someone be so smart and honest too?" she said. "You're not the least bit embarrassed, and you don't play games like other men. Are you gay?"

"No, I'm not gay, but we are playing a game, Allison. What else would you call this?"

The next forty minutes were more of the same banter. After the call—and not at my request—she texted photos of her shaved naked crotch and a nipple on her breast.

> **ME:** Would these be yours?

> **ALLISON:** Yes.

> **ME:** I hope you're not looking for the same from me, because you're not going to get them.

No response.

Geez ... this is weird, said The Boys.

Before the evening was out, she sent several more short, cryptic texts. They turned out to be answers to questions she had asked me but then refused to answer herself.

> **ALLISON:** 13

> **ME:** What's 13?

> **ALLISON:** Men I've had sex with.

A few more answers were texted, but I stopped responding, turned off the phone, and went to sleep.

The next week, I had a meeting in Richmond, so I texted her with an idea.

> **ME:** Do you want to meet next week? I could drive to you after my board meeting in Richmond on Wednesday. We could meet for an hour or so before I have to drive home.

> **ALLISON:** No

> **ALLISON:** Maybe

> **ALLISON:** Okay

> **ALLISON:** I'm not going to have sex with you.

> **ME:** We are definitely not having sex.

As strange as it was, something was familiar about her. I sensed someone trying hard to reach out, to make a small bridge and connection, while at the same time, trying to burn it down so it would fail. I knew this scenario all too well from the struggles of my late wife. I also assumed that Allison was on some powerful medications for mental health issues, and they might be the cause of the unwanted weight gain she alluded to in our call. I also surmised this was the reason she had no photo in her dating profile.

But Allison certainly had her wits and sense of humor about her—as raw as it was at times—and was seemingly now successful in business too. Still, she clearly struggled, kind of like Eeyore in *Winnie the Pooh*—pessimistic, gloomy, and depressed. While there seemed little I could do, I thought I heard a cry for help and felt the need to respond. When you are in the depths of depression, it's pure hell—indescribable, really. I knew it only from being on the outside, but I was all too aware of its ability to destroy a person's life.

I arrived at Allison's store in Washington, Virginia, at five o'clock after my all-day board meeting in Richmond. She told me to park in the back and use the rear door, but when I went into the bakery, no one was there, and the store was closed. I saw ovens and other baking equipment in the back, a large bulletin board with different colored Post-it notes tacked to it with what looked like the month's deliveries planned out for each day, and a small front area for walk-in retail customers. It appeared that most of her business was for events, and retail was only a small part of it. Feeling like an intruder in the empty shop, I went back out and sat in my car.

Fifteen minutes later, an SUV slowly approached in the parking lot and stopped as far away as possible. I got out of my car, and after a few moments of looking at me, Allison got out too, looking nervously at the ground. She tugged at her sweater to pull it down and make it neat on her overweight body. She was unrecognizable from the old photograph she had sent. As I watched, she walked toward me, mostly looking at the ground, with only the occasional glance up.

Clearly embarrassed at how she looked, she greeted me quietly. I said a few things to help her get past the awkward moment and make her feel comfortable. It seemed to work as we walked inside.

She showed me the store, told me how it all worked, and described some of her incredible edible creations; she was quite the talented baker. She allowed me to taste a few things, and they were nothing short of amazing.

She then talked about her depression, her medications, the story of her business, and how she had pulled her life out of a terrible tailspin. I shared with her aspects of my wife's struggles and a few details of her passing. Allison then looked at me with *the look* I knew all too well.

As I mentioned before, whenever I told the true story of my wife's passing, I often felt like I was treated as some sort of wounded bird. People looked at me—or rather, studied me—looking for any visible cracks in my heart, my soul, and my spirit.

Looking me up and down as she searched for those cracks, Allison made note of how I was dressed—my custom dress shirt from Hong Kong, my dapper socks, and my woven leather dress shoes.

"You're so damn gay! You are! Look at your clothes. You don't *fuck* women!"

"You can go with that if you want, but I'm not gay."

"I could *never* have sex with you. I want a rough-looking guy to go at me. You're too nice. You *have* to be gay!"

After a bit more of this back and forth, we transitioned into a conversation about her. She talked about what she wanted to do with her life and what she wanted to do to feel better about herself.

I mentioned beginning an exercise routine, but she said she didn't know how to start and that she was too embarrassed to try. I said she needed to take baby steps at first—to schedule walks and go from there. I told her a tangible reminder might help her get into a regular schedule.

I walked to her bulletin board that had the days of the month laid out with different colored Post-it notes.

"This is perfect," I said. "Let's figure out your days and plug some exercise time into your master schedule here. If you see it written out in front of you, maybe that'll help you do it."

We talked through her calendar for a few minutes, then I grabbed a pad of bright pink Post-it notes. I wrote, "Allison Exercise" on several and, with thumb tacks, stuck them to the bulletin board on the afternoons of Tuesdays and Thursdays. She looked at the board, said nothing at first, but then said she'd try. After that, we began a slow walk back to my car.

I shared a few things my late wife had said during her struggles, things said during the more desperate times.

Allison said, "So she was like me, a glass-half-empty kind of person?"

"No," I said, pausing with emotion now beginning to well up inside. "She wasn't a glass-half-empty person; she was a glass-broken person ... and you're not that."

She looked at me, and her eyes said thank you.

We said goodbye to each other, I offered a supportive hug, and I left.

During the ninety-minute drive home, a thousand thoughts swirled through my head, but one was clearest among all others. *I'm done.*

I'm done.

I'm done ... no more dating ... I'm done!

A few days later, Allison texted and said she took the "Allison Exercise" Post-it notes off the bulletin board. I said it was her call and wished her luck. After that, I blocked her number.

And that was it—Venus was over.

CHAPTER 21

Leaving Venus

WHAT HAPPENED TO BRING AN end to my journey to Venus? The short of it, I think, is that I finally got my act together. But the longer explanation goes something like this.

I mentioned earlier that I booked a week's stay in mid-February at Canyon Ranch in Arizona. I was sorely in need of a rest and reboot in the aftermath of my mother-in-law's passing, everything that had happened the year before, and *everything in total* that had happened in the four and a half years since my wife's death.

That week away to work on everything—mind, body, spirit, and life—seemed to do its job. I came home in late February with newfound energy, a much clearer head, and a sense that life was there for me where it hadn't been before. I couldn't remember the last time I had felt so good, so hopeful, and just plain excited about life.

As I waded back into the online dating scene upon my return, it felt odd and ill-fitting. Even though I continued it with fervor for another three months, unbeknownst to me, the clock was ticking.

A part of feeling that *life was there for me* was the dawning realization of how blessed I was; I had a great family, wonderful friends, and really, a very good life. Instead of seeking a future to be found, I came to better understand and appreciate the many blessings I had.

I was one *very* lucky guy.

For whatever reason, my meeting with Allison made it all click into place. Plus, The Boys had been suggesting I stop. Well, okay ... more like they'd been screaming at the top of their lungs for quite a while.

So as spring transitioned into summer, I let the remaining matches and various dates play out and wrapped things up as neatly as possible.

However, there was another important reason I left Venus.

With family being first and foremost, I wanted to be in Massachusetts, closer to the school for my son with special needs. Four months after I left Venus, I rented an apartment in Massachusetts. For the next three years, I divided my time between there and my home in northern Virginia. I crafted a work plan that wrapped itself around my new split-state existence. It allowed me to devote more time to my son's future but, by default, less on mine. However, it did give me time to start writing this book.

As I wrote this final chapter—four years after having left Venus—time had obviously afforded me the chance for a fair amount of reflection on those three years, and from that, I gathered a few thoughts I'd like to share.

First—and this is no great revelation—as much as you want life to be simple, dating and relationships are c-o-m-p-l-i-c-a-t-e-d. It's complicated anywhere and everywhere, not just across an ocean. Add online dating into the mix, and it's exponentially more complicated.

Second, and this is related to the first, it's a hard and indisputable fact that you can't be a middle-aged woman or man without having baggage. When you've lived four or five decades, the baggage accumulates; that's all there is to it. People who say they want someone *without baggage* aren't being realistic. It's a unicorn that doesn't exist.

Third, because of how the whole online dating process evolved, much to my shock and dismay, I became the dreaded *serial dater* without realizing it. I was always looking ahead to the next one, and the next one, and the next one—a treadmill to nowhere of mind-numbing repetition. The juggling of dates and women was nuts too—one here, one there, a phone call at seven, another at nine. One date on a Friday night, a brunch on Saturday morning, a date on Saturday night ... and this was the *norm* in the digital-dating world. Even nuttier was pretending it *wasn't* nuts!

Fourth, if something crazy happened, I *way* overanalyzed, trying to make sense of it.

Is it me? I too often asked myself.

The lesson learned? If it *seems* crazy, it is. The totality of all the wacky things that some women thought were normal or okay to do was, well … just crazy, sometimes bat-shit crazy!

Fifth, on many first dates that began online, it was a loathsome process to have to work my way up from being the assumed cheating scumbag, snake-under-a rock, stalker, or potential serial killer. I mentioned early in the book that all men were assumed to be such until proven otherwise, and I get why women have to be cautious. But it always felt like such a hole to work my way out of, and quite frankly, I came to hate it.

Sixth, and this is a big one, is the enormous black cloud of judgment that envelopes you when you're immersed in online dating; it's baked into the DNA. It's amplified and cuts in all the most hurtful ways. Of course, appearance was always the first judgment that took place, given that photos in online dating profiles were always front and center, but it wasn't the only one. It was such a relief when I left Venus to be free of the black cloud of judgment that cloaked me and became me.

Finally—after all was said and done—out of the fifty-four women I met on Venus, I only connected with four or five in any meaningful way. It was a lousy track record for all the investment of time, money, and effort. The rest of the women were … well … you know because you just read about some of them.

Thinking I was missing out on life two years after my wife's passing, I threw myself into this dating project (as I called it) and learned that a lot of what I was missing out on was actually something best to be avoided. I also accumulated *more* baggage at a rapid and astonishing rate, but at least now I knew I wasn't missing out on anything.

I don't regret my time on Venus. It showed me so much about people out there in this great big crazy world—a real eye-opener, to be sure. I'm a better, more confident person for it. I do regret all the time I wasted when I could have been doing other—perhaps better—things. But in the end, I realized it was time that had to be spent for me to move down the road in my particular journey of life.

Do I understand women better because of my journey? A qualified yes. I have a newfound appreciation and awareness of what motivates women in dating and relationships, and I know it's so varied that I can't possibly understand it all. But I do understand more.

I want to touch on something that, in itself, could be the subject of another book (one that will never be written). A couple of times, I alluded to—but wondered often—if I was somehow broken from my experiences with my wife's depression and suicide. I wondered if I was broken in spirit and in my ability to engage with others, to love, to be loved, and to even care anymore about anything.

I can say with certainty that I changed as a person, and I *am* a little more c-o-m-p-l-i-c-a-t-e-d, of that there is no doubt. But broken? No. I'm consciously more protective of my heart, to be sure, and that in itself might make it harder for me to give love in the way some might need, or for me to receive love in the way some may have to give. Emily hit upon it a few times in her scathing emails during our breakup. I can't say she was entirely wrong, but I can say with certainty that I did the right thing for both of us.

But in a yin-yang sort of way, I'm also much more open, generous, and, hopefully, a kinder person. I absolutely treasure my family and friends and will drop everything to be there for them. Also excitingly, some of my new filters are wide open to live life to the fullest.

If I haven't been there, I want to go.

If I haven't seen it, I want to see it.

If I haven't done it, I want to do it.

If I haven't experienced it, I want to experience it—and that might explain the reason for my three-year journey to Venus.

As for my three years in Massachusetts, they concluded several years ago. I'm now back in my home in northern Virginia, outside Washington, D.C. Probably the biggest thing to come out of both my time on Venus and my time after is that I finally *can* answer the previously elusive questions of "What do I want?" and "Where do I see myself in ten or fifteen years?"

In the dedication at the front of this book, the initials "BB" are those of my late wife. She once asked, totally out of the blue, why I loved her. What I told her then, I shared in my eulogy upon her death.

"You make me better than what I am; yet you make what I am okay to be."

She loved that in only a few words—and needing no time to think about it—I was able to tell her how vital she was to my being. It also spoke to the magic we found in each other, something so many seek in a relationship.

Where do I stand now on matters of the heart? The words of Loretta Young sum it up pretty well. She was a young movie actress who had a torrid off-screen love affair in 1935 with the legendary leading man, and very married, Clark Gable. Asked to comment on the affair decades later, she was insightfully philosophical.

"Love isn't something you find; it's something that finds you."

And, in fact, that's exactly what happened to me not more than five months after I threw in the towel on dating and left Venus. While that story will remain private and untold—I'm not entirely a kiss-and-tell kind of guy—I will share that we met at church.

Who is *that woman?* The Boys and I said at once, upon seeing her for the first time. These many years later, we're still happily together.

Acknowledgements

MY STORY AND THIS BOOK would not be possible without the encouragement, support, and guidance from so many people. Many shared with me how honored they were to get an in-progress and early glimpse of the final manuscript and to feel the thrill of being a voyeur in the reading of my story. In the end, however, like me and the women I write about in the book, they preferred to remain anonymous. Nevertheless, I wish to give them—and you know who you are—my most heartfelt gratitude.

I would like to publicly acknowledge and thank my three editors, Dawn Brotherton, Nellwyn Lampert, and Jennifer Jas. In addition to expressing their shock and sometimes laughing themselves silly at the stories they were editing, they approached their work with vigor, professionalism, and unwavering support. They took a rookie writer's story and helped craft it into a worthy literary creation.

I would also like to thank Polly Letofsky (Publishing Mama), of My Word Publishing, for her phenomenal guidance, support, and encouragement in bringing my book to publication.

Lastly, I want to give a special thank you to the members of my local writers club. Amazing writers and published authors, they helped me believe I could do this when I wasn't sure I could. Without them, this book would not be here. You all are simply the best.

Want to Chat with Turner?

Turner Grant is available for virtual and in-person book club visits, podcasts, and other media appearances.

To contact, please visit: **TurnerGrantAuthor.com**

CPSIA information can be obtained
at www.ICGtesting.com
Printed in the USA
BVHW031709100223
658305BV00006B/73